IMPERIALISM

Modern Scholarship on European History
Henry A. Turner, Jr.   General Editor

Imperialism:

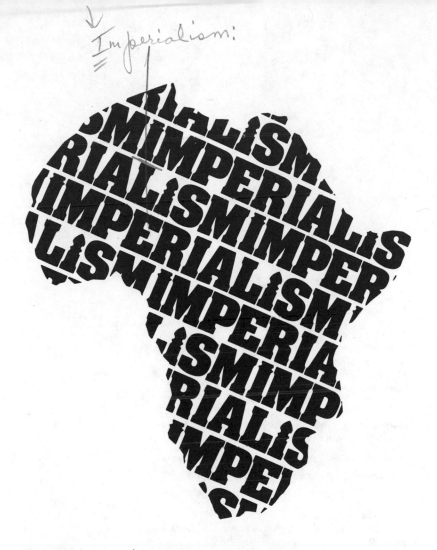

The Robinson and Gallagher Controversy
Edited with an Introduction by
WM. ROGER LOUIS
Modern Scholarship on European History

New Viewpoints
A Division of Franklin Watts
New York   London   1976

New Viewpoints
A Division of Franklin Watts
730 Fifth Avenue
New York, New York 10019

Library of Congress Cataloging in Publication Data
Main entry under title:

Imperialism: the Robinson and Gallagher controversy.

(Modern scholarship on European history)
"Selected works of Robinson and Gallagher": p.
Bibliography: p.
Includes index.
1. Colonies in Africa. 2. Imperialism. 3. Gallagher,
John, 1919-   4. Robinson, Ronald Edward, 1920-
I. Louis, Wm. Roger. II. Robinson, Ronald Edward,
1920-   III. Gallagher, John, 1919-
JV246.I43   325'.341'096   75-26730
ISBN 0-531-05375-X
ISBN 0-531-05582-5 pbk.

To Ronald Robinson and Jack Gallagher

CONTENTS

PREFACE

It is probably no exaggeration to say that the Robinson and Gallagher controversy has produced the most substantial debate among historians of imperialism since Parker T. Moon and William L. Langer wrote on the subject in the interwar years. This volume discusses the critical issues. I hope that it also serves a useful purpose by bringing together the basic interpretative writings of Robinson and Gallagher, though of course anyone truly interested in the controversy will want to read their major collaborative work, *Africa and the Victorians.*

There are in fact two important controversies. The debate about "The Imperialism of Free Trade" has taken place mainly among economic historians in the *Economic History Review.* Africanists and students of imperialism in Africa have discussed various aspects of *Africa and the Victorians* above all in the *Journal of African History.* This symposium links the two debates. It attempts to indicate that there is a logic to the work of Robinson and Gallagher that unifies the entire field of the expansion of Europe. For them it is not enough to criticize hypotheses of broad and intellectual significance without offering another set to take their place. Robinson and Gallagher believe that their explanation is nearer the evidence and more sophisticated than the traditional interpretations of imperialism. Some historians regard their unified theory of imperialism as a valid alternative to the Marxist interpretation.

I will not attempt to list my colleagues who in one way or another have helped to bring this project to its completion, but I would like to convey my thanks to all of them. I greatly regret that rising printing costs prohibit the republishing of major essays by Jean Stengers, Oliver Macdonagh, A. G. Hopkins, V. G. Kiernan, Colin Newbury,

Ronald Hyam, and Noel Garson, and critiques of *Africa and the Victorians* by Roland Oliver, John Hargreaves, A. P. Thornton, and David Fieldhouse. References to these works may be found in the footnotes of the introductory essay. I would welcome comment on the usefulness of the present volume both for teaching purposes and as a means of carrying forward the debate.

After reading the introductory essay, Jean Stengers has told me that the reader should be warned about the contrast between the way Robinson and Gallagher write history and the way I have presented their ideas. Actually I have merely tried to make explicit the implicit argumentation of Robinson and Gallagher, and I would like to thank them for their assistance through correspondence and conversation.

There are times when one hesitates to criticize Robinson and Gallagher for fear of having missed the joke. The "excentric" theory, for example, is a pun to be taken seriously. Their work as a whole repays serious and close study. At Oxford Harold Macmillan once said in good-natured vein when introduced to Ronald Robinson, "Oh yes, Africa and the Victorians, couldn't understand a word of it." Without the acrimony that has characterized some of the controversy, the introductory essay to this volume and the comments at the end have been written with a genuine effort to understand the arguments of the participants, as well as to criticize their ideas.

Wm. Roger Louis
The University of Texas at Austin
Easter 1975

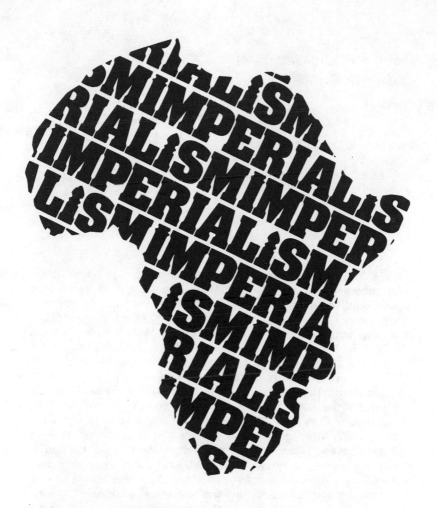

PART I

Introduction

Robinson and Gallagher
and Their Critics

In 1953 John A. Gallagher and Ronald E. Robinson published their celebrated article "The Imperialism of Free Trade," in which they argued that the nature of British imperialism in the nineteenth century remained constant. Seven years later appeared their magnum opus, *Africa and the Victorians*. The subtitle of the English edition, "The Official Mind of Imperialism," reflects the content of the book. The subtitle of the American edition, "The Climax of Imperialism in the Dark Continent," dramatizes the theme of continuity. In 1962 they sharply distilled their views on nineteenth-century expansion in a chapter in the *New Cambridge Modern History*, which, like "The Imperialism of Free Trade," is republished in this volume. A decade later, in 1972, in an article also included in this volume, Ronald Robinson advanced the argument into an "excentric" or collaborative theory of imperialism, which holds that imperialism in large part is the function of non-Western collaboration and resistance.[1] More than anything else, collaboration and resistance determine the incidence, the form, and the rise and fall of imperialism.

The accomplishment of Robinson and Gallagher has been hailed by Eric Stokes of Cambridge University as no less than a historiographical revolution, a new viewpoint in the history of the subject.[2] They themselves believe that they have achieved a unified theory of imperialism that is sustained in the case study of *Africa and the Victorians*. However one judges the work of Robinson, now the Beit Professor of the History of the British Commonwealth at Oxford University, and Gallagher, now Vere Harmsworth Professor of Imperial and Naval History at Cambridge University, there can be no question that their influence has been far-reaching.

In general, Robinson and Gallagher have attempted to replace traditional interpretations of imperialism with a new set of hypotheses which, they believe, is nearer the facts. They have tried to bridge the gap between theory and the historical evidence. The bedrock idea which underlies all their later work is to be found in the 1953 article. It argues continuity of British expansion and policy; but it also suggests discontinuity of imperialist activity and form or mode of expansion, according to circumstances in countries beyond Europe. Increasingly in their later work, they stress the trigger-action of non-European resistance. Response and collaboration introduce a random element into the process of imperialism, which, before Robinson and Gallagher, had been regarded from a narrow, Eurocentric point of view. Some of their critics have charged that they have merely inverted the old chronology of mid-Victorian anti-imperialism and late-Victorian imperialism, paradoxically producing the "Imperialism of Free Trade" and late-Victorian indifference to empire. What they have done, in fact, is something far more sophisticated and fundamental:

1. They have asserted that the urge to imperialism in Europe was merely one factor governing the timing and scope of imperialist activity abroad. Thereby they have challenged virtually all existing theories.

2. As they have developed their theories, they have argued that the process was governed as much if not more by non-European politics and economics as by European.

3. They have concluded that the phasing and changing forms of imperialism were unlikely to have conformed to chronological periods of opinion and policy in the expanding societies of Europe.

Africa and the Victorians was conceived as the acid test for this argumentation. It led them to unanticipated conclusions. In their investigation they discovered that strategic considerations were the highest common denominator in the calculations of the men who did the carving up of Africa. These strategic calculations were to an extent phantasmagorical. Strategic ideas reflected subjective interpretations of the history of European expansion. British statesmen in fact suffered from neuroses about holding what they had inherited. Misapprehension and blunders in dealing with non-European crises without understanding them often inadvertently turned decisions not to advance into advances; very often high-flying strategic notions were covers for these blunders.

The result of *Africa and the Victorians* as a test case can be summed up in these propositions:

1. The highest common denominator in the partitioners' calculations was the search for strategic security in the world.

2. What compelled them to expand, however, were not these strategic interests as such but crises in Egyptian and South African politics which seemed to dictate that these interests must be secured by extension of territory.

3. The changes in Anglo-French relations and in the diplomacy within the European power balance which stemmed from the Egyptian crisis drove the partitioners in the same direction.

4. A distinction must be made between the "motives" of the partitioners and the "causes" of the African partition. The most compelling motives were strategic, although of course they did not exclude commercial interests or philanthropic interests in some regions. The causes of the partition of Africa, on the other hand, lie in the changes in Egyptian and South African domestic politics rather than in intensified drives to expansion in European society. These changes resulting from African crises in turn produced changes in the relations of Britain, France, and Germany.

The chapter in the *New Cambridge Modern History* attempts to generalize on these points from the British to the other European participants in the "Scramble for Africa." The chapter is an elaboration of the book. Robinson's 1972 essay develops the argument to its full implications, from acquiring empires to ruling and losing them.

More specifically, Robinson and Gallagher attack the traditional notion that "imperialism" is the formal rule or control by one people or nation over others. In their view, historians have been mesmerized by formal empire and maps of the world with regions colored red. The bulk of British emigration, trade, and capital went to areas outside the formal British Empire. A key to the thought of Robinson and Gallagher is the idea of empire "informally if possible and formally if necessary." In *Africa and the Victorians* they develop the argument of imperialism and subimperialisms, in other words, forces not fully amenable to metropolitan control such as the foreign community and bondholders in Egypt, Cecil Rhodes in South Africa, and monopolistic commercial enterprises such as those of George Goldie on the Niger and King Leopold on the Congo. They argue that to understand late-nineteenth-century imperialism it is important to grasp the significance of certain key events such as the occupation of

Egypt by the British in 1882. In this case in particular British imperialism should be seen to some extent as a response to indigenous nationalism. The essay in the *New Cambridge Modern History* extends the argument of unanticipated local resistance which drags in the metropolitan powers. What alters is not British policy but conditions abroad. Robinson and Gallagher do not deny that steadily mounting economic pressures led to a steady increase of colonies, but that the spectacle of the Scramble can be understood fully only by perceiving the difficulty of reining back subimperialisms and dealing with protonationalist movements. As the arguments develop and the emphasis shifts, it is useful to bear in mind that continuity is one of the dominant principles of "the official mind." Another is that of parsimony or economy. British statesmen persistently exercised economy of effort and expense. The official mind itself can be described as the way in which the bureaucracy perceives its own history, the memory of past triumphs and past disasters. It possesses its own self-image and aspirations. It appraises present problems obliquely and subjectively. It is capable of translating economic interests into strategic concepts. It is a force in itself. It can be a cause of imperialism.

Theses of the "Imperialism of Free Trade": Continuity and Regionalism
The point of overriding importance in "The Imperialism of Free Trade" is the argument of continuity: "a fundamental continuity in British expansion throughout the nineteenth century." The character of this continuity or the nature of imperialism itself is determined by the changing circumstances at various times and in different regions—in their words, imperialism "is largely decided by the various and changing relationships between the political and economic elements of expansion in any particular time and place." The product of this interaction is *imperialism,* which remains constant. This interpretation constitutes a challenge to the basic idea of periodization in history and flies in the face of traditional views. Taking on at once the major analysts of the subject, Robinson and Gallagher attack the concept of the "new imperialism" espoused by such diverse writers as John A. Hobson, V. I. Lenin, Leonard Woolf, Parker T. Moon, Robert L. Schuyler, and William L. Langer. Those students of imperialism, whatever their purpose in writing, all saw a fundamental difference between the imperialist impulses of the mid- and late-Victorian eras. Langer perhaps best summarized the importance of making the distinction of late-nineteenth-century imperial-

ism when he wrote in 1935: "Centuries hence, when interests in the details of European diplomacy in the pre-war period will have faded completely, this period will still stand out as the crucial epoch during which the nations of the western world extended their political, economic and cultural influence over Africa and over large parts of Asia. . . . in the larger sense the story is more than the story of rivalry between European imperialisms; it is the story of European aggression and advance in the non-European parts of the world."[3] In most important accounts, the partition of Africa in twenty years' time stands as the very symbol of new forces of imperialism and as a watershed in modern history.

With this watershed Robinson and Gallagher will have nothing to do. On the contrary, they demonstrate the disadvantages to the concept of the "New Imperialism." Looking at maps in imperial colors in order to judge the nature of imperialism, they argue, is like gauging the size of icebergs only by the parts above the waterline. With this remarkable analogy they are able immediately to expose the central error of earlier historians such as John R. Seeley and Hugh Edward Egerton and untold numbers of historians of the British Empire whose interpretations have been guided by constitutional and racial concepts—the same as those which originally inspired the imperial federation movement. The mid-Victorian empire was informal as well as formal, economic as much as it was political. Leaving aside for the moment the powerful argument of informal expansion and control, it is important to point out that Robinson and Gallagher rightly criticize many conventional historians who see the mid-Victorian empire almost exclusively as one of indifference toward colonial activity. Again, this time by use of an arresting series of facts, Robinson and Gallagher in a few sentences launch a frontal attack on the myth of the static nature of the mid-Victorian empire in even its formal and constitutional structure:

> Between 1841 and 1851 Great Britain occupied or annexed New Zealand, the Gold Coast, Labuan, Natal, the Punjab, Sind and Hong Kong. In the next twenty years British control was asserted over Berar, Oudh, Lower Burma and Kowloon, over Lagos and the neighborhood of Sierra Leone, over Basutoland, Griqualand and the Transvaal; and new colonies were established in Queensland and British Columbia.[4]

They thus provide a dazzling reminder that there should be nothing especially surprising about additional territorial acquisition during the last two or three decades of the century. The question is whether the case is strong enough to destroy the old concept of a "New Imperialism," or whether their theory of continuity can be applied—

as later in the *New Cambridge Modern History* they emphatically imply it can—to the colonial experiences of other countries as well as to Great Britain. The force of the argument of "The Imperialism of Free Trade" derives from the history of the British Empire. The test of its universality must lie in explaining not only the unique features of Great Britain as the greatest imperial power of the nineteenth century but also the imperialism of Europe and of the United States and Japan as well. The phenomenon of late-nineteenth-century imperialism was worldwide.

No one has more clearly expressed doubts about the universality of the Robinson and Gallagher concept than has Professor Geoffrey Barraclough:

> The central fact about the "new imperialism" is that it was a world-wide movement, in which all the industrialized nations, including the United States and Japan, were involved. If it is approached from the angle of Great Britain, as historians have largely been inclined to do, it is easy to underestimate its force and novelty; for the reactions of Britain, as the greatest existing imperial power, were primarily defensive, its statesmen were reluctant to acquire new territories, and when they did so their purpose was usually either to safe-guard existing possessions or to prevent the control of strategic routes passing into the hands of other powers. But this defensive, and in some ways negative, attitude is accounted for by the special circumstances of Great Britain, and was not typical. It was from other powers that the impetus behind the "new imperialism" came—from powers that calculated that Britain's far-flung empire was the source of its might and that their own new-found industrial strength both entitled them to and necessitated their acquiring a "place in the Sun."[5]

As Barraclough points out, no one would deny the importance of the expansion of Europe's economy, technology, languages, and ideas throughout the world. The result probably constitutes the major revolution of our times. The legacies of European imperialism are undeniable. The question is whether there can be a single explanation and whether the theory of continuity has universal applicability. Put a different way, the question is whether late-nineteenth-century imperialism manifested an unprecedented urge to empire, or whether, for example, the partition of Africa merely represented the culmination of earlier expansionist tendencies. There lie some of the crucial areas of controversy raised by Robinson and Gallagher.

Themes of *Africa and the Victorians* and "The Partition of Africa." Imperial Security. Subimperialisms and Protonationalisms. Comprehensive Criticisms.
If the imperialism of the 1880s and 1890s represented no real

break with previous patterns of expansion, what then were the immediate causes of the Scramble? The answer can be found in part in the phrase "subimperialisms" or in other words the actions of the local agents of imperialism and their indigenous collaborators in such places as on the frontiers of southern British Africa. "Local crises" at the peripheries of the empire precipitate the intervention of the imperial power. Despite the importance of this theme, it is crucial to note that it is subordinate to the grand design of the book, which may be summed up as "imperial security." British statesmen acted on strategic calculations in a way quite differently from what they would have done had they based their decisions on economic advantages as such. Economic interests were involved but were not determinative. "The official mind" translated economic calculations into strategic concepts drawn from long-rooted experience of the worldwide empire. Thus Robinson and Gallagher differ radically from those historians who emphasize designs for economic exploitation. Their view is also the reverse of those who hold that the calling of the "white man's burden" played a central part in the European advance into the interior of Africa. Leaving aside for the moment their implicit attack on the theorists of economic imperialism, Robinson and Gallagher believe, as Sydney Kanya-Forstner has pointed out, that, far from espousing the "civilizing mission," British statesmen saw that Africa could not be transformed in the British image. Lord Salisbury, like Lord Milner in the later era of the First World War, pessimistically adopted the policy of "We hold what we have." To protect the existing empire in the East, the British were driven into strategic annexations and spheres of influence that eventually extended British power and lines of communication through the "Southern British World" from the Cape to Cairo to Singapore.

In "The Partition of Africa" Robinson and Gallagher extend their arguments to apply to the European powers as well as the British, and they expand the dimension of their analysis to take account of the African (and Asian) side of the equation. The countertheme of subimperialism is protonationalism, which plays an even greater role in the chapter than in the book. In the long run it develops into their ultimate argument that nationalism is a continuation of imperialism, which subsumes the argument of imperial security.

In both the book and the chapter they hold that the character of European imperialism fundamentally did not change but responded to non-European nationalist resistance of both neo-traditional and modern kinds. While taking into account rivalry with France and other powers in such areas as West Africa and the Congo, they contend that African resistance more than anything else brought about the transition from informal to formal empire and helped to trigger the Scramble. "Imbroglios with Egyptian proto-nationalists and thence with Islamic revivals across the whole of the Sudan drew the powers into an expansion of their own in East and West Africa. Thousands of miles to the south, English efforts to compress Afrikaner nationalists into an obsolete imperial design set off a second sequence of expansion in southern Africa."[6] As Eric Stokes has pointed out, this proposition reverses the Eurocentric interpretation of historians such as Moon, Langer, and A. J. P. Taylor, who hold that tensions within Europe generated the Scramble for colonies.[7] After the dramatic insight of *Africa and the Victorians* and "The Partition of Africa," Africa can no longer be seen as a blank map on which Europeans freely wrote their will.[8] In overturning the traditional historiographical assumption that pressures within Europe produced European imperialism in Africa, Robinson and Gallagher attempt to prove that the idea of economic exploitation came after the event of political takeover, as if almost by afterthought.[9]

This polemical argument against the theories of economic imperialism leads Robinson and Gallagher along with David Fieldhouse into a direct assault on Hobson, who viewed British expansion as synonymous with attempts at exploitation.[10] Here the point should be emphasized that Hobson's theory of imperialism differed from Lenin's. Lenin gave a more subtle explanation. According to Eric Stokes:

> . . . [I]t is too easily forgotten that the theory of economic or capitalist imperialism does not stand or fall on the authority of Hobson but of Lenin. A scrutiny of Lenin's principal writings reveals that no error could be more fundamental than to suppose that he was putting forward the same model of imperialism as Hobson. In the vital question of chronology Lenin made it plain that the era of monopoly finance capitalism did not coincide with the scramble for colonies between 1870 and 1900 but came after it.[11]

In this view Robinson and Gallagher as well as Fieldhouse err in seeing "the conflation of arguments of Hobson and Lenin . . . [as] a single model." After reviewing Lenin's writings and concluding that he was less concerned with providing a theoretical analysis of the scramble for colonies than in explaining the genesis of the First World War, Stokes goes on to isolate the economic argument of Robinson and Gallagher, thereby putting it into perspective:

> Robinson and Gallagher rightly pour scorn on the notion that economic interests were anything like powerful enough to bring about a historical

phenomenon so remarkable as the scramble for Africa, but it is another thing to say they had no place at all, and sub silentio they admit their importance. . . .

Only in Egypt and East Africa were commercial interests clearly of subordinate importance. The "official mind" may have placed considerations of strategy and security uppermost in its calculations of African policy, but it would be difficult to show that it acted very differently in that part of the world where Robinson and Gallagher regard the British economic stake as preponderant, and for whose strategic defence they argue Britain's African policy was shaped. . . . in Asia, as in Africa, the agencies of expansion were essentially economic and provoked the crises that drew the statesmen on to the scene. . . . when free of the elements of exaggeration Lenin's account of the colonial scramble is not one of narrow economic determinism, nor is Robinson's and Gallagher's one of simple non-economic motivation.[12]

Reduced from complexity, the interpretations both of Lenin and of Robinson and Gallagher have similarities. "[W]hen the arguments of both Lenin and of Robinson and Gallagher have been freed from the elements of caricature," Stokes concludes, "their general analyses of European colonialism between 1870 and 1914 exhibit a surprising degree of correspondence. Lenin, it would appear, was no Leninist; he too stands the classical model of economic imperialism on its head."[13] If this interpretation is accurate, then Robinson and Gallagher might be considered non-Leninist Leninists, and their contemptuous rejection of Marxist interpretation of imperialism deserves rescue from the relegation of a single footnote in *Africa and the Victorians.*[14] It is a good point about Lenin and a good joke on Robinson and Gallagher. They are anything but Leninists.

With vivid recognition of the seriousness of the attack, V. G. Kiernan in the *Socialist Register* commented on the way Robinson and Gallagher have left Lenin's bones "bleaching in the Sahara."[15] Where else except at the North and South poles could one find less evidence of capitalist exploitation? According to this engaging and sardonic critique, Robinson and Gallagher have failed to meet Hobson and Lenin fairly on their own ground. In a supremely sophisticated manner the evidence has been rigged. Robinson and Gallagher have based their interpretation on "the official mind," which they erroneously assume is the originator of policy. "It is . . . a delusion of archive-searchers, who inhale a subtly intoxicating atmosphere and need its stimulus to keep them going, to suppose that ministers and under-secretaries are careful to leave behind them all the documents required for a verdict on their actions."[16] Laying the ground rules that evidence must consist mainly of the official records, Robinson and Gallagher next select the part of the world where the capitalists could least expect to make a profit. Kiernan thus blasts what he believes to be Robinson and Gallagher's specious reasoning.

> [O]ne acquittal leads easily to another. Capitalism did not really covet its neighbour's sand. Therefore capitalism cannot really have coveted its neighbour's oil, or his coal, or his rubber, or his ox, or his ass, or his man-servant, or his maid-servant, or anything that was his. Henry VIII did not chop off the head of his last wife. Therefore Henry VIII cannot have chopped off the heads of any of his wives. Twice two is not five. Therefore twice three cannot be six.[17]

With logic of this sort, Robinson and Gallagher find that the defense of India is the guiding thread through the diplomatic labyrinth. But Kiernan believes it to be a subtly misleading explanation:

> What it overlooks is that the cry of 'India in danger' was a convenient one for financiers and concession-hunters, as well as historians; for anyone with an eye on Burmese timber, Yunnan railways, Malayan rubber, or Persian oil. It was a plausible excuse for all businessmen found in compromising situations, an unanswerable claim for official backing. If there had been space-travellers in those days India would have been a compulsory reason for Britain to take part in the race to the moon. . . .[18]

Using official sources that echo the strategic defense of India, Robinson and Gallagher treat the policy-makers as political computers with no recognition of the immense influence of the financiers. Their account of local crises thus in Kiernan's judgment totally misrepresents the real forces at work:

> The assertion that the British Government did not desire to occupy Egypt only amounts to saying that it would have preferred to go on with the cheaper and discreeter method of letting Egypt be exploited through a native puppet; just as U.S. marines are only sent into a banana-republic when the local dictator fails to deliver the bananas. Business interests wanting intervention could always provoke a situation, or help a situation to take shape, where ministers would have no choice about intervening, and could do so with a good or at least a brave conscience.[19]

In South Africa Kiernan finds their explanation even more unsatisfactory than in Egypt. He makes his point in regard to Lord Salisbury, who at the end of his career wrote bitterly that Britain had to go to war "for people whom we despise, and for territory which will bring no profit and no power to England." Salisbury, in Kiernan's view, did not know why the Boer War was fought, and neither do Robinson and Gallagher because they have been content "to look through his spectacles." Certainly they would not find the evidence in official documents, nor would their method lead them to it.

> If Lenin deals out too summary a drumhead justice to capitalism, Robinson and Gallagher go to the opposite extreme. On their rules of evidence no conviction could ever be secured against any business lobby. Capitalism to be found guilty would have to be caught in flagrante delicto with a signed confession in its pocket properly witnessed by three ministers of the Crown.[20]

To Kiernan, Robinson and Gallagher give away their case when they acknowledge that British Africa was merely "a gigantic footnote to the Indian Empire." In India can be found the true and unabashed economic motives for empire, which Robinson and Gallagher have obscured by their analysis of strategy in Africa.[21] Kiernan thus emerges as the preeminent critic who charges that Africa and the Victorians is a whitewash of economic imperialism.

Writers who acknowledge the originality of Robinson and Gallagher's work, including Kiernan and Stokes, find themselves in at least implicit conflict with George Shepperson, coauthor of The Independent African.[22] Just as Robinson and Gallagher emphasize the continuity of development of the British Empire, so Shepperson sees Africa and the Victorians as the logical and not especially earthshaking extension of ideas of previous writers. Writing in that elite journal of historical journals, La Revue Belge de Philologie et d'Histoire,[23] Shepperson points out in an essay included in this volume that Robinson and Gallagher build the subtlety of their argument on works such as W. K. Hancock, Wealth of Colonies,[24] and he indicates that their enquiry overlaps with that of such writers as Hannah Arendt and Karl Deutsch, both of whom in different ways have made exceedingly important contributions to the subject of imperialism and nationalism.[25] It can be said that none of these writers was particularly concerned with non-European elements of imperialism, but it is true that their work finds little reflection in Africa and the Victorians. Above all, Shepperson judges Robinson and Gallagher weakest in that area in which they claim to have made a major contribution, the theory of imperialism. "If, perhaps, there had been a preliminary review of the subject," writes Shepperson, who objects to economic theory being dismissed in a mere footnote, "terms could have been defined at the start and subsequent theorization made easier."[26] As it stands Africa and the Victorians suffers from lack of analysis of economic motivation where it might have been most illuminating. For example, Robinson and Gallagher devote very little attention to the Berlin Congo Conference of 1884–85, the whole point of which was trade, and they neglect the role of King Leopold, whose founding of the Congo Free State at that time later made a mockery of the very phrase "free trade." If grand strategy more than hope of economic gain guided British statesmen, then "It is strange . . . that there is no mention of Cecil Rhodes's attempts to secure Katanga, the overruling of which by the British government affords a striking demonstration of the authors' thesis."[27] In cautious words Shepperson accepts *Africa and the Victorians* as a contribution to the history of the expansion of Europe, and indeed to the history of Africa, but by no means a revolutionary contribution. He sees the possibility of assimilating the arguments of Robinson and Gallagher with the ideas of such diverse writers as Schumpeter, Veblen, and Mannoni into "The Theory of Imperialism and European Partition of Africa."[28]

No one recently has made more substantial contributions to the analysis of the theories of imperialism than has David Fieldhouse, a historian who has devoted his career to the study of the economic factor in the expansion of Europe. He does not so much dissent from the views of Robinson and Gallagher as to see their work essentially as an investigation into the political causes of the expansion of Europe. *Africa and the Victorians* confirms his own view that the partition of Africa occurred not only because of the dynamics of power politics and European diplomacy but also because of subimperialisms and crises in colonial areas. In 1962 Fieldhouse regarded *Africa and the Victorians* as "perhaps the sanest and most convincing interpretation yet published of the real character of British imperialism in the late nineteenth century."[29] More than any other commentator he emphasized the Schumpeterian essence of the work—"the root of imperialist policies in this period was to be found in the special attitudes of the European aristocracy. . . ."[30] the division of Africa showed how little British statesmen were interested in the acquisition of new colonies for purely economic reasons, which were always subordinated to strategic considerations."[31] As for the contribution of Robinson and Gallagher to the theory of imperialism, Fieldhouse in *The Theory of Capitalist Imperialism* in 1967 classified it as "peripheral"—not in the sense of failing to get at the heart of the problem but in the sense of explaining imperialism by forces at the circumference of empires.[32] "By no means all colonial acquisitions resulted from crises at the perimeter, and where the peripheral approach fails, the historian must turn back to Europe for his explanation."[33] As will be seen in the bibliographical note in this volume, Fieldhouse has emerged in 1973 as a protagonist in the Robinson and Gallagher controversy by integrating the "Eurocentric" and the peripheral theories. No other writer has given such powerful independent support to the general analysis of Robinson and Gallagher, though he does not accept all of their arguments. It is important to note that, in the historiography of the controversy, this is an original development and should be regarded as distinct from his interpretation in *The Theory of Capitalist Imperialism*. At the time, *The Theory* was significant, among other reasons, because it provoked Ronald Robinson into an elucidation of the Robinson and Gallagher position.

"The Thinker"[34] Clarifies the Argument

The idea of Robinson and Gallagher is precisely the opposite of Fieldhouse's ultimate resort in *The Theory of Capitalist Imperialism* of finding the explanation of European imperialism within Europe. They aim to replace the Eurocentric approach with a more satisfactory explanation of non-European elements of imperialism. Thus Fieldhouse's assessment as "peripheral" (and perhaps the connotation) caused Ronald Robinson to elucidate the Robinson and Gallagher theory. Here is the interpretation that may be taken as their most recent thoughts on the subject:

> [I]t is what might be called an 'excentric' approach to European imperialism. To borrow a figure from geometry, there was the Eurocentric circle of industrial strategy making varying intersections with circles centred in the implacable continuities of African and Asian history. Imperialism, especially in its time scale, was not precisely a true function of either circle. It was in many ways excentric to both. It should be emphasized that the Afro-Asian crises which evoked imperialism were often not essentially the products of European forces but of autonomous changes in African and Asian domestic politics. Changing over to a mechanical analogy, imperialism was in another sense the 'centre of mass' or resultant of both circles. Hence the motivation and modes of imperialism were functions of collaboration, non-collaboration, mediation and resistance of varying intersections of the two circles.[35]

Imperialism is thus in part a function of indigenous politics of the non-European world. The argument is an expansion and reenforcement of the one first put forward in "The Imperialism of Free Trade," that imperialism is the political function of the process of integration of various countries at various times into the world's economy. Their position is thus consistent.

D. C. M. Platt and the Attacks on "The Imperialism of Free Trade"

Of the economic historians, D. C. M. Platt far and away remains the most persistent critic of Robinson and Gallagher. He is the author of the pioneering work *Finance, Trade, and Politics in British Foreign Policy 1815–1914*.[36] Setting for himself the goal of estimating the extent to which commerce influenced foreign relations, Platt analyzes the continuity of British foreign policy during the nineteenth century as an overriding concern for national security with a closely linked corollary of creation and preservation of British trading opportunities. He thus finds himself more or less in agreement with the main theme of *Africa and the Victorians*. "The official mind," bent on security of the routes to the east, gave way to other expansionist powers in the western part of the continent but nevertheless tried to safeguard trading interests there. But Platt questions whether Robinson and Gallagher have not distorted African problems at the expense of those of other regions. One of the merits of his detailed work is the examination of British policy throughout the world:

> There is . . . a danger that the new explanation of British official motives in Africa during the 'Age of Imperialism,' while stressing, legitimately enough, such factors as the security of the routes to the East and of the Empire itself, will under-emphasize the part played in British policy by the need to protect the relative position of British trade in world markets. This need, which has already served as a constant, underlying theme in the description of British policy in Egypt, Turkey, and Persia, will be shown to have been of even greater importance in determining British policy in China and Latin America. Could it, then, have been so relatively unimportant in the Partition of Africa? . . .
>
> The point has been made by Robinson and Gallagher . . . that the minimal economic value of the new territories divided among the Powers during the Partition shows how slight a part economics must have played in determining international policy. . . . The point is well taken, but it was the fear of being excluded from prospective *as well as* existing markets which prompted H.M. Government's policy in West and Central Africa, and nobody at the time could estimate precisely what these markets might be worth in future.[37]

On this well-taken point Platt's criticism is identical with that of most prominent critics of Robinson and Gallagher. African dividends may eventually have been small, but this fact does not necessarily explain the motives for the partition; territories that remained largely unexplored during the Scramble might or might not eventually have paid large financial returns. On the whole, however, Platt's study of Africa (which is less extensive than that of other regions) confirms the resounding themes of *Africa and the Victorians:* "The importance of British interests in India in the formulation of British policy in Uganda and the Upper Nile region is now undeniable."[38]

Before turning to Platt's evaluation of "The Imperialism of Free Trade," perhaps it would be well to restate the ideas of Robinson and Gallagher in relation to "informal empire."[39] According to them, "the imperialism of free trade" covers one or more of the following links between an expanding and a receiving political economy:

1. The exertion of power or diplomacy to impose and sustain free trading conditions on another society against its will;

2. The exertion of capital or commercial attraction to bend economic organization and direction of growth in directions complementary to the needs and surpluses of the expanding economy;

3. The exertion of capital and commercial attraction directly upon foreign governments to influence them toward cooperation and alliance with the expanding country;

4. The direct intervention or influence of the export-import sector interests upon the politics of the receiving country in the direction of collaboration and political-economic alliance with the expanding power;

5. The taking over by European bankers and merchants of sectors of non-European domestic economies under cover of imposed free trade without accompaniment of large capital or export inputs from Europe, as in China.

If any one passage in "The Imperialism of Free Trade" sums up their argument, perhaps it is this:

> British policy followed the principle of extending control informally if possible and formally if necessary. To label the one method 'anti-imperialist' and the other 'imperialist', is to ignore the fact that whatever the method British interests were steadily safeguarded and extended. The usual summing up of the policy of the free trade empire as 'trade not rule' should read 'trade with informal control if possible; trade with rule when necessary'.[40]

It is remarkable, as Platt points out, that no historian took serious issue with that proposition during the 1950s, and, even after the publication of *Africa and the Victorians,* few historians appeared to recognize that the theory of continuity and its corollary of informal empire had profound implications for the historiography of the era.

"[T]he point is that the character of this expansion *had* changed," Platt exclaimed in April 1968 in *Past and Present,* as almost in a plea for sanity among fellow historians.

The fashionable theory that British expansion was designed simply to maintain the security of the existing Empire against a new threat from the Continental Powers can explain a great deal. . . . But the new threat which Britain faced in and after the 1880s was not confined to imperial frontiers and communications; it extended also to the security of British trade and finance. . . . Before 1880 British statesmen had not been especially worried by foreign colonial expansion. Nor were they worried by expansion after that date provided that the markets remained open to British trade and investment and that no strategic interests were damaged.

So long as there were no restrictions on trade, the British Government tolerated foreign annexations.

. . . H.M. Government's part in the 'New Imperialism' might have been restricted entirely to areas of strategic interest if it had not been for the revival of European Protectionism and the threat to the fair and equal treatment of British trade and finance. . . . Imperial expansion was only the most spectacular, and in Whitehall the least popular, of the remedies supplied. It was as simple as that.[41]

In the same year, 1968, in the *Economic History Review*, Platt began to take on Robinson and Gallagher on grounds of his own especial expertise, Latin America. His criticism here is especially interesting because Latin America serves as one of the main props of their argument. It is simply not true, Platt argues, that mid-Victorian statesmen acted vigorously to open markets and to keep them open, in Latin America, in China, or anywhere else. British policy in Latin America, for example, aimed at preserving neutrality, often in opposition to British financiers. After an abundance of examples from Latin America and China:

Non-intervention and laissez-faire were the characteristic attitudes of mid-Victorian officialdom, and these attitudes were faithfully reflected overseas. It is not true, for example, that British government policy in Latin America was to obtain 'indirect political hegemony over the new regions for the purposes of trade', or to create 'a new and informal empire' in the interests of future British commercial expansion.[42]

In *Finance, Trade, and Politics:*

It is not true, for example, that H.M. Government was prepared to exercise informal control in Latin America, whatever the provocation, and the examples quoted by Gallagher and Robinson go nowhere to prove their case.[43]

And again in still "Further Objections" (included in this volume), in the *Economic History Review*, in a full-blown reconsideration of the issue:

The British government's role, in mid-Victorian England, was limited, and

it was forced into an active promotional policy towards trade and invest-
ment overseas only under international pressure in the last decades of the
century. Late-Victorian governments were not applying the same methods,
under new conditions, to achieve what remained the same goals. The
whole concept of what was a 'legitimate' function for the Foreign Office
and the Diplomatic Service had had to be altered and transformed under
the competitive conditions and active foreign diplomacy of the 'eighties.[44]

According to Platt's view, the "submerged part of the iceberg" of informal empire becomes less significant the more it is scrutinized and more and more the product of the fanciful imagination of Robinson and Gallagher. The "informal empire" presumably existed above all in Latin America, the Levant, and China. Yet these are precisely the areas where, in the mid-nineteenth century, absence of returns checked expansion of trade. Arguing that "the Imperialism of Free Trade" is an anachronism because it antedates by several decades the relative importance of the "informal empire" as a place for investment and a source of raw materials and foodstuffs, Platt contends that the incentives for economic expansion simply did not exist. If "The Imperialism of Free Trade" once served as a salutary corrective to the stereotyped conceptions of mid-Victorian empire, then Platt's articles are equally useful in keeping a balanced—and *relative*—view of mid-nineteenth-century imperialism.[45]

The first of the case studies testing the general ideas of Robinson and Gallagher is by Oliver MacDonagh, "The Anti-Imperialism of Free Trade."[46] It is about the ideas of Richard Cobden and the Manchester School in the years 1840–70. The general comments and conclusions are especially helpful in clearing up semantic and conceptual confusions that have run through the entire controversy. What after all do Robinson and Gallagher mean by "informal empire"? To MacDonagh it can be summed up by stating that both formal and informal empires are to some extent identical and interchangeable. The two kinds of empire express variable political functions of the extending patterns of overseas trade, investment, migration, and culture (a seminal idea later reenforced in the "excentric" theory). MacDonagh argues that this reasoning merely replaces old conceptual difficulties with new and unanticipated ones. Since the United States received much of British capital and emigrants during the nineteenth century, should the United States be included in the "informal empire"? Even apart from the United States, a drastic recoloring of the imperial map might be required. "We might find ourselves constrained to drain Canada of colour while the Balkans were being painted off-red." And some cases defy categories. For example, was Ireland imperializing or being imperialized?

Ireland was indeed the prime exporter of population from the United Kingdom; but she was also the major exporter of French Revolutionary ideology, Roman Catholic religion and anti-British sentiment. In fact, 'overseas trade, investment, migration and culture' were not four battalions in the same regiment: they did not even march in the same direction.[47]

Even apart from the difficult question of where to place and how to describe Ireland in any commentary on imperialism, is there perhaps a danger in not only the universality but also the depersonalization of the theory of Robinson and Gallagher? It did make a very real difference, as MacDonagh points out, that opportunity gave Disraeli and not Gladstone the chance to purchase the Suez canal shares in 1875. Gladstone probably would have refused, and the Egyptian crisis leading to the occupation in 1882 would have taken a substantially different form, whatever the role of the Egyptian nationalists. The idea of a constant and aggressive mid-Victorian imperialism has to be considered in relation to personalities and movements. Here MacDonagh develops his thesis: the free traders of the 1840–70 period clearly perceived the informal empire; but to imply that they promoted the growth of empire is basically to misread the history of the era.

It is true that the pre-eminent free traders of the period 1840–70 were well aware of the development of 'informal empire', and discerned many of the features which Mr. Gallagher and Dr. Robinson have re-discovered. But they also pronounced them to be a sin against free trade, and opposed them with all the resources at their command.[48]

Free trade means, as MacDonagh clearly explains, the doctrine of specific associations and persons, of which the Manchester School and Richard Cobden in particular were at the center. Cobden stood against all imperialism, formal and informal. The free-trade movement represented a force of Victorian society in perpetual conflict with the aristocracy and those principles associated with the aristocracy: unnecessary governmental expenditures, bellicosity, war as a solution to problems of colonial and international relations. The free trade movement was more than a movement concerned with mere trade: it espoused moral principles and the idea of a society that would regulate itself if free from governmental interference. Not least it was a movement for peace, including support of international arbitration and disarmament. For Robinson and Gallagher to say that imperialism characterized the era of free trade, in other words mid-Victorian England, is one thing, and to them goes the credit of destroying once and for all the myth of the mid-nineteenth century as anti-imperialist.[49] But for them to imply at least by ambiguity that the free-trade movement supported the forces of imperialism is misleading if not mischievous. The distinction is fundamental. In Mac-Donagh's judgment the meaning conveyed by the phrase "Imperialism of Free Trade" is the opposite of the truth.[50]

In "The Imperialism of Free Trade—Peru, 1820–70," W. M. Mathew examines the viability of the thesis in a case study of an especially significant Latin American country.[51] Peru is a happy choice because one can evaluate the ideas of Robinson and Gallagher against a specific mid-Victorian problem in which the British Government remained aloof, and then proceed to the eve of the First World War, when Britain did intervene. Mathew asks whether the British Government employed economic and military measures in order to place Peru in a position of imperial subordination, which is one way to test the straightforward idea of the Imperialism of Free Trade (though not, perhaps, the "excentric theory"). During the nineteenth century Peru's guano trade with Britain reached sizable proportions. In the 1850s and 1860s the British imported more fertilizer from Peru than from any other Latin American country. And in the decade and a half of 1851–65 loans to Peru ranked greater than to any other Latin American country. But Peru behaved in a way that should have angered the free-trade imperialists of Robinson and Gallagher. The Peruvian Government demanded artificial prices for the guano and defaulted on obligations to British bondholders. How did the British respond?

> Farmers, agricultural commentators, and government alike in the early and mid-1850's all appear to have concurred that lower guano prices and more regular guano supplies would greatly assist the process of agricultural improvement in Britain—and to have accepted, too, that these could be secured through a degree of coercion which British governments, as it turned out, were simply not prepared to apply.[52]

About the defaults to the bondholders? "In July 1857 Clarendon told a party of bondholders in London that 'it would be inconsistent with the policy of the British government to enter into territorial guarantees with foreign governments.' "[53] When the British Government did contemplate intervention, it appears to have been to redress breaches of international law, not to promote economic exploitation. Mathew concludes "there is little in the historical record to justify viewing Peru as a victim of British imperialism, as part of Britain's 'invisible empire of informal sway.' " The history of mid-nineteenth-century Peru, in Mathew's view, does not sustain the themes of "The Imperialism of Free Trade."[54] Nor do any of the major themes of "The Imperialism of Free Trade" or *Africa and the Victorians* help to explain why Britain did intervene in Peru half a century later, in the era of the rubber atrocities. After the turn of the century the Peruvian Amazon Company, which was in fact a private British company, exploited the Indians of the upper Amazon, in the Putumayo region, even more viciously than in the Congo. Rumors of atrocities appeared in the British press, and the Aborigines Protection Society pressed the Foreign Office for intervention. The Foreign Office felt sufficient humanitarian pressure to despatch the British Consul in Brazil to investigate. The resulting report of 1912 constituted a damning indictment of the rubber regime of the Putumayo. Neither the Foreign Office nor the British public sympathized with rubber ruffians. Under parliamentary and public pressure, the company disbanded. There is no explanation of this episode other than humanitarian. This particular incident of course lies beyond the confines of their investigation, but it seems fair to say that the influence of the humanitarians and crusaders on "the official mind" is a neglected dimension in the later works of Robinson and Gallagher.[55]

Historians of Latin America are deeply divided over the concept of "Imperialism of Free Trade." Along with Platt and Mathew, H. S. Ferns in *Britain and Argentina in the Nineteenth Century* argues that the word "imperialism" to be used in a meaningful sense must imply political subordination. "If we accept the proposition that imperialism embraces the fact of control through the use of political power, then the verdict for Britain is unquestionably 'Not Guilty.' "[56] Ferns holds that the Argentine government always possessed sufficient strength to shape the course of British-Argentine relations and that the economic facts of Argentina's financial power "make nonsense of myths about British imperialism and Argentina as a semi-colony of a great and powerful state."[57] In an article of lasting importance on "Britain's Informal Empire in Argentina," written in the same year as Robinson and Gallagher's *démarche* in 1953, Ferns contended that Britain's policy of political restraint had allowed Argentina to develop without the political friction that had characterized British relations with India, China, and Egypt. "In a very real sense Argentina was the first community, substantially dependent economically on Great Britain, to achieve Dominion status."[58] This positive interpretation would probably go beyond Platt's, but both are adamant that Britain pursued a policy of political neutrality.

By contrast, the writings of other Latin American historians such as Peter Winn and Richard Graham can be associated with Robinson and Gallagher. They stress "informal empire" both as a British policy and a Latin American reality.[59] Along with Robinson and Gallagher, Graham emphasizes the importance of the role of the collaborator. Graham's interpretation in some ways is the opposite of Ferns's. Brazil may or may not have been on its way toward Dominion status, but in Graham's view there can be no doubt about the subordination of Brazil in the informal empire. It involved a transfer of values as well as economic exploitation.

> . . . the force of the imperial power is to be measured not only or even primarily by the overt acts of political control but by the degree to which the values, attitudes and institutions of the expansionist nation infiltrate and overcome those of the recipient one. In this process the native collaborator or sepoy is indispensable. It is when influential publicists and local politicians become convinced that the way of life of the imperial power is the best one imaginable that the strength of that nation is at its greatest, although the evidence may then be least noticeable. In nineteenth-century Brazil there were both institutional and personal reflections of this mechanism of imperial control.[60]

Like Robinson and Gallagher, Graham sees the founts of British expansion as constant. "The same forces that in the 1840's demanded the opening of Chinese ports had earlier taken a keen interest in breaking down the monopolies maintained by Spain and Portugal in the New World."[61] Regardless whether one endorses the interpretation of Ferns or Graham, it is important to keep the problem of the "informal empire" in Latin America in worldwide perspective. Case studies may seem to prove Robinson and Gallagher both wrong and right, depending on other circumstances. To return to the case of Peru, for example, Clarendon made his statement of nonintervention in July 1857, when the British government faced the necessity of sending every available man to India to deal with the mutiny. It was a time immediately following the Persian expedition, the China war, and not long after the Crimean war. Intervention in South America had to be conceived on a different order from that in Asia. In addition there was the possibility that intervention might interfere with relations with the United States. As in the case of Africa, British actions in Latin America have to be viewed as part of the problems facing British foreign policy and the British Empire as a whole.

In "Economic Imperialism in West Africa: Lagos, 1880–92," by A. G. Hopkins, the interests of the economic historians and the African historians begin to mesh.[62] It is an illuminating article. The topic is specialized but the view is large. Hopkins argues that critics of the theory of economic imperialism including Robinson and Gallagher have been so eager to destroy conventional concepts that they fail to see the truly operative economic elements in the Scramble. This is especially true of West Africa, treatment of which most critics see as the weakest in *Africa and the Victorians*. Hopkins begins by asking the narrow and useful question: Why did the Europeans partition not only Africa in general, but West Africa in particular? He is of course by no means the first to ask that question but his line of reasoning is enlightening. The answer given by Robinson and Gallagher, he argues, has the advantages but also the disadvantages of seeing the connection between West Africa and other parts of the world; once they commit themselves to explaining the partition of West Africa for reasons of grand strategy that have nothing to do with that particular area, then they do not permit themselves to see the full force of the economic reasons why the European powers partitioned West Africa. Another way of putting it is that Robinson and Gallagher help us to understand why the British failed to paint all of West Africa red, but their explanation falls short of explaining how Britain managed to hold on to two of the richest areas, Nigeria and the Gold Coast. They underplay the significance of the economic depression of the 1880s because the very existence of a depression seems sufficient evidence to dispose of the aggressive economic imperialism of Hobson, for example, as a dynamic in the partition of West Africa. Robinson and Gallagher therefore search for and find non-West African explanations. On the other hand, if one starts with another set of suppositions:

> [S]uppose that the widespread depression in West African trade had a dynamic rather than a static effect on British and French interests; suppose that it upset the status quo, increased commercial rivalries, and led merchants and local officials to press for an alternative policy, a forward policy, in West Africa. There is a striking anticipation of this hypothesis in the history of Tudor England, for it was an economic crisis in the middle of the sixteenth century which encouraged English merchants to seek markets in new regions, including West Africa. If an economic crisis led the Elizabethans to the west coast, is it not possible that a similar motive encouraged the Victorians to move from the coast to the interior?[63]

The economic depression of the 1880s caused crises in commercial and manufacturing industries; British traders favored partition as a means to prevent occupation by other powers. In sum, economic strategy played a major part in the Scramble for West Africa and cannot be cavalierly dismissed in the fashion of Robinson and Gallagher. In the course of his inquiry Hopkins comes into collision with the views of Professor J. F. A. Ajayi of the University of Ibadan and with the Emin Pasha Professor of African history at the University of Chicago, Ralph Austen. They disagree with Hopkins about the internal history of the Yoruba states in the nineteenth century and the extent to which British intervention was caused by the West African merchants, whose influence Ajayi and Austen believe to be exaggerated.[64] But they do not dispute Hopkins's major conclusion, which in part takes exception to Ronald Robinson's description of "the decrepit, mythological beast of economic imperialism."[65] According to Hopkins:

> In the last analysis, the partition of West Africa may be thought of as a political act carried out to resolve the economic conflicts which had arisen as a result of the meeting of two disparate societies, one developing, the other underdeveloped. Seen in these terms, economic imperialism was not a mythical beast, a paper tiger, but a real, live creature after all.[66]

This is a rich investigation, important for changes in the economic structure of West Africa as well as for the ideas it generates about theories of economic imperialism and the value of the Robinson and Gallagher thesis.

The Arguments Recapitulated. Ronald Robinson Expands the Theory in "Non-European Foundations."

Before this present discussion passes from aspects of the controversy that have preoccupied economic historians and goes on to points that have aroused the interest of historians of Africa as well as of European imperialism generally, perhaps it would be well to recapitulate the basic themes of the three works of "The Imperialism of Free Trade," *Africa and the Victorians,* and the chapter in the *New Cambridge Modern History* in relation to each other. In the recapitulation can be seen the development of a basic idea undergoing considerable modification over a period of nine years. "The Imperialism of Free Trade" essentially is an explanation of nineteenth-century British imperialism. Its basic theme is continuity. It makes no pretense of explaining the imperialisms of France or Germany, and it is entirely Anglocentric in outlook. It speaks of "pseudonationalist" movements in Africa. Its ideas provide the framework of *Africa and the Victorians* as a case study. "The Imperialism of Free Trade" becomes "The Spirit of Victorian Expansion" as the authors restate their case "more cautiously."[67] With the premise of continuity we are given what the economic historians refer to as "equilibrium analysis." The European balance of power is disturbed and the result is the partition of Africa. The authors are not inclined to accept the theory of economic imperialism as an explanation and do not emphasize increasing economic competition in western Africa as a major cause of the partition. In order to explain the upsetting of the equilibrium they point to the Egyptian uprising, which threatens Britain's short route to the East. Here we come to their main thesis. The consequent British occupation of Egypt in 1882 directly causes the Scramble for Africa. The wording of their argument is explicit: "By altering the European balance, the occupation of Egypt inflated the importance of trivial disputes in tropical Africa and set off a scramble." The shattering of the Anglo-French entente results in French aggressive moves especially in West Africa in compensation. Bismarck, in his own phrase, using the "Egyptian baton," joins the Scramble, essentially for traditional diplomatic reasons. All of this, they now argue, can only be understood by grasping the interaction between European and African societies. In *Africa and the Victorians,* which appeared at a time when African history came of age as a recognized academic discipline, the "pseudonationalist" movements of "The Imperialism of Free Trade" become "protonationalist" movements. The Egyptians in the north and the Boers in the south suck the British into the extremities of the continent. The overriding purpose of the British presence is the protection of their routes to the East, not economic exploitation. "They moved into Africa, not to build a new African empire, but to protect the old empire in India. ... The decisive motive behind late-Victorian strategy in Africa was to protect the all-important stakes in India and the East."[68] In the article in the *New Cambridge Modern History* the argument appears in its most extreme and aggressive form. The authors repeat the conclusion of "The Imperialism of Free Trade" that the imperialists in Africa were scraping the bottom of the barrel. The partition is described as a remarkable freak. The imperialists, including Bismarck and Ferry, felt no new impulses to imperialize, the latter now being dragged into places such as Tunisia by Muslim rebellion and the former still wielding the Egyptian baton.[69] This is history written with a vengeance. It is out for the blood of the theorists of economic imperialism. As an alternative theory it puts forward the signal hypothesis of European imperialism as a reflex to protonationalist movements not only in northern and southern Africa but now also in such places as the western Sudan and Ethiopia.[70] They see the interaction of western imperialism and indigenous polities in places such as China and India. Here is the bid of Robinson and Gallagher for an explanation of imperialism as a worldwide phenomenon.

> *The defter nationalisms of Egypt and the Levant, the 'Scholars of New Learning' in Kuang-Hsü China, the sections which merged into the continental coalition of the Indian Congress, the separatist churches of Africa—in their different ways, they all planned to re-form their personalities and regain their powers by operating in the idiom of the westerners.*[71]

In sum, imperialism becomes a powerful engine of social change. Nationalism becomes a continuation of imperialism.[72]

The argument is clarified, developed, and modified in Robinson's "Non-European Foundations." Here is the clarification:

> *Any new theory must recognise that imperialism was as much a function of its victims' collaboration or non-collaboration—of their indigenous politics, as it was of European expansion. The expansive forces generated in industrial Europe had to combine with elements within the agrarian societies of the outer world to make empire at all practicable.*[73]

Imperialism occurs when the expansive forces of the west interact with indigenous polities. There are three parts to the formula: European strategy and economics make two components, indigenous collaboration or resistance the third. Here Robinson more explicitly develops the idea of collaboration:

> *Without the voluntary or enforced cooperation of their governing elites, economic resources could not be transferred, strategic interests protected or xenophobic reaction and traditional resistance to change contained. Nor without indigenous collaboration, when the time came for it, could Europeans have conquered and ruled their non-European empires. From the outset that rule was continuously resisted; just as continuously native mediation was needed to avert resistance or hold it down.*[74]

Thus the central mechanism of imperialism is collaboration. The collaborative elements in nonwestern societies succeed or fail in integrating western and nonwestern economies. Their success leads eventually to conversion against alien rule and the ousting of the Europeans. Here the theory is modified in that it becomes more distinctly a-historical. Imperialism is best understood by use of geometrical or mechanical analogies that can be applied regardless of time or place. The element of collaboration makes the mechanism work. Imperialism is thus a formula or a static concept. As a conceptual tool it can be used to comprehend the European takeover, the period of colonial rule, decolonization, and even "neocolonialism." Robinson's concept is free from the shackles of historical causality that make *Africa and the Victorians* such an intensely fascinating work. The "excentric" theory has the advantages of the insight of social science but the disadvantage of attempting to deal with such colorful personalities as Rosebery or Goldie with a formula. In *Africa and the Victorians* the artistic brilliance of the pen portraits unique to the Victorian age is at war with the proclivity to search for an underlying principle or determining chain of events.

The Onslaught against *Africa and the Victorians*

The breadth and sweep of *Africa and the Victorians* in all its originality and complexity can best be examined by reviewing specific attacks. If critics of the book are agreed upon any one point, it is that Robinson and Gallagher overargue their case in regard to Egypt. They attempt to establish a direct, causal relationship between the British occupation in 1882 and the subsequent partition of the continent. In the vanguard against this interpretation, Jean Stengers pointed out in one of the first major commentaries on the book that commercial and political rivalry in the basin of the Congo existed independently from the Egyptian question.[75] Merely to give a precis of his essay is to present an entirely different idea of how the history of the Scramble might be written. It restores vitality to the notion of the "New Imperialism" so warmly scorned by Robinson and Gallagher. Are we to believe, Stengers asks, that the Scramble was merely a myth, that circumstances change but not the spirit of the times? Did the imperialists casually partition Africa merely because of a chain of circumstances beginning in Egypt? Not in the least. First of all the European powers scrambled not only for Africa but also for the Pacific, which geographically strains the credibility of the Egyptian argument. Furthermore the atmosphere of international relations concerning Africa had changed in a short period of time, as Stengers illustrates in a comment of Lord Salisbury: "When I left the Foreign Office in 1880, nobody thought about Africa. When I returned to it in 1885, the nations in Europe were almost quarrelling with each other as to the various portions of Africa which could obtain."[76] Who took the initiative and where? One might well suspect King Leopold in the Congo, but his earlier schemes aimed at commercial exploitation, not political sovereignty. We must look to France for the explanation, and two episodes are instructive. In 1882 De Brazza unfurled the French flag on the Congo and in 1883 France embarked on a protectorate policy on the western coast. Brazza had concluded a treaty with an African chief at Stanley Pool, an area of strategic and commercial importance because it commands the head of the navigable Congo. The French Parliament approved this treaty in the autumn of 1882 and this act began the political appropriation of central Africa. What moved the French Parliament? In a phrase, "public opinion"—a theme that runs profoundly contrary to the interpretation of Robinson and Gallagher. The Egyptian issue raised its head south of the Equator in a way not perceived in *Africa and the Victorians*. The occupation of Egypt wounded French national pride. With a sense of humiliation in Egypt, the press clamored for success in the Congo. Journalists proclaimed De Brazza a national hero defending French commerce and civilization. "National pride, national amour-propre, and chauvinism, all poured into colonial affairs with unprecedented force." In the autumn of 1882 the flames of colonial enthusiasm waxed intense for the first time in modern history. The sparks soon ignited public opinion in other countries. Even Bismarck eventually felt the heat of the public's passion for colonies. Did England remain isolated from the colonial "fire," "fever," "mania," or whatever phrase one might use to describe the phenomenon that swept Europe during the 1880s? According to Stengers, definitely not. There may have been a lag in the force with which colonial enthusiasm hit England, and British statesmen such as Salisbury may have acted primarily for defensive reasons of strategy. But the appropriation of the non-Western world fascinated even Salisbury, whose political study of African cartography fired such participants as Harry Johnston. In other words, there was an emotional dimension of the Scramble, not least to the builders of the British Empire in Africa. In Stengers' view, *Africa and the Victorians* emphasizes the slowness, the deliberation, and the indifference of British statesmen at the expense of the sense of mission or "sacred fire" motivating such men as Cecil Rhodes. The charge is fundamental. Robinson and Gallagher have failed to convey that intangible but all important element in history, the spirit of the times.

According to historians of West Africa, the general thesis of imperialism as a political phenomenon and the specific argument of Egypt setting off the Scramble founders on the complexities of economic history.[77] No one has written with greater authority on trade and commerce in West Africa than has Dr. Colin Newbury.[78] "If it is true," he wrote in the *Journal of African History,* quoting the resounding conclusion of Robinson and Gallagher, "that 'the theory of economic imperialism puts the trade before the flag, the capital before the conquest, the cart before the horse', then the theory requires modification and a reappraisal of its terms, at least in the West African context. But neither was any 'horse' goaded into the interior by a *bâton égyptien.* And until a history of West African trade and commerce has been written the question of motive at any point in the expansion of Europe in that area is still open."[79] There was no direct connection between the Egyptian issue and the partition, as he indicates by an extensive examination of both French and British documents. Robinson and Gallagher may be right in saying the trade followed the flag—with this important qualification: "But not quite all trade or all capital." And not necessarily the national flag.[80] Contradictions abound whether in the theories of economic imperialism or of Robinson and Gallagher. The fundamental argument put forward by Newbury is that the scramble for West Africa did not originate merely in political or military calculations by the strategy makers in London or Paris. Fear of rising tariff barriers played an important part.

Anglo-French trade rivalry in West Africa forms one of the main themes of John D. Hargreaves's *Prelude to the Partition of West Africa,*[81] which appeared shortly after *Africa and the Victorians.* As Ronald Hyam has pointed out in a major critical essay, the two works complement each other.[82] In straightforward and noncontroversial vein Hargreaves traces the commercial negotiations that shaped the colonial boundaries after 1885. Though he does not explicitly enter the lists with Robinson and Gallagher, he has noted the exaggeration of the Egyptian thesis and their "very British view." In his review of *Africa and the Victorians,* he made the superb observation that the detailed research at the Public Record Office produces an effect "as if *Ulysses* had been compiled from the records of the Dublin police force."[83] Hargreaves's own work, in contrast to Robinson and Gallagher's, manifests a diligent effort fully to take account of the French as well as the British side and to evaluate without preconceptions the objectives and methods of African rulers during the partition. Henri Brunschwig, who reviewed the *Prelude* in the *Journal of African History,* commented that if one took together the works of Hargreaves, Stengers, and Newbury, the consensus does not favor Robinson and Gallagher: whatever the emphasis, France, not Britain, set in motion the partition of the continent.[84] Essentially in agreement with Stengers, Brunschwig argues in his own work that deals with the subject, *L'Avènement de l'Afrique Noire,*[85] that De Brazza on the Congo with his treaty of 1882, not the British with the occupation of Egypt, sparked the chain of events of the political partition. "So much for Robinson and Gallagher!" exclaimed Professor Roland Oliver in the *Journal of African History.*[86]

Hence a controversy within a controversy. Though emphasizing the British invasion of Egypt as the direct cause of the partition of

West Africa, Robinson and Gallagher find themselves in agreement with Stengers and Brunschwig that French naval and consular initiatives in the Gulf of Guinea in the winter of 1882–83 stimulated the immediate scramble in that region.[87] Colin Newbury and A. S. Kanya-Forstner, however, have reviewed the entire question on the basis of extensive research in French archives and have challenged this view. Their article in the *Journal of African History* in 1969 is remarkable for its comprehensive grasp of the basic issues of French expansion.[88] The crucial change in French policy, they argue, did not occur in 1882 but in 1879–80. At this time Charles de Freycinet (Minister of Public Works and later Prime Minister) and Admiral Jean Jauréguiberry (Minister of Marine and Colonies) inaugurated the era of French imperialism in West Africa by making specific decisions to establish French political as well as economic claims to territory and to assume military burdens of responsibility. The result of this investigation leads the authors to adjust the themes of Robinson and Gallagher to the counterpoint of French imperialism:

> The policies of Freycinet and Jauréguiberry contained the very essence of late-nineteenth century imperialism; they were the Gallic 'doctrine of tropical African estates' enunciated fifteen years before Chamberlain came to office. And this difference in timing was vital. By 1895 the scramble for West Africa was virtually over; in 1880 it had yet to begin. Chamberlain's doctrine may have 'inspired the beginning of . . . modern administration' in Britain's African territories; its French counter-part inspired the actual process of expansion. The beginnings of British imperialism in West Africa may have been a consequence of the partition; the beginnings of French imperialism were its cause.[89]

Though it alters crucial causes and dates, this interpretation supports the thesis of continuity of Robinson and Gallagher: "the initiatives of 1882–3 were a less radical departure from previous policies than has hitherto been assumed. . . ." With a French twist it also expands the dimension of the argument. It is an ingenious analysis of "the official mind" of French imperialism. It helps immensely in clarifying the chronology of the partition. Henri Brunschwig, again acting as moderator, suggests that at least everyone can be agreed that responsibility for the Scramble rests with France. He draws the distinction between the terms "Scramble" and "Course au Clocher" (steeplechase), the latter phrase appearing in the vocabulary of politics later than the former. For the decisive dates in the *dual* Anglo-French rivalry and the French initiative, Newbury and Kanya-Forstner correctly point to the years 1879–80. In 1882 the Scramble became truly *multinational,* a steeplechase whose competitors included King Leopold and eventually Bismarck.[90]

The years 1879–82 also represent the shattering of the *dual* Anglo-French control in Egypt and the beginning of the subsequent *multinational* competition in tropical Africa. Robinson and Gallagher are undoubtedly correct in emphasizing the way in which the emergency of the Egyptian crisis loomed over the minor issues of the partition. The question is whether they correctly establish a causal relationship between the Egyptian invasion and the partition and whether they are right in their interpretation of Egyptian nationalism or "protonationalism." On the latter point the student of this controversy might do well to remember the balanced interpretation of Professor Langer:

> It would be erroneous . . . to regard the troubles which arose in Egypt in 1881 and 1882 purely as a mutinous movement of discontented officers. . . . A native press sprang up, and before long something resembling a national, constitutional party appeared on the scene. Of course, one must not look for absolute unity of purpose or for consistency in a rudimentary movement of this sort. Religious, political, and social factors were all intertwined in it, and within the group itself there were ill-concealed contradictions and antagonisms. The ecstatic partisanship of European Arabophils, like Wilfrid Scawen Blunt, harmed the movement perhaps more than it helped it, for by idealizing it these men made it rather ridiculous in the disillusioned eyes of the Westerner. . . . The movement was, in fact, directed primarily against the domination of the country by foreign interests.[91]

The interpretation of Robinson and Gallagher does not contradict Langer's, but it is much more insistent. The emphasis is different: "A recognisably modern nationalist revolution was sweeping the Nile Delta by 1882."[92] Where lies the correct balance? In Langer's view that *if one event more than another* gave impetus to British imperialism in the late nineteenth century it was the *British* occupation of Egypt? Or in the thesis of Robinson and Gallagher, that the occupation was the *decisive event* caused by *Egyptian nationalism?* Miss Agatha Ramm, as an authority probably more familiar with Gladstone's foreign policy that anyone else, and with no particular ax to grind in this controversy, has given her judgment in regard to those questions. In a full review of the collapse of the Anglo-French condominium, she examines British policy in the context of the distinct traditions of Palmerston and Gladstone and the varying French responses. Noting that in the *New Cambridge Modern History* Robinson and Gallagher call attention to national and Muslim revolt against alien and Christian rule in Tunisia[93] as well as Egypt, Miss Ramm points out that Frenchmen saw this revolt more clearly than the British, who remained more skeptical. In the historiography of the subject Robinson and Gallagher have performed a valuable service in giving greater dimension to the indigenous north African part of the problem. But essentially her own interpretation comes closer to Langer's rather than the one of Robinson and Gallagher. "The ultimate causes of the establishment and of the end of the Dual Control in Egypt lay in the foreign policies of the Great Powers. The immediate causes lay in Egypt itself."[94] In regard to the connection between the occupation of Egypt and the Scramble for Africa, Miss Ramm endorses the explanation of Robinson and Gallagher without accepting their premise of a causal relationship: "[t]he partition of Africa took place in the context of Anglo-French ill feeling. Bismarck was able to embark upon a colonial policy with a much greater degree of freedom than he would have enjoyed had the Anglo-French entente and the Anglo-French condominium in Egypt continued to exist."[95]

European Imperialisms and African Nationalisms

Historians probably have spilled more ink over Bismarck's colonial policy than any other episode of the Scramble. Perhaps because of this extensive treatment, Robinson and Gallagher treat it in the same manner as the theories of economic imperialism and give it short shrift in two pages.[96] They merely accept the conclusions of the works of diplomatic historians, including A. J. P. Taylor's *Germany's First Bid for Colonies,* which is the epitome of the diplomatic approach.[97] In 1967 Henry A. Turner delivered a scathing attack on Taylor, and, since Robinson and Gallagher accept his interpretation, on them as well.[98] Turner denounces the Taylor and Robinson-Gallagher position as an acceptance of the *Primat der Aussenpolitik,* or in other words the idea that foreign affairs governed Bismarck's actions. The Taylor and Robinson-Gallagher thesis explains within the framework of international diplomacy Bismarck's sudden conversion from a staunch opponent of colonial expansion to the founder of Germany's overseas empire. At a time when Bismarck pursued reconciliation with France, he quarreled with Britain over colonial issues such as South West Africa in which he had no real interest. France and Germany would unite together against the imperialism of Great Britain. This explanation takes account to some extent of Bismarck's exploitation of a popular issue for electioneering purposes, and his personal pique at Gladstone and Lord Granville, the Foreign Secretary.[99] But it fails to encompass the powerful economic reasons for Bismarck's abrupt change of course. Though he remained skeptical, who was to say that the colonial enthusiasts in Germany might not be right in maintaining that colonies would eventually prove to be valuable? According to Turner, "Bismarck was also not immune to the *Torschlusspanik* that was to play such an important role in the partition of the non-European world—the fear that the gate was rapidly closing and that the last chance was at hand."[100] Bismarck aimed to protect German merchants who faced rising protective tariffs abroad, and he sought to secure economic opportunities overseas at a time when the other western nations were appropriating the rest of the nonwestern world. Hans-Ulrich Wehler gives massive support to this interpretation in *Bismarck und der Imperialismus,* a landmark in the economic history of modern Europe as well as a conclusive examination of the socioeconomic and political ingredients of Bismarck's imperialism.[101] He also specifically attacks the explanation of Robinson and Gallagher. German imperialism can be seen in no other way than as the result of socioeconomic forces within Europe and by no means as a response to indigenous nationalist movements abroad. Robinson and Gallagher, Wehler argues, uncritically take over the "simplistic theory" of Taylor because it suits their purpose.[102] Bismarck aimed to support Germany's foreign trade in pragmatic style; he tried to unite the German people by picking up the theme of colonial enthusiasm and Anglophobism; and he attempted to defend the traditional social structures of the Prussian state by diverting abroad the forces of social imperialism. All of this complex explanation of Bismarck's imperialism must be seen within the context of European history. So far as Bismarck is concerned, African nationalism as a causal factor in European imperialism did not exist.

In the view of Jean Stengers, African nationalism played no part in the imperialism of King Leopold and the creation of the Congo Free State. Probably the Congo State more than any other example can be put forward as a case in which the imperialists partitioned Africa in total disregard of the wishes or influences of the indigenous inhabitants.

> The Congo is the archetype of a political entity brought into being on African soil completely by the will of a European. One would seek in vain for any African substructure, any autochthonous base for this state as it appeared toward the end of the nineteenth century. It had nothing in common—save the name—with the Congo of former times, the Congo that had two or three centuries earlier been an important African kingdom. Its origins are to be found entirely in the will of one man—Leopold II of Belgium.

In 1884–5 Leopold traced its boundaries firmly on the map of Africa. These extended to the very heart of the Black Continent and included regions largely unexplored up to that time. These borders were recognized by the powers and thus the Congo was born.[103]

King Leopold was motivated by greed, economic and territorial. He dreamed of an empire on the Nile as well as on the Congo. His imagination knew no bounds. He combined the idealism of a Rhodes with the business acumen of a Rockefeller. He was a patriotic imperialist, his purpose the exploitation of the Congo for the embellishment and glory of Belgium. So idiosyncratic and indeed unique was King Leopold's blend of imperialism that it defies classification by theory.[104] Nor can King Leopold's imperialism in any way be regarded as a response to local conditions in Africa, protonationalistic or other. "All the features peculiar to the Free State . . . derived their origin from the person of its sovereign. The influence of the African environment was negligible, that of the metropolitan milieu scarcely less so."[105]

Henri Brunschwig makes the same point of the imperialists' disregard of African conditions by beginning *Le Partage d'Afrique Noire* with reference to the disposal of Poland, Finland and the Baltic states by Hitler and Stalin in 1939.[106] Blatant violation of Europe's own political and national boundaries puts into perspective the lack of scruple in drawing boundaries in black Africa. It is no doubt true that Africans influenced the course of the partition more than has been commonly recognized.[107] But most critics would argue that to shift the emphasis and impetus of nationalism from Europe to Africa is to produce a distortion of history. It is to caricature a fundamental truth of the modern expansion of Europe. European imperialism originated in Europe. No one is more insistent about the ultimate causes of French nationalism and imperialism than is Brunschwig: Galvanized by the defeat of 1871, "the French people as a whole were not interested in colonization for its own sake but only in relation to everyone's major preoccupation—the German menace."[108]

While the historians of European imperialism have criticized Robinson and Gallagher for distorting the non-European dimension of the nationalist theme, the Africanists have attacked them for basically misinterpreting early nationalist or resistance movements. T. O. Ranger has analyzed the subject in an essay which Robinson and Gallagher themselves regard as among the most stimulating of the commentaries by their critics.[109] Ranger recapitulates the argument as it is especially developed in "The Partition of Africa." Nationalism is a continuation of imperialism; but primary resistance movements were essentially backward-looking and traditional. Recalcitrance represented the reactionary element of tribal life. In Robinson and Gallagher's own words resistance movements were "romantic reactionary struggles against the facts, the passionate protest of societies which were shocked by a new age of change and would not be comforted." In his full-scale critique of this view, Ranger first points out that recent studies by other scholars, including Thomas Hodgkin, would greatly qualify this interpretation in West Africa. There was an immediate significance of the resistance for later nationalist movements by, for example, not only the memory of the earlier struggles but also the surviving structure of the anti-European movements. Ranger goes on to indicate at length the ways in which Robinson and Gallagher should be challenged in central and eastern Africa:

> [H]aving made this point of the continuing significance of memories of defeat, it is at once necessary to go on to say that not all resistances were doomed to total failure and crushing suppression. Some of them preserved liberties, wrung concessions or preserved pride. In so doing they made their own very important contributions to the creation of the environment in which later politics developed.[110]

The Hehe in German East Africa, for example, did not twist the colonial situation particularly to their advantage, but they certainly maintained their pride. Resistance movements contributed to the environment of later, modern nationalist politics. Thus Robinson and Gallagher's contrast between the backward-looking resistance movements and forward-looking "defter nationalisms" is overdrawn. Nevertheless Ranger has obviously found the concept extraordinarily useful in formulating his own basic ideas on the subject even though he arrives at almost the opposite conclusion: Resistance movements, even in the form of witchcraft, were "often revolutionary in method and in purpose and sought to transcend tribal limitations."[111]

One could argue that the theme of nationalism also goes askew in relation to the major "protonationalist" movements of *Africa and the Victorians*. Even if one grants the attractiveness of the argument of Egyptian provocation in the north, Afrikaner nationalism as the catalyst of British imperialism is open to doubt. According to Professor Leonard Thompson, Afrikaner national consciousness did not exist before the 1870s. British intervention created the combination of nationalistic fear and pride—not vice versa.[112] This view is upheld by one of the leading Afrikaner historians of the subject, F. A. van

Jaarsveld. British imperialism stimulated Afrikaner nationalism.[113] In the judgment of C. F. Goodfellow, whose book is an extensive study of South Africa in the 1870s, British policy "arose from no unforeseen incident, and was in reaction against no nationalist challenge." Again, the reverse of the thesis of Robinson and Gallagher is true: "So far as the inter-relationship between British imperialism and Afrikaner nationalism is concerned, it seems much more plausible to say that the nationalism of the 1880s and later was in reaction against the impact of British imperialism during the 1870s."[114] The same conclusion is reached by D. M. Schreuder, whose *Gladstone and Kruger* aims in part at testing the idea of Afrikaner nationalism as a stimulus of British imperialism. He concludes that Afrikaner unity was no more than a mirage: "What Professor Gallagher and Dr. Robinson have taken as a major theme of their *Africa and the Victorians* . . . was no more than a momentary aberration in Afrikaner behaviour in the nineteenth century."[115] In fact one can conclude in regard to nationalism in Schreuder's words. He writes about Victorians and Afrikaners, but the same might be said of Robinson and Gallagher: "The historian is left with a supreme irony." Upon careful examination, the general themes of *Africa and the Victorians* still flash brilliantly, but the more the specific cases are studied the more luminous appear the older and more traditional accounts of the expansion of Europe.

The Achievement of Robinson and Gallagher

Let it be said at once and finally that whatever reservations one might have about the themes of *Africa and the Victorians* they do not detract from the accomplishment of Robinson and Gallagher. Anyone who writes about imperialism must take account of their work. *Africa and the Victorians* is a classic. Like most masterpieces, it bears the stamp of the age in which it was written. No one would want to exaggerate the extent to which historians are prisoners of their eras, but perhaps it is helpful in explaining the more exuberant inspirations of Robinson and Gallagher to remember that "The Imperialism of Free Trade" was written during the time of Marshall Aid and that the chapter on the British occupation of Egypt was drafted during Nasser's nationalization of the canal and the Suez crisis of 1956.[116] Ronald Robinson's more sober reassessment of the occupation and its consequences is a modification but by no means a repudiation: The breakdown of collaborative indirect rule was the "imperative" for the British invasion "and incidentally for much of the subsequent rivalry impelling the partition of Africa."[117] The element of collaboration is the vital key.[118] The work of Robinson and Gallagher has made it clear—above all—that indigenous collaboration and recalcitrance helped to shape European penetration into some non-Western societies, that collaboration guided the direction and form of colonial control, and, by extension, that the inversion of collaboration into noncooperation determined in large part the process of decolonization. Their insights can be applied to various regions and different eras.[119] Whatever the merit of the critics' objections, Robinson and Gallagher have provided an intellectual framework in which an array of difficult problems can fruitfully be discussed. Their work carries the study of "imperialism" a long way forward.

Unresolved Problems: Imperialism and War. Imperialism in Worldwide Perspective. The Work of Robinson and Gallagher as Social Science or History as Art?

The unresolved problems can be defined by comment on Robinson and Gallagher's method. If there is paradox in such central concepts as "Imperialism of Free Trade," considerable sophistication also characterizes their handling of the general themes of economic motives during the Scramble and imperialism as a cause of war. Though *Africa and the Victorians* can be read as a polemic against the theorists of economic imperialism, nowhere do Robinson and Gallagher deny the economic essence of empire. In the accounts of the Fashoda crisis,[120] and the origins of the Boer War,[121] the reader can rightly draw the general conclusion that the continental powers subordinated their colonial activity to European concerns. Colonial expansion was no more than a marginal activity for France and Germany and never of any substantial economic importance. This truth holds true as well for the British, for whom imperialism in Africa was clearly more than a fringe activity yet always subordinate to Britain's noncolonial role. Robinson and Gallagher do not emphasize the poisoning of international relations by internecine rivalry in Africa, and it is beyond their scope to examine the extent to which the emotions generated by the Boer War contributed to the atmosphere of the decade before the war. We will not know the answers to such problems until thorough studies are made of the changing climate of opinion. To what extent did contemporaries alter their views about the problems and consequences of colonial expansion as a result of the Boer War? Robinson and Gallagher probably would minimize the significance of such an investigation, just as Jean Stengers would affirm its fundamental importance. The split is between those who wish to stress the continuity of historical experience and those who emphasize the changing perceptions of fundamental historical problems. There can be no ultimate resolution of the issue of continuity—one of the major differences, in other words, between Robinson and Gallagher and some of their critics—because it hinges on approach and temperament as well as the answers sought.

The Robinson and Gallagher controversy provides insight into the universality of the problems of imperialism even in such areas as Japanese expansion in the Far East,[122] while it also indicates that the debate about continuity is by no means restricted to British imperialism. The controversy about American expansion has similarities. William Appleman Williams, Walter La Feber, and Thomas McCormick emphasize the conscious pursuit of informal empire as a constant theme in American history,[123] while Ernest May espouses an analogous interpretation to Stengers's explanation of imperialism as a phenomenon most usefully associated with a particular era.[124] On the one hand, imperialism can be seen as an ever-present, all-pervasive and perhaps even unconscious urge for empire. Perhaps a universal formula or satisfactory theory of imperialism may never be found, but the search is worthwhile. On the other hand, some historians are as much interested in the differences as the similarities of historical eras and are more concerned to paint the last two decades of the nineteenth century as possessing unique characteristics of an age which will be remembered for its exuberant enthusiasm for colonies, the racial arrogance of the Europeans, and the belief that Europeans were somehow divinely destined to rule the world. The controversy is at least in part a collision between those with the approach and temperaments of social scientists who believe in the search for universal explanations or theory and historians who believe that history is best considered an art and not a science. In the works of Robinson and Gallagher there are elements of both.

NOTES

[1]John Gallagher and Ronald Robinson, "The Imperialism of Free Trade," *Economic History Review,* Second Series, VI, 1 (1953), pp. 1–15; Ronald Robinson and John Gallagher with Alice Denny [Mrs. Robinson], *Africa and the Victorians: the Official Mind of Imperialism* (London, 1961) (for the transition between "The Imperialism of Free Trade" and the book, see "Imperial Problems in British Politics" by Ronald Robinson in *Cambridge History of the British Empire,* III, pp. 127–80); R. E. Robinson and J. Gallagher, "The Partition of Africa," in *New Cambridge Modern History,* XI, chapter 22; Ronald Robinson, "Non-European Foundations of European Imperialism: Sketch for a Theory of Collaboration," in eds. E. R. J. Owen and R. B. Sutcliffe, *Studies in the Theory of Imperialism* (London, 1972), chapter 5.

[2]Eric Stokes, "Imperialism and the Scramble for Africa: The New View," a pamphlet published by the Historical Association of Rhodesia and Nyasaland (Local Series 10, 1963); see by the same author also especially "Late Nineteenth-Century Colonial Expansion and the Attack on the Theory of Economic Imperialism: A Case of Mistaken Identity?" *Historical Journal,* XII, 2 (1969), pp. 285–301.

[3]William L. Langer, *The Diplomacy of Imperialism* (New York, 1956 edn.), pp. 67 and 96.

[4]"Imperialism of Free Trade," pp. 2–3. For an interesting review of the historiographical debate about the Free Trade era, see C. C. Eldridge, *England's Mission: The Imperial Idea in the Age of Gladstone and Disraeli, 1868–1880* (University of North Carolina Press, 1973). In general, Eldridge's book gives support to the Robinson and Gallagher thesis that events in the overseas world caused a defensive reaction and brought about a transformation of attitude toward empire. For another valuable recent survey, see B. A. Knox, "Reconsidering Mid-Victorian Imperialism," *Journal of Imperial and Commonwealth History,* I, 2 (January 1973). See also D. A. Low, *Lion Rampant* (London, 1973) and A. G. L. Shaw, ed., *Great Britain and the Colonies, 1815–1865* (London, 1970). One other recent publication also merits special com-

ment in relation to Robinson and Gallagher's effort to reverse the traditional ethnocentric vision of the partition of Africa. G. N. Uzoigwe, in an account significant in his own view as the first attempt by an African to provide a comprehensive analysis of the Scramble, describes the approach of Robinson and Gallagher as only "a more serious way of reasserting Seeley's thesis that Britain acquired its empire in a state of absentmindedness." *Britain and the Conquest of Africa* (University of Michigan Press, 1974), p. 24.

[5]Geoffrey Barraclough, *An Introduction to Contemporary History* (Penguin, 1967 edn.), pp. 56–67.

[6]"The Partition of Africa," p. 594.

[7]For example, here is a classic statement of Europe's imperialism in Africa being no more than a "safety valve" of Europe's energies and explosive troubles: "All the Great Powers except Austria-Hungary found a safe channel for their exuberance outside Europe. They stumbled on this solution by chance, without foresight." A. J. P. Taylor, *The Struggle for Mastery in Europe* (Oxford, 1954), p. 256. Mr. Taylor has remained singularly consistent in his argument that "the age of imperialism" merely postponed the final struggle for mastery of Europe. See his comment below, "The Meanings of Imperialism."

[8]See Stokes, "Late Nineteenth-Century Colonial Expansion," especially pp. 286–87 for the other principal assumptions that Stokes believes the authors have successfully challenged. Like Robinson and Gallagher's interpretation of Victorian statesmen, there may be a subjective element of what Stokes thinks they *should* have attacked.

[9]*Ibid.* "[I]t was first and foremost a political phenomenon. . . ." For clear objections to the political interpretation of Robinson and Gallagher in favor of one of economic factors being important but not determinative, see W. J. Mommsen, "Nationale und ökonomische Faktoren im britischen Imperialismus vor 1914," *Historische Zeitschrift*, 206, 3 (1968). For another German commentary especially valuable for the perspective on continuity, Karl Rohe, "Ursachen und Bedingungen des modernen britischen Imperialismus vor 1914," in Wolfgang J. Mommsen, ed., *Der moderne Imperialismus* (Stuttgart, 1971).

[10]See D. K. Fieldhouse, " 'Imperialism': An Historiographical Revision," *Economic History Review*, Second Series, XIV, 2 (1961); see also Harvey Mitchell, "Hobson Revisited," *Journal of the History of Ideas*, XXVI, 3 (July–Sept. 1965); Bernard Porter, *Critics of Empire: British Radical Attitudes to Colonialism in Africa 1895–1914* (London, 1968); and Hugh Stretton, *The Political Sciences* (London, 1969), chapter 4.

[11]Stokes, "Late Nineteenth-Century Colonial Expansion," p. 289.

[12]*Ibid.,* p. 292–93.

[13]*Ibid.,* p. 301.

[14]*Africa and the Victorians*, p. 15, n. 1. For a Marxist critique of Robinson and Gallagher, see Tom Kemp, *Theories of Imperialism* (London, 1967), p. 154. Since so many critics have commented on the theories of economic imperialism being compressed into a single note, perhaps it is of interest to

note that in the original manuscript the authors had devoted an entire chapter exposing what they believe to be the Eurocentric and false assumptions of existing theories of imperialism. They argued that these theories are not based on empirical historical study but are theories about European societies. The publishers, however, insisted on reducing the manuscript by one third. The chapter was reduced to a note. Robinson and Gallagher did this on grounds that it was more important to present the historical evidence than to debate, in their view, already discredited theories. I am indebted to Professor Robinson for information on this point.

[15]V. G. Kiernan, "Farewells to Empire," *The Socialist Register, 1964* (New York, 1964), pp. 259–79.

[16]*Ibid.,* p. 265. For similar comment see Christopher Fyfe in *Irish Historical Studies,* XIII (40) March 1962, pp. 93–94. In Fyfe's view, *Africa and the Victorians* "smells of the Public Record Office (a nice but limited smell), not at all of Africa."

[17]Kiernan, "Farewells to Empire," p. 269.

[18]*Ibid.,* p. 270.

[19]*Ibid.,* p. 266.

[20]*Ibid.,* pp. 267–68.

[21]*Ibid.,* p. 270. In this regard Tom Kemp comments: "However useful the new information available from such a work, no real analytical advance has been made, nor has the 'theory' of imperialism been refuted. In fact, as far as these authors are concerned, the question remains largely open because they do see African expansion as being a direct result of an already existing imperialist interest in India. Clearly, any full analysis of British imperialism in this period would have to take into account India, what these authors have called the 'informal empire', as well as the newly-annexed territories which, if of little or no economic importance at the time, subsequently were economically appraised and became privileged markets and investment fields for British capitalism." Kemp, *Theories of Imperialism,* p. 154. For Robinson and Gallagher's assessment of the importance of India, see *Africa and the Victorians,* pp. 10–13.

[22]George Shepperson and Thomas Price, *Independent African* (Edinburgh, 1958).

[23]"Africa, the Victorians and Imperialism," *Revue Belge de Philologie et d'Histoire,* XL, 4 (1962).

[24]Cambridge, 1950. For another major critical essay that also stresses the antecedents of Robinson and Gallagher's arguments, see A. P. Thornton, "The Partition of Africa," in *For the File on Empire* (London, 1968). Thornton identifies the assumptions of Robinson and Gallagher with those of J. S. Keltie, *The Partition of Africa* (London, 1895).

[25]Hannah Arendt, *Origins of Totalitarianism* (London, 1958 edn.); Karl W. Deutsch, *Nationalism and Social Communication* (New York, 1953).

[26]*English Historical Review,* LXXVIII (April 1963), pp. 345–47.

[27]*Ibid.*

[28]This is the title of a conference held at the Centre of African Studies,

University of Edinburgh, in November 1967 for the purpose, in Shepperson's words, to "provide a group of recent case studies in certain aspects of the European partition of Africa, which may provide material for those historians and sociologists who believe theory to be possible." The proceedings of the conference make fascinating reading on various aspects of imperialism, but the conference did not entirely succeed in moving toward a general theory. In Professor John Hargreaves' summing up: "I fear some of our members may have been disappointed to find us apparently lost in the jungle of historical particulars." *The Theory of Imperialism and the European Partition of Africa* (Centre of African Studies, University of Edinburgh, 1967). By contrast, *Studies in the Theory of Imperialism* (cited note one) organizes the theme of discussion around Marxist interpretations of imperialism. It is a stimulating debate.

²⁹See D. K. Fieldhouse, ed., *The Theory of Capitalist Imperialism* (London, 1967); *Economics and Empire* (Cornell University Press, 1973).

³⁰*Economic History Review,* Second Series, XIV, 3 (April 1962), pp. 574–76. In *Africa and the Victorians,* pp. 20–21, Robinson and Gallagher acknowledge Schumpeter's writings as brilliant. Following his analysis they write: "The aristocrat by right, the official by *expertise,* both felt socially superior and functionally detached from those who pushed trade and built empires. . . . England's rulers had inherited not only a world empire but the experience gained in bringing it together, and the assumptions and prejudices accumulated from past successes and failures inevitably influenced their behaviour in the partition." For criticism of this interpretation, see especially Kiernan, "Farewells to Empire," p. 265: "A . . . fallacy is the treatment of the governing class as a separate caste of mandarins, aloof from the vulgar preoccupations of mere businessmen and absorbed in their 'high calling'. . . . what the book fails to reckon with, just as it turns a blind eye to the transformation of capitalism in that epoch, was the development of a consolidated plutocracy in Britain and in Europe: a social stratum within which Scottish earls and Prussian junkers married Jewish heiresses, and politicians collected directorships in the City, and old-fashioned notions of gentility survived with less and less distinct meaning. . . . Without reference to this process of fusion at the top of society, this mixing of the cream, the new imperialism cannot be comprehended." For another observation on the influence of Schumpeter on Robinson and Gallagher, see George Lichtheim, *Imperialism* (New York, 1971), p. 97, n. 1, where he remarks that "The Imperialism of Free Trade" is "an attempt to show that the partition of the globe among rival powers after 1880 had no rational economic motivation."

³¹Fieldhouse in the *Economic History Review, ibid.*

³²In this connection see also John S. Galbraith, "The 'Turbulent Frontier' as a Factor in British Expansion," *Comparative Studies in Society and History,* II, 2 (January 1960); and W. David McIntyre, *The Imperial Frontier in the Tropics, 1865–75* (London, 1967).

³³Fieldhouse, *Theory of Capitalist Imperialism,* p. 193. See below, "Suggestions for Further Reading," for comment on Fieldhouse's latest

work, *Economics and Empire,* in which he has adopted an almost entirely peripheral interpretation.

[34]As Ronald Robinson is known in some circles. See J. M. Lee, *Colonial Development and Good Government* (Oxford, 1969), p. 102.

[35]Robinson, "Non-European Foundations of European Imperialism," pp. 139–40. The circle analogy is also used by John Fage in his essay in eds. Prosser Gifford and Wm. Roger Louis, *Britain and Germany in Africa: Imperial Rivalry and Colonial Rule* (Yale University Press, 1967). At the two Yale conferences which produced this and the companion volume, *France and Britain in Africa: Imperial Rivalry and Colonial Rule* (Yale University Press, 1971), the ideas of Robinson and Gallagher were discussed from time to time in regard to both imperial history and African history. Prosser Gifford draws the conclusion: "One important aspect of *Africa and the Victorians* is that the framework for imperial thought was established in the Cabinet and Parliament, often by reference to modes of thought developed in dealing with problems in Ireland or India that had little to do with Africa—or by reference to domestic political needs and alliances. This point is crucial because it explains why *British* interests shaped British imperialism. There were indeed national, rather than European, responses to imperial situations. To concentrate upon African situations as Robinson and Gallagher do when they speak of collaboration is equally valid in explaining the final result, but the force of the original book is that it points to the origins of assumptions in the imperial mind."

[36]Oxford, 1968. For an analysis of the book in relation to the Robinson and Gallagher thesis, see Zara Steiner in the *Historical Journal,* XIII, 3 (1970), pp. 545–52.

[37]Platt, *Finance, Trade, and Politics,* pp. 256–59.

[38]*Ibid.,* p. 260.

[39]Robinson and Gallagher attribute the phrase "informal empire" to C. R. Fay, but it is no exaggeration to say that it now has passed into the vocabulary of imperial history as a Robinsonian and Gallagherian concept. For discussion of early usage of the phrase, Robin W. Winks, "Toward a Theory on Decolonizing an Informal Empire," a paper presented at the meeting of the American Historical Association in December 1973.

[40]"Imperialism of Free Trade," p. 13. The argument continues that in Africa the imperialists scraped "the bottom of the barrel." On this point David Landes has made an astute observation: "While accepting this point about the persistence and indeed primacy of the economic pressures toward empire, especially informal empire, in nineteenth-century Britain, I would dissent from this interpretation on a ground . . . that it will account for only a part —an important but nevertheless insufficient part—of the facts. In particular, it will not account for a major historical phenomenon, the occupation of large areas of the world for noneconomic reasons. The correct observation that Africa was 'the bottom of the [imperialist] barrel,' far from disposing of the significance of this occupation, only heightens it." David S. Landes, "Some Thoughts on the Nature of Economic Imperialism," *Journal of Economic*

History, XXI, 4 (1961). Landes's theory of imperialism perhaps can best be conveyed by the phrase "dynamic equilibrium model," by which he means that the expansion of empire, whether direct or indirect, formal or informal, into unprofitable as well as profitable areas, is inherent in the nature of imperialism as a response to disparity of power.

[41]D. C. M. Platt, "British Policy during the 'New Imperialism,' " *Past and Present*, 39 (April 1968), pp. 134–38. The article is mainly an attack on Fieldhouse, who along with Robinson and Gallagher also stresses continuity rather than change. See Fieldhouse's "Historiographical Revision." For further support of the interpretation of continuity, see Bernard Semmel, *The Rise of Free Trade Imperialism* (Cambridge, 1970). "From the standpoint of ideology, . . . from the perspective of theory and policy no less than from that of activities, it is possible to see continuity, rather than an interlude of anti-imperialism" (p. 4). Within the context of his earlier work, *Imperialism and Social Reform* (London, 1960), Semmel offered this criticism of "The Imperialism of Free Trade": "It tends too much to regard imperialism as all of one piece with the different imperialisms as responses to different conditions, one succeeding the other in almost mechanical fashion . . ." (p. 133). Semmel's contribution to the debate about the imperialism of free trade has been summed up by D. R. Sardesai as providing "a predominantly economic-oriented theoretical cushioning to the Robinson-Gallagher argument . . ." (*American Historical Review*, 77, 2, April 1972, p. 514).

[42]D. C. M. Platt, "The Imperialism of Free Trade: Some Reservations," *Economic History Review*, Second Series, XXI, 2 (August 1968), p. 305.

[43]*Finance, Trade, and Politics*, p. 361.

[44]D. C. M. Platt, "Further Objections to an 'Imperialism of Free Trade,' 1830–60," *Economic History Review*, Second Series, XXVI, 1 (February 1973), p. 87.

[45]One might argue that the difficulty is partly semantic, that Platt and Robinson and Gallagher are talking about two different things. To some extent this is true. Platt seeks to explain the differences between mid and late Victorian expansion, while Robinson and Gallagher seek to explain the similarities of the two eras by the concept of imperialism as a function, but not a necessary function, of an expanding economy, and, as the concept is elaborated in the "excentric theory," as the interaction between the expansive forces of the West and the collaborative elements of non-Western societies at no particular time. Platt is also clearly interested in establishing the purpose of British policy at given times, while Robinson and Gallagher are as much concerned with the reality of imperialism as they are with varying questions of motive. The ambiguity or ingenuity of the phrase "Imperialism of Free Trade" can be blamed for its share of semantic confusion. But the area of controversy is real enough. Platt emphasizes that the two eras distinctly differed; Robinson and Gallagher speak of the "so called New Imperialism." There are also true differences about the meaning of "informal" that go beyond semantics. See Steiner's review article cited in note 36.

⁴⁶Oliver MacDonagh, "The Anti-Imperialism of Free Trade," *Economic History Review*, Second Series, XIV, 3 (April 1962), pp. 489–501.

⁴⁷*Ibid.*, p. 489, n. 3.

⁴⁸*Ibid.*, p. 490.

⁴⁹See, in this connection, John S. Galbraith, "Myths of the 'Little England' Era," *American Historical Review*, LXVII, 1 (October 1961).

⁵⁰See however R. J. Moore, "Imperialism and 'Free Trade' Policy in India, 1853–4," *Economic History Review*, Second Series, XVII, 1 (August 1964), critical of MacDonagh. For the theory in regard to India see also especially Peter Harnetty, *Imperialism and Free Trade: Lancashire and India in the Mid-Nineteenth Century* (University of British Columbia Press, 1972), which uses the idea as a "conceptual tool." The implicit rejoinder of Robinson and Gallagher to MacDonagh's line of argument can be found particularly in Robinson's expansion of the theory, that the mechanism of collaboration operates at various times in various regions, not necessarily in fixed historical eras or in regard to individuals, in "Non-European Foundations of European Imperialism." Even within the context of the 1953 essay it could be argued that MacDonagh has not taken all of the argument fully into account. When he speaks of the inclusion of the United States in the informal empire as the *reductio ad absurdum* of their logic, it could be maintained that this is precisely what Robinson and Gallagher have in mind.

⁵¹W. M. Mathew, "The Imperialism of Free Trade: Peru, 1820–70," *Economic History Review*, Second Series, XXI, 3 (December 1968).

⁵²*Ibid.*, p. 574.

⁵³*Ibid.*, p. 577.

⁵⁴Again, as in the case of the MacDonagh article, the implicit retort is that imperialism is not necessarily a function of economic expansion. See "Imperialism of Free Trade," p. 6.

⁵⁵This is not to deny the value of, for example, the chapter on "Moral Suasion in Guinea and Zanzibar." It is rather to say that in *Africa and the Victorians* Robinson and Gallagher are more interested in explaining why British statesmen intervened so infrequently instead of following the lead of the humanitarians. "[A]s the ambitious schemes of the humanitarians broke one by one against the facts of Africa, statesmen became more and more hard-headed. They saw clearly that no concrete national interest would be served by serious state intervention in tropical Africa." *Africa and the Victorians*, p. 27. Compare with J. Gallagher, "Fowell Buxton and the New African Policy, 1838–1842," *Cambridge Historical Journal*, X (1950), p. 58, where the emphasis is on "the great political force which the humanitarians could employ." The conclusion is of fundamental importance in understanding the sporadic influence of the humanitarians on governmental policy: "Granted a weak Government and a stirring cause, they could for a time bend colonial policy away from its general pattern, and could force politicians who thought West Africa not worth the bones of one British Grenadier, to risk far more than that."

[56]H. S. Ferns, *Britain and Argentina in the Nineteenth Century* (Oxford, 1960), p. 487. By the same author, *Argentina* (New York, 1969); and *The Argentine Republic* (New York, 1973).

[57]Ferns, *Britain and Argentina,* p. 489.

[58]H. S. Ferns, "Britain's Informal Empire in Argentina, 1806–1914," *Past and Present,* 4 (November 1953), p. 63.

[59]Peter Winn, "Uruguay and British Economic Expansion, 1880–1893," (Cambridge University Ph.D. Thesis, 1972); Richard Graham, *Britain and the Onset of Modernization in Brazil, 1850–1914* (Cambridge, 1968).

[60]Richard Graham, "Sepoys and Imperialists: Techniques of British Power In Nineteenth-Century Brazil," *Inter-American Economic Affairs,* 23, 2 (Autumn, 1969), pp. 23–37.

[61]*Ibid.,* p. 24.

[62]A. G. Hopkins, "Economic Imperialism in West Africa: Lagos, 1880–92," *Economic History Review,* XXI, 3 (December 1968).

[63]*Ibid.,* pp. 583–84.

[64]A. F. A. Ajayi and R. A. Austen, "Hopkins on Economic Imperialism in West Africa," *Economic History Review,* Second Series, XXV, 2 (May 1972), pp. 303–06; and A. G. Hopkins, "Economic Imperialism in West Africa: a Rejoinder," *ibid.,* pp. 307–12. For Austen's views on Robinson and Gallagher within the context of African economic history, see Ralph A. Austen, "Economic History," *African Studies Review,* XIV, 3 (December 1971).

[65]*Journal of African History,* II (1961), p. 158.

[66]Hopkins, "Economic Imperialism in West Africa," p. 606; for Hopkins' enlarged analysis, *An Economic History of West Africa* (Longman and Columbia University Press, 1973). The interpretation in the book has much in common with Robinson's "Non-European Foundations of European Imperialism."

[67]W. L. Burn, *History,* XLVIII, 163 (June 1963), p. 250.

[68]*Africa and the Victorians,* p. 464.

[69]"The Partition of Africa," pp. 595 and 604.

[70]*Ibid.,* pp. 609–10 and p. 626. For important critical assessment of the theory in regard to the Western Sudan, see A. S. Kanya-Forstner, *The Conquest of the Western Sudan: A Study in French Military Imperialism* (Cambridge, 1969), especially pp. 268–69.

[71]"The Partition of Africa," p. 640.

[72]On the imperialism-nationalism theme, see especially Anil Seal, *The Emergence of Indian Nationalism* (Cambridge, 1968), chapter 8.

[73]"Non-European Foundations of European Imperialism," p. 118.

[74]*Ibid.,* p. 120. The word "collaboration" is not, of course, used in a pejorative sense. "It is as false to interpret the 'collaborating class' as a dependent compradore 'quisling' element as it is to suppose . . . that it hoisted itself into the saddle and rose the blinkered imperial war horse as it chose." Eric Stokes, "Traditional Resistance Movements and Afro-Asian Nationalism: the Context of the 1857 Mutiny Rebellion in India," *Past and Present,* 48 (August 1970), p. 102. For an example of work done in the field of nationalism, see

T. O. Ranger, "African Reactions to the Imposition of Colonial Rule in East and Central Africa," in eds. L. H. Gann and Peter Duignan, *Colonialism in Africa*, I (Cambridge, 1969). Stokes discusses the "populist" conception of Ranger in contrast to the "elitist" conception of Robinson and Gallagher in "Traditional Resistance Movements and Afro-Asian Nationalism." For a list of relevant articles see the notes in Robinson, "Non-European Foundations of European Imperialism."

[75]Jean Stengers, "L'Impérialisme Colonial de la Fin du XIXe Siècle," *Journal of African History*, III, 3 (1962).

[76]*Ibid.*, p. 471.

[77]See for example John E. Flint, "Nigeria: the Colonial Experience," in *Colonialism in Africa*, I, pp. 224–25, n. 1: The view of "territorial partition of Africa as a 'repercussion' of the British occupation of Egypt in 1882 . . . would not be acceptable to most scholars who have worked in the West African documents in detail; they would regard it as an over-simplification." Flint has developed this line of criticism into a major attack in the Festschrift for Gerald Graham, where he attempts "to show that an almost exactly opposite thesis can provide a more acceptable explanation for Britain's West African role in the partition; that the British occupation of Egypt in 1882 was not a basic consideration of British strategy in West Africa during partition; that far from neglecting her role in West Africa, or conceding claims there in return for Nile security, British decisions in West Africa were based solidly on considerations of commercial advantage; and that the territorial expansion of Britain in West Africa may be regarded as a classic case study of commercial imperialism." John E. Flint, "Britain and the Partition of West Africa," in *Perspectives of Empire*, eds. John E. Flint and Glyndwr Williams (London, 1973).

[78]See for example Colin W. Newbury, "Trade and Authority in West Africa from 1850 to 1880," in *Colonialism in Africa*, I.

[79]Newbury, "Victorians, Republicans, and the Partition of West Africa," *Journal of African History*, III, 3 (1962), p. 501.

[80]Newbury, "The Tariff Factor in Anglo-French West African Partition," in eds. Prosser Gifford and Wm. Roger Louis, *France and Britain in Africa* (Yale University Press, 1971), p. 221.

[81]London, 1963.

[82]Ronald Hyam, "The Partition of Africa," *Historical Journal*, 7, 1 (1964).

[83]John D. Hargreaves, "British and French Imperialism in West Africa, 1885–1898," in *France and Britain in Africa*, p. 276, n. 42; his review of *Africa and the Victorians* is "Victorians in Africa," *Victorian Studies*, VI (1962/63), pp. 75–80.

[84]Henri Brunschwig, "Les Origines du Partage de l'Afrique Occidentale," *Journal of African History*, V, 1 (1964), pp. 121–25.

[85]Paris, 1963.

[86]*Journal of African History*, V, 1 (1964), p. 134. Oliver's review of *Africa and the Victorians* is in the *Observer* of 27 August 1961. Here he makes the point, among others, that Robinson and Gallagher's preoccupation with strategy has led them to misinterpret the Scramble in East Africa. "The strategic

importance of Kenya and Uganda was a secondary discovery, made only when it was known that the chartered company was failing. It was an excuse to hold on rather than an incentive to go in."

[87] *Africa and the Victorians*, p. 166.

[88]C.W. Newbury and A. S. Kanya-Forstner, "French Policy and the Origins of the Scramble for West Africa," *Journal of African History*, X, 2 (1969), pp. 253–76.

[89]*Ibid.*, 275.

[90]Henri Brunschwig, " 'Scramble' et 'Course au Clocher,' " *Journal of African History*, XII, 1 (1971), pp. 139–41; *Le Partage de l'Afrique Noire* (Paris 1971), pp. 153–56.

[91]William L. Langer, *European Alliances and Alignments* (New York, 1956 edn.), pp. 262–64. It should be noted that Langer himself found the arguments of *Africa and the Victorians* persuasive. He wrote in 1962: "A new analysis of the partition of Africa contends convincingly that Britain, concerned by the disturbance of the European balance of power by the German victories of 1870–1871, was driven primarily by concern for its communications with India to assume control of Egypt, and that this move in turn had such repercussions on international relations as to precipitate the 'scramble for Africa.' " *William L. Langer, "Farewell to Empire," Foreign Affairs*, 41, 1 (October, 1962).

[92]"The Partition of Africa," p. 597.

[93]For the Tunisian question in relation to the Egyptian, see Jean Ganiage, "France, England, and the Tunisian Affair," in *France and Britain in Africa;* and *Les origines du protectorat français en Tunisie, 1861–1881* (Paris, 1959).

[94]Agatha Ramm, "Great Britain and France in Egypt, 1876–1882," in *France and Britain in Africa*, p. 77. For the Egyptian argument in relation to Egyptian and African history, see specially Roger Owen, "Egypt and Europe: From French expedition to British occupation," in *Studies in the Theory of Imperialism*. As an expert on the Middle East, Owen believes that the Arabi movement, far from being indigenous, was in fact the result of a long period of interaction between Europe and Egypt. Therefore Robinson and Gallagher must be wrong in their argument that Africa's history is autonomous. See his comment below, "Robinson and Gallagher and Middle Eastern Nationalism."

[95]Ramm, "Great Britain and France in Egypt," p. 119.

[96]*Africa and the Victorians*, pp. 173–174.

[97]London, 1938.

[98]Henry Ashby Turner, Jr., "Bismarck's Imperialist Venture: Anti-British in Origin?" in eds. Prosser Gifford and Wm. Roger Louis, *Britain and Germany in Africa* (Yale University Press, 1967), chapter 2.

[99]"I now incline to believe that the principal explanation lay in Bismarck's bad temper, when the British government failed to do what he wanted. This explanation sounds trivial, but there is more evidence for it than for any other." A. J. P. Taylor in response to Turner's attack, *English Historical Review*, LXXXIV (October 1969), p. 816.

[100]Turner, "Bismarck's Imperialist Venture," p. 51.

[101]Hans-Ulrich Wehler, *Bismarck und der Imperialismus* (Cologne, 1969).

[102]According to Wehler, even apart from the uncritical and entirely unsatisfactory account of German imperialism: "Their model cannot successfully be defended either theoretically or empirically; even British imperialism during those years poses numerous questions which are excluded by their model. Apart from the fact that the description of policy in South Africa undercuts the authors' theories, their theories take no account of the many domestic and foreign interests which everywhere are the basis of certain stereotypes of political language and which condition the political horizon of ruling élites—the self-evident economic importance of India, for instance. In many respects their book is an exercise in belated historicism, with subtle apologetics." Note 11, pp. 125–26 in Hans-Ulrich Wehler, "Bismarck's Imperialism 1862–1890," *Past and Present,* 48 (August 1970), which is a synopsis of the main interpretations of *Bismarck und der Imperialismus.*

[103]Jean Stengers, "The Congo Free State and the Belgian Congo before 1914," in *Colonialism in Africa,* I, p. 261.

[104]See Jean Stengers, "King Leopold's Imperialism," in *Studies in the Theory of Imperialism,* chapter 11.

[105]Stengers, "The Congo Free State and the Belgian Congo before 1914," p. 287.

[106]*Le Partage d'Afrique Noire,* p. 21. The observation holds true for Africa as well. The imperialists still envisaged a repartition as late as the 1930s. See Klaus Hildebrand, *Vom Reich zum Weltreich* (Munich, 1969); for the British side, W. R. Louis, "Colonial Appeasement, 1936–1938," *Revue Belge de Philologie et d'Histoire,* XLIX, 4 (1971).

[107]See, for example, John D. Hargreaves, "West African States and the European Conquest," in *Colonialism in Africa,* I, chapter 6.

[108]Henri Brunschwig, "French Exploration and Conquest in Tropical Africa from 1865 to 1898," in *Colonialism in Africa,* I, p. 141; on the general theme, Henri Brunschwig, *French Colonialism 1871–1914* (London, 1966), with an introduction by Ronald Robinson. Cf. Raoul Girardet, *L'Idée coloniale en France* (Paris, 1972).

[109]T. O. Ranger, "Connexions between 'Primary Resistance' Movements and Modern Mass Nationalism in East and Central Africa," *Journal of African History,* IX, 3 (1968).

[110]*Ibid.,* p. 441.

[111]*Ibid.,* p. 452.

[112]Leonard Thompson, in eds. Monica Wilson and Leonard Thompson, *Oxford History of South Africa,* II (Oxford, 1971), p. 301.

[113]F. A. Van Jaarsveld, *The Awakening of Afrikaner Nationalism, 1868–1881* (Cape Town, 1961).

[114]Clement Francis Goodfellow, *Great Britain and South African Confederation 1870–1881* (Oxford University Press, 1966), p. 218.

[115]D. M. Schreuder, *Gladstone and Kruger: Liberal Government and Coloni-*

al *'Home Rule' 1880–85* (London, 1969), p. 475, n. 2. For a commentary on the validity of the argument in regard to the Western Sudan, see Kanya-Forstner, *The Conquest of the Western Sudan,* p. 269.

In fairness to Robinson and Gallagher, it should be added that the complexities of South African history as illuminated by such historians as Goodfellow and Schreuder also can be interpreted to give support to other interpretations of *Africa and the Victorians.* For example, Goodfellow clearly establishes that British policy in the 1870s was essentially imperialist in the sense of pursuing a federal goal, and he thus indicates a continuity in imperial policy that links earlier imperialists such as Carnarvon and Frere to the imperialists of the 1890s such as Chamberlain and Milner. On Schreuder's argument that Afrikaner nationalism was a "mirage," Afrikaner republicanism and the will for its defense did exist during the war of 1880–81. If Afrikaner nationalism seemed to be a mirage in the 1880s it was in part because of the Liberal policy of conciliating the Afrikaners by restoring their independence. After the Jameson Raid, when Afrikaner nationalism definitely ceased to be a mirage, the general themes of both Schreuder and Robinson and Gallagher hold true: Britain as a world power in relative decline had not only to respond to the imperialism of her European rivals but also to crises of local nationalisms throughout the Empire. I am indebted to Professor Noel Garson for his comments on these points. For his contribution to the Robinson and Gallagher debate, see his essay, "British Imperialism and the Coming of the Anglo-Boer War," *South African Journal of Economics,* 30, 2 (June 1962).

[116]I am grateful to Professor Gallagher for discussion of these points.

[117]Robinson, "Non-European Foundations of European Imperialism," p. 130.

[118]Collaboration is the vital key to Robinson and Gallagher, but not to historians such as T. O. Ranger who hold that *resistors* rather than collaborators are more significant in the colonial situation. For comment on Robinson and Gallagher perhaps inadvertently opening the floodgates of ideological history in this regard, see Donald Denoon and Adam Kuper, "The 'New Historiography' in Dar Es Salaam," *African Affairs,* 69, 277 (October 1970).

[119]For example, Keith Sinclair, "Hobson and Lenin in Johore: Colonial Office policy towards British concessionaires and investors, 1878–1907," *Modern Asian Studies,* I, 4 (October 1967), p. 352: "One need merely mention the route to the East and the tendency of established colonies to expand their borders to see that Robinson and Gallagher are more at home in Johore than Hobson and Lenin." Wm. Roger Louis, *Great Britain and Germany's Lost Colonies, 1914–1919* (Oxford, 1967), p. 159: "The powerful theme of *Africa and the Victorians* is even more true of British statesmen of the First World War period than for those of the partition era: 'Over and over again, they show an obsession with security, a fixation on safeguarding the routes to the East.' "

[120]The key work to be compared with Robinson and Gallagher is G. N. Sanderson, *England, Europe and the Upper Nile, 1882–1899* (Edinburgh, 1965). Sydney Kanya-Forstner has written: "Throughout his treatment of Brit-

ish policy, Professor Sanderson's implicit intention has been at least in part to challenge the whole interpretation of *Africa and the Victorians:* that British policy on the Upper Nile was from beginning to end determined by the need to protect the security of Egypt and was formulated by an *élite* largely immune from outside influences. This is why he stresses the influence of private interest and public opinion." (*Historical Journal*, 9, 2, 1966, pp. 251–54). See also Jean Stengers, "Aux Origines de Fachoda; L'Expedition Monteil," *Revue Belge de Philologie et d'Histoire*, XXXVI (1958), pp. 436–50; XXXVIII (1960), pp. 366–404 and 1040–65; R. G. Brown, *Fashoda Reconsidered* (London, 1970); and Marc Michel, *La Mission Marchand, 1895–1899* (Paris, 1972). For an important review article, see J. Stengers, "Une Facette de la Question du Haut-Nil: Le Mirage Soudanais," *Journal of African History*, X, 4 (1969), which has references useful for the Robinson-Gallagher controversy.

[121]See J. S. Marais, *The Fall of Kruger's Republic* (Oxford, 1961), which is compared with Robinson and Gallagher by N. G. Garson in a major review article cited in note 115; see also L. M. Thompson, *The Unification of South Africa, 1902–1910* (Oxford, 1960); G. H. L. Le May, *British Supremacy in South Africa, 1899–1907* (Oxford, 1965); and G. Blainey, "Lost Causes of the Jameson Raid," *Economic History Review*, Second Series, XVIII, 1 (August 1965), which, by contrast to Robinson and Gallagher, argues that Rhodes risked political power in order to preserve economic power. Other important recent articles are: J. S. Galbraith, "The British South Africa Company and the Jameson Raid," *Journal of British Studies*, X, 1 (1970); Robert V. Kubicek, "The Randlords in 1895: A Reassessment," *Journal of British Studies*, XI, 2 (1972); Andrew Porter, "Lord Salisbury, Mr. Chamberlain and South Africa 1895–9," *Journal of Imperial and Commonwealth History*, I, 1 (1972); and A. N. Porter, "Sir Alfred Milner and the Press, 1897–1899," *Historical Journal*, XVI, 2 (1973).

[122]The book to be read in this regard to the Robinson and Gallagher controversy is Akira Iriye, *Pacific Estrangement: Japanese and American Expansion, 1897–1911* (Cambridge, Mass., 1972).

[123]William Appleman Williams, *The Tragedy of American Diplomacy* (New York, 1962 edn.); Walter La Feber, *The New Empire: An Interpretation of American Expansion, 1860–1898* (Ithaca, 1963); and Thomas J. McCormick, *China Market: America's Quest for Informal Empire, 1893–1901* (Chicago, 1967).

[124]Ernest R. May, *American Imperialism: a Speculative Essay* (New York, 1968).

PART II

**Selected Works of
Robinson and Gallagher**

The Imperialism of
Free Trade

JOHN GALLAGHER AND
RONALD ROBINSON

The concluding lines of an essay written by Professor Gallagher in 1951 provide an interesting prologue to "The Imperialism of Free Trade":

> There can be no doubt that the main line of policy in the mid-nineteenth century was opposed to colonial expansion in all but special cases; but it is interesting to speculate how many qualifications would be injected into that generalization by the study of the temporary aberrations of policy forced on governments by humanitarians, business men and politicians in opposition. The years 1838–42, for example, witnessed not only the new policy in Africa, but the forward move in the Pacific, the protection of Morocco and Tahiti, the occupation of Aden, and the war with China. Not all of these were expansionist moves in the formal sense, but they all played their part in the 'informal empire' which was a consequence of the status of Great Britain in the world. (J. Gallagher, "Fowell Buxton and the New African Policy, 1838–1842," Cambridge Historical Journal, *1, 1950, p. 58).*

The quotation is useful in seeing that the theory of continuity as developed in "The Imperialism of Free Trade" is as much thematic as it is chronological. It is the continuity between the two parts of the iceberg, the formal and informal empires. This mode of interpreting the essay becomes all the more clear if Ronald Robinson's later essay "Non-European Foundations" is read in conjunction with it.

Since the argument of "The Imperialism of Free Trade" is the foundation for all their subsequent work—and since the theme is such a vexed question—perhaps it is useful to spell out the main points in the argument as unequivocally as possible:

1. British expansion of trade and investment is continuous, as is the exertion of power to protect it when and where necessary.

2. The timing and place of imperial intervention depends in part on local conditions. The non-European factor in European imperialism varies on time scales of African and Asian history and not necessarily on the expansive forces of Europe.

3. Therefore the mode or form of European expansion will not be mainly formal in one period of European history and informal or anti-imperialist at another. The form is determined in large part by the circumstances in particular overseas countries, and in any one period of European expansion, some countries will pass from informal to formal modes of imperial influence while others will be passing from formal to informal forms. For example, in 1830 to 1870, while India is still being taken into the formal empire, the white colonies are passing from formal to informal empire through responsible government.

In sum, their thesis is continuity of expansion, but flexibility in forms of political intervention and control depending on local circumstances.

For examples of objections to the propositions put forward in the essay, see Owen and Sutcliffe, Studies in the Theory of Imperialism. *Roger Owen remarks in the introduction that the authors "were all in disagreement with the position taken in respect of Britain by Robinson and Gallagher in their 'The imperialism of free trade'."*

"The Imperialism of Free Trade" was first published in the Economic History Review, *Second Series, VI, 1 (1953). It is reprinted with permission from the authors and the Editors of the* Review.

I

It ought to be a commonplace that Great Britain during the nineteenth century expanded overseas by means of 'informal empire'[1] as much as by acquiring dominion in the strict constitutional sense. For purposes of economic analysis it would clearly be unreal to define imperial history exclusively as the history of those colonies coloured red on the map. Nevertheless, almost all imperial history has been written on the assumption that the empire of formal dominion is historically comprehensible in itself and can be cut out of its context in British expansion and world politics. The conventional interpretation of the nineteenth-century empire continues to rest upon study of the formal empire alone, which is rather like judging the size and character of icebergs solely from the parts above the water-line.

The imperial historian, in fact, is very much at the mercy of his own particular concept of empire. By that, he decides what facts are of 'imperial' significance; his data are limited in the same way as his concept, and his final interpretation itself depends largely upon the scope of his hypothesis. Different hypotheses have led to conflicting conclusions. Since imperial historians are writing about different empires and since they are generalizing from eccentric or isolated aspects of them, it is hardly surprising that these historians sometimes contradict each other.

The orthodox view of nineteenth-century imperial history remains that laid down from the standpoint of the racial and legalistic concept which inspired the Imperial Federation movement. Historians such as Seeley and Egerton looked on events in the formal empire as the only test of imperial activity; and they regarded the empire of kinship and constitutional dependence as an organism with its own laws of growth. In this way the nineteenth century was divided into periods of imperialism and anti-imperialism, according to the extension or contraction of the formal empire and the degree of belief in the value of British rule overseas.

Ironically enough, the alternative interpretation of 'imperialism', which began as part of the radical polemic against the Federationists, has in effect only confirmed their analysis. Those who have seen imperialism as the high stage of capitalism and the inevitable result of foreign investment agree that it applied historically only to the period after 1880. As a result they have been led into a similar preoccupation with formal manifestations of imperialism because the late-Victorian age was one of spectacular extension of British rule. Consequently, Hobson and Lenin, Professor Moon and Mr. Woolf[2] have confirmed from the opposite point of view their opponents' contention that late-Victorian imperialism was a qualitative change in the nature of British expansion and a sharp deviation from the innocent and static liberalism of the middle of the century. This alleged change, welcomed by one school, condemned by the other, was accepted by both.

For all their disagreement these two doctrines pointed to one interpretation; that mid-Victorian 'indifference' and late-Victorian 'enthusiasm' for empire were directly related to the rise and decline in free-trade beliefs. Thus Lenin wrote: 'When free competition in Great Britain was at its height, i.e. between 1840 and 1860, the leading British bourgeois politicians were . . . of the opinion that the liberation of the colonies and their complete separation from Great Britain was inevitable and desirable.'[3] Professor Schuyler extends this to the decade from 1861 to 1870: '. . . for it was during those years that tendencies toward the disruption of the empire reached their climax. The doctrines of the Manchester school were at the height of their influence.'[4]

In the last quarter of the century, Professor Langer finds that 'there was an obvious danger that the British [export] market would be steadily restricted. Hence the emergence and sudden flowering of the movement for expansion. . . . Manchester doctrine had been belied by the facts. It was an outworn theory to be thrown into the discard.'[5] Their argument may be summarized in this way: the mid-Victorian formal empire did not expand, indeed it seemed to be disintegrating, therefore the period was anti-imperialist; the later-Victorian formal empire expanded rapidly, therefore this was an era of imperialism; the change was caused by the obsolescence of free trade.

The trouble with this argument is that it leaves out too many of the facts which it claims to explain. Consider the results of a decade of 'indifference' to empire. Between 1841 and 1851 Great Britain occupied or annexed New Zealand, the Gold Coast, Labuan, Natal, the Punjab, Sind and Hong Kong. In the next twenty years British control was asserted over Berar, Oudh, Lower Burma and Kowloon, over Lagos and the neighbourhood of Sierra Leone, over Basutoland, Griqualand and the Transvaal; and new colonies were established in Queensland and British Columbia. Unless this expansion can be explained by 'fits of absence of mind', we are faced with the paradox that it occurred despite the determination of the imperial authorities to avoid extending their rule.

This contradiction arises even if we confine our attention to the formal empire, as the orthodox viewpoint would force us to do. But if we look beyond into the regions of informal empire, then the difficulties become overwhelming. The normal account of South African policy in the middle of the century is that Britain abandoned any idea of controlling the interior. But in fact what looked like withdrawal from the Orange River Sovereignty and the Transvaal was based not on any *a priori* theories about the inconveniences of colonies but upon hard facts of strategy and commerce in a wider field. Great Britain was in South Africa primarily to safeguard the routes to the East, by preventing foreign powers from acquiring bases on the flank of those routes. In one way or another this imperial interest demanded some kind of hold upon Africa south of the Limpopo River, and although between 1852 and 1877 the Boer Republics were not controlled formally for this purpose by Britain, they were effectually dominated by informal paramountcy and by their dependence on British ports. If we refuse to narrow our view to that of formal empire, we can see how steadily and successfully the main imperial interest was pursued by maintaining supremacy over the whole region, and that it was pursued as steadily throughout the so-called anti-imperialist era as in the late-Victorian period. But it was done by shutting in the Boer Republics from the Indian Ocean: by the annexation of Natal in 1843, by keeping the Boers out of Delagoa Bay in 1860 and 1868, out of St Lucia Bay in 1861 and 1866, and by British intervention to block the union of the two Republics under Pretorius in 1860.[6] Strangely enough it was the first Gladstone Government which Schuyler regards as the climax of anti-imperialism, which annexed Basutoland in 1868 and Griqualand West in 1871 in order to ensure 'the safety of our South African Possessions'.[7] By informal means if possible, or by formal annexations when necessary, British paramountcy was steadily upheld.

Are these the actions of ministers anxious to preside over the liquidation of the British Empire? Do they look like 'indifference' to an empire rendered superfluous by free trade? On the contrary, here is a continuity of policy which the conventional interpretation misses because it takes account only of formal methods of control. It also misses the continuous grasp of the West African coast and of the South Pacific which British seapower was able to maintain. Refusals to annex are no proof of reluctance to control. As Lord Aberdeen put it in 1845: '. . . it is unnecessary to add that Her Majesty's Government will not view with indifference the assumption by another Power of a Protectorate which they, with due regard for the true interests of those [Pacific] islands, have refused.'[8]

Nor can the obvious continuity of imperial constitutional policy throughout the mid- and late-Victorian years be explained on the orthodox hypothesis. If the granting of responsible government to colonies was due to the mid-Victorian 'indifference' to empire and even a desire to be rid of it, then why was this policy continued in the late-Victorian period when Britain was interested above all in preserving imperial unity? The common assumption that British governments in the free-trade era considered empire superfluous arises from over-estimating the significance of changes in legalistic forms. In fact, throughout the Victorian period responsible government was withheld from colonies if it involved sacrificing or endangering British paramountcy or interests. Wherever there was fear of a foreign challenge to British supremacy in the continent or subcontinent concerned, wherever the colony could not provide financially for its own internal security, the imperial authorities retained full responsibility, or, if they had already devolved it, intervened directly to secure their interests once more. In other words, responsible government, far from being a separatist device, was simply a change from direct to indirect methods of maintaining British interests. By slackening the formal political bond at the appropriate time, it was possible to rely on economic dependence and mutual good-feeling to keep the colonies bound to Britain while still using them as agents for further British expansion.

The inconsistency between fact and the orthodox interpretation arises in yet another way. For all the extensive anthologies of opinion supposedly hostile to colonies, how many colonies were actually abandoned? For instance, the West Africa Committee of 1865 made a strong and much quoted case for giving up all but one of the West African settlements, but even as they sat these settlements were being extended. The Indian empire, however, is the most glaring gap in the traditional explanation. Its history in the 'period of indifference' is filled with wars and annexations.

Moreover, in this supposedly *laissez-faire* period India, far from being evacuated, was subjected to intensive development as an economic colony along the best mercantilist lines. In India it was possible, throughout most of the period of the British Raj, to use the governing power to extort in the form of taxes and monopolies such valuable primary products as opium and salt. Furthermore, the characteristics of so-called imperialist expansion at the end of the nineteenth century developed in India long before the date (1880) when Lenin believed the age of economic imperialism opened. Direct governmental promotion of products required by British industry, government manipulation of tariffs to help British exports, railway construction at high and guaranteed rates of interest to open the continental interior—all of these techniques of direct political control were employed in ways which seem alien to the so-called age of *laissez-faire*. Moreover, they had little to do, particularly in railway finance, with the folk-lore of rugged individualism. 'All the money came from the English capitalist' as a British official wrote, 'and, so long as he was guaranteed five per cent on the revenues of India, it was immaterial to him whether the funds which he lent were thrown into the Hooghly or converted into bricks and mortar.'[9]

To sum up: the conventional view of Victorian imperial history leaves us with a series of awkward questions. In the age of 'anti-imperialism' why were all colonies retained? Why were so many more obtained? Why were so many new spheres of influence set up? Or again, in the age of 'imperialism', as we shall see later, why was there such reluctance to annex further territory? Why did decentralization, begun under the impetus of anti-imperialism, continue? In the age of *laissez-faire* why was the Indian economy developed by the state?

These paradoxes are too radical to explain as merely exceptions which prove the rule or by concluding that imperial policy was largely irrational and inconsistent, the product of a series of accidents and chances. The contradictions, it may be suspected, arise not from the historical reality but from the historians' approach to it. A hypothesis which fits more of the facts might be that of a fundamental continuity in British expansion throughout the nineteenth century.

II

The hypothesis which is needed must include informal as well as formal expansion, and must allow for the continuity of the process. The most striking fact about British history in the nineteenth century, as Seeley pointed out, is that it is the history of an expanding society. The exports of capital and manufactures, the migration of citizens, the dissemination of the English language, ideas and constitutional forms, were all of them radiations of the social energies of the British peoples. Between 1812 and 1914 over twenty million persons emigrated from the British Isles, and nearly 70 per cent of them went outside the Empire.[10] Between 1815 and 1880, it is estimated, £1,187,000,000 in credit had accumulated abroad, but no more than one-sixth was placed in the formal empire. Even by 1913, something less than half of the £3,975,000,000 of foreign investment lay inside the Empire.[11] Similarly, in no year of the century did the Empire buy much more than one-third of Britain's exports. The basic fact is that British industrialization caused an ever-extending and intensifying development of overseas regions. Whether they were formally British or not, was a secondary consideration.

Imperialism, perhaps, may be defined as a sufficient political function of this process of integrating new regions into the expanding economy; its character is largely decided by the various and changing relationships between the political and economic elements of expansion in any particular region and time. Two qualifications must be made. First, imperialism may be only indirectly connected with economic integration in that it sometimes extends beyond areas of economic development, but acts for their strategic protection. Secondly, although imperialism is a function of economic expansion, it is not a necessary function. Whether imperialist phenomena show themselves or not, is determined not only by the factors of economic expansion, but equally by the political and social organization of the regions brought into the orbit of the expansive society, and also by the world situation in general.

It is only when the polities of these new regions fail to provide satisfactory conditions for commercial or strategic integration and when their relative weakness allows, that power is used imperialistically to adjust those conditions. Economic expansion, it is true, will tend to flow into the regions of maximum opportunity, but maximum opportunity depends as much upon political considerations of security as upon questions of profit. Consequently, in any particular region, if economic opportunity seems large but political security small, then full absorption into the extending economy tends to be frustrated until power is exerted upon the state in question. Conversely, in proportion as satisfactory political frameworks are brought into being in this way, the frequency of imperialist intervention lessens and imperialist control is correspondingly relaxed. It may be suggested that this willingness to limit the use of paramount power to establishing security for trade is the distinctive feature of the British imperialism of free trade in the nineteenth century, in contrast to the mercantilist use of power to obtain commercial supremacy and monopoly through political possession.

On this hypothesis the phasing of British expansion or imperialism is not likely to be chronological. Not all regions will reach the same level of economic integration at any one time; neither will all regions need the same type of political control at any one time. As the British industrial revolution grew, so new markets and sources of supply were linked to it at different times, and the degree of imperialist action accompanying that process varied accordingly. Thus mercantilist techniques of formal empire were being employed to develop India in the mid-Victorian age at the same time as informal techniques of free trade were being used in Latin America for the same purpose. It is for this reason that attempts to make phases of imperialism correspond directly to phases in the economic growth of the metropolitan economy are likely to prove in vain. The fundamental continuity of British expansion is only obscured by arguing that changes in the terms of trade or in the character of British exports necessitated a sharp change in the process.

From this vantage point the many-sided expansion of British industrial society can be viewed as a whole of which both the formal and informal empires are only parts. Both of them then appear as variable political functions of the extending pattern of overseas trade, investment, migration and culture. If this is accepted, it follows that formal and informal empire are essentially interconnected and to some extent interchangeable. Then not only is the old, legalistic, narrow idea of empire unsatisfactory, but so is the old idea of informal empire as a separate, non-political category of expansion. A concept of informal empire which fails to bring out the underlying unity between it and the formal empire is sterile. Only within the total framework of expansion is nineteenth-century empire intelligible. So we are faced with the task of re-fashioning the interpretations resulting from defective concepts of organic constitutional empire on the one hand and Hobsonian 'imperialism' on the other.

The economic importance—even the pre-eminence—of informal empire in this period has been stressed often enough. What was overlooked was the inter-relation of its economic and political arms; how political action aided the growth of commercial supremacy, and how this supremacy in turn strengthened political influence. In other words, it is the politics as well as the economics of the informal empire which we have to include in the account. Historically, the relationship between these two factors has been both subtle and complex. It has been by no means a simple case of the use of gunboats to demolish a recalcitrant state in the cause of British trade. The type of political lien between the expanding economy and its formal or informal dependencies, as might be expected, has been flexible. In practice it has tended to vary with the economic value of the territory, the strength of its political structure, the readiness of its rulers to collaborate with British commercial or strategic purposes, the ability of the native society to undergo economic change without external control, the extent to which domestic and foreign political situations permitted British intervention, and, finally, how far European rivals allowed British policy a free hand.

Accordingly, the political lien has ranged from a vague, informal paramountcy to outright political possession; and, consequently, some of these dependent territories have been formal colonies whereas others have not. The difference between formal and informal empire has not been one of fundamental nature but of degree. The ease with which a region has slipped from one status to the other helps to confirm this. Within the last two hundred years, for example, India has passed from informal to formal association with the United Kingdom and, since World War II, back to an informal connexion. Similarly, British West Africa has passed through the first two stages and seems to-day likely to follow India into the third.

III

Let us now attempt, tentatively, to use the concept of the totality of

British expansion described above to restate the main themes of the history of modern British expansion. We have seen that interpretations of this process fall into contradictions when based upon formal political criteria alone. If expansion both formal and informal is examined as a single process, will these contradictions disappear?

The growth of British industry made new demands upon British policy. It necessitated linking undeveloped areas with British foreign trade and, in so doing, moved the political arm to force an entry into markets closed by the power of foreign monopolies.

British policy, as Professor Harlow has shown,[12] was active in this way before the American colonies had been lost, but its greatest opportunities came during the Napoleonic Wars. The seizure of the French and Spanish West Indies, the filibustering expedition to Buenos Aires in 1806, the taking of Java in 1811, were all efforts to break into new regions and to tap new resources by means of political action. But the policy went further than simple house-breaking, for once the door was opened and British imports with their political implications were pouring in, they might stop the door from being shut again. Raffles, for example, temporarily broke the Dutch monopoly of the spice trade in Java and opened the island to free trade. Later, he began the informal British paramountcy over the Malacca trade routes and the Malay peninsula by founding Singapore. In South America, at the same time, British policy was aiming at indirect political hegemony over new regions for the purposes of trade. The British navy carried the Portuguese royal family to Brazil after the breach with Napoleon, and the British representative there extorted from his grateful clients the trade treaty of 1810 which left British imports paying a lower tariff than the goods of the mother country. The thoughtful stipulation was added 'that the Present Treaty shall be unlimited in point of duration, and that the obligations and conditions expressed or implied in it shall be perpetual and immutable'.[13]

From 1810 onwards this policy had even better chances in Latin America, and they were taken. British governments sought to exploit the colonial revolutions to shatter the Spanish trade monopoly, and to gain informal supremacy and the good will which would all favour British commercial penetration. As Canning put it in 1824, when he had clinched the policy of recognition: 'Spanish America is free and if we do not mismanage our affairs sadly she is *English*.'[14] Canning's underlying object was to clear the way for a prodigious British expansion by creating a new and informal empire, not only to redress the Old World balance of power but to restore British influence in the

New. He wrote triumphantly: 'The thing is done . . . the Yankees will shout in triumph: but it is they who lose most by our decision . . . the United States have gotten the start of us in vain; and we link once more America to Europe.'[15] It would be hard to imagine a more spectacular example of a policy of commercial hegemony in the interests of high politics, or of the use of informal political supremacy in the interests of commercial enterprise. Characteristically, the British recognition of Buenos Aires, Mexico and Colombia took the form of signing commercial treaties with them.

In both the formal and informal dependencies in the mid-Victorian age there was much effort to open the continental interiors and to extend the British influence inland from the ports and to develop the hinterlands. The general strategy of this development was to convert these areas into complementary satellite economies, which would provide raw materials and food for Great Britain, and also provide widening markets for its manufactures. This was the period, the orthodox interpretation would have us believe, in which the political arm of expansion was dormant or even withered. In fact, that alleged inactivity is seen to be a delusion if we take into account the development in the informal aspect. Once entry had been forced into Latin America, China and the Balkans, the task was to encourage stable governments as good investment risks, just as in weaker or unsatisfactory states it was considered necessary to coerce them into more co-operative attitudes.

In Latin America, however, there were several false starts. The impact of British expansion in Argentina helped to wreck the constitution and throw the people into civil war, since British trade caused the sea-board to prosper while the back lands were exploited and lagged behind. The investment crash of 1827 and the successful revolt of the pampas people against Buenos Aires[16] blocked further British expansion, and the rise to power of General Rosas ruined the institutional framework which Canning's strategy had so brilliantly set up. The new regime was unco-operative and its designs on Montevideo caused chaos around the Rio de la Plata, which led to that great commercial artery being closed to enterprise. All this provoked a series of direct British interventions during the 1840's in efforts to get trade moving again on the river, but in fact it was the attractive force of British trade itself, more than the informal imperialist action of British governments, which in this case restored the situation by removing Rosas from power.

British policy in Brazil ran into peculiar troubles through its tactless attempt to browbeat the Government of Rio de Janeiro into abolishing slavery. British political effectiveness was weakened, in spite of economic predominance, by the interference of humanitarian pressure groups in England. Yet the economic control over Brazil was strengthened after 1856 by the building of the railways; these—begun, financed and operated by British companies—were encouraged by generous concessions from the government of Brazil.

With the development of railways and steamships, the economies of the leading Latin American states were at last geared successfully to the world economy. Once their exports had begun to climb and foreign investment had been attracted, a rapid rate of economic growth was feasible. Even in the 1880's Argentina could double her exports and increase sevenfold her foreign indebtedness while the world price of meat and wheat was falling.[17] By 1913, in Latin America as a whole, informal imperialism had become so important for the British economy that £999,000,000, over a quarter of the total investment abroad, was invested in that region.[18]

But this investment, as was natural, was concentrated in such countries as Argentina and Brazil whose governments (even after the Argentine default of 1891) had collaborated in the general task of British expansion. For this reason there was no need for brusque or peremptory interventions on behalf of British interests. For once their economies had become sufficiently dependent on foreign trade the classes whose prosperity was drawn from that trade normally worked themselves in local politics to preserve the local political conditions needed for it. British intervention, in any case, became more difficult once the United States could make other powers take the Monroe doctrine seriously. The slackening in active intervention in the affairs of the most reliable members of the commercial empire was matched by the abandonment of direct political control over those regions of formal empire which were successful enough to receive self-government. But in Latin America, British governments still intervened, when necessary, to protect British interests in the more backward states; there was intervention on behalf of the bond holders in Guatemala and Colombia in the 'seventies, as in Mexico and Honduras between 1910 and 1914.

The types of informal empire and the situations it attempted to exploit were as various as the success which it achieved. Although commercial and capital penetration tended to lead to political co-operation and hegemony, there are striking exceptions. In the United States, for example, British business turned the cotton South into a colonial economy, and the British investor hoped to do the same with the Mid-West. But the political strength of the country stood in his way. It was impossible to stop American industrialization, and the industrialized sections successfully campaigned for tariffs, despite the opposition of those sections which depended on the British trade connexion. In the same way, American political strength thwarted British attempts to establish Texas, Mexico and Central America as informal dependencies.

Conversely, British expansion sometimes failed, if it gained political supremacy without effecting a successful commercial penetration. There were spectacular exertions of British policy in China, but they did little to produce new customers. Britain's political hold upon China failed to break down Chinese economic self-sufficiency. The Opium War of 1840, the renewal of war in 1857, widened the inlets for British trade but they did not get Chinese exports moving. Their main effect was an unfortunate one from the British point of view, for such foreign pressures put Chinese society under great strains as the Taiping Rebellion unmistakably showed.[19] It is important to note that this weakness was regarded in London as an embarrassment, and not as a lever for extracting further concessions. In fact, the British worked to prop up the tottering Pekin regime, for as Lord Clarendon put it in 1870, 'British interests in China are strictly commercial, or at all events only so far political as they may be for the protection of commerce'.[20] The value of this self-denial became clear in the following decades when the Pekin government, threatened with a scramble for China, leaned more and more on the diplomatic support of the honest British broker.

The simple recital of these cases of economic expansion, aided and abetted by political action in one form or other, is enough to expose the inadequacy of the conventional theory that free trade could dispense with empire. We have seen that it did not do so. Economic expansion in the mid-Victorian age was matched by a corresponding political expansion which has been overlooked because it could not be seen by that study of maps which, it has been said, drives sane men mad. It is absurd to deduce from the harmony between London and the colonies of white settlement in the mid-Victorian age any British reluctance to intervene in the fields of British interests. The warships at Canton are as much a part of the period as responsible government for Canada; the battlefields of the Punjab are as real as the abolition of suttee.

Far from being an era of 'indifference', the mid-Victorian years were the decisive stage in the history of British expansion overseas, in that the combination of commercial penetration and political influence allowed the United Kingdom to command those economies which could be made to fit best into her own. A variety of techniques adapted to diverse conditions and beginning at different dates were employed to effect this domination. A paramountcy was set up in Malaya centered on Singapore; a suzerainty over much of West Africa reached out from the port of Lagos and was backed up by the African squadron. On the east coast of Africa British influence at Zanzibar, dominant thanks to the exertions of Consul Kirk, placed the heritage of Arab command on the mainland at British disposal.

But perhaps the most common political technique of British expansion was the treaty of free trade and friendship made with or imposed upon a weaker state. The treaties with Persia of 1836 and 1857, the Turkish treaties of 1838 and 1861, the Japanese treaty of 1858, the favours extracted from Zanzibar, Siam and Morocco, the hundreds of anti-slavery treaties signed with crosses by African chiefs—all these treaties enabled the British government to carry forward trade with these regions.

Even a valuable trade with one region might give place to a similar trade with another which could be more easily coerced politically. The Russian grain trade, for example, was extremely useful to Great Britain. But the Russians' refusal to hear of free trade, and the British inability to force them into it, caused efforts to develop the grain of the Ottoman empire instead, since British pressure at Constantinople had been able to hustle the Turk into a liberal trade policy.[21] The dependence of the commercial thrust upon the political arm resulted in a general tendency for British trade to follow the invisible flag of informal empire.

Since the mid-Victorian age now appears as a time of large-scale expansion, it is necessary to revise our estimate of the so-called 'imperialist' era as well. Those who accept the concept of 'economic imperialism' would have us believe that the annexations at the end of the century represented a sharp break in policy, due to the decline of free trade, the need to protect foreign investment, and the conversion of statesmen to the need for unlimited land-grabbing. All these explanations are questionable. In the first place, the tariff policy of Great Britain did not change. Again, British foreign investment was no new thing and most of it was still flowing into regions outside the formal empire. Finally the statesmens' conversion to the policy of extensive annexation was partial, to say the most of it. Until 1887, and only occasionally after that date, party leaders showed little more enthusiasm for extending British rule than the mid-Victorians. Salisbury was infuriated by the 'superficial philanthropy' and 'roguery' of the 'fanatics' who advocated expansion.[22] When pressed to aid the missions in Nyasaland in 1888, he retorted: 'It is not our duty to do it. We should be risking tremendous sacrifices for a very doubtful gain.'[23] After 1888, Salisbury, Rosebery and Chamberlain accepted the scramble for Africa as a painful but unavoidable necessity which arose from a threat of foreign expansion and the irrepressible tendency of trade to overflow the bounds of empire, dragging the government into new and irksome commitments. But it was not until 1898 that they were sufficiently confident to undertake the reconquest of so vital a region as the Sudan.

Faced with the prospect of foreign acquisitions of tropical territory hitherto opened to British merchants, the men in London resorted to one expedient after another to evade the need of formal expansion and still uphold British paramountcy in those regions. British policy in the late, as in the mid-Victorian period preferred informal means of extending imperial supremacy rather than direct rule. Throughout the two alleged periods the extension of British rule was a last resort —and it is this preference which has given rise to the many 'anti-expansionist' remarks made by Victorian ministers. What these much quoted expressions obscure, is that in practice mid-Victorian as well as late-Victorian policy makers did not refuse to extend the protection of formal rule over British interests when informal methods had failed to give security. The fact that informal techniques were more often sufficient for this purpose in the circumstances of the mid-century than in the later period when the foreign challenge to British supremacy intensified, should not be allowed to disguise the basic continuity of policy. Throughout, British governments worked to establish and maintain British paramountcy by whatever means best suited the circumstances of their diverse regions of interest. The aims of the mid-Victorians were no more 'anti-imperialist' than their successors', though they were more often able to achieve them informally; and the late-Victorians were no more 'imperialist' than their predecessors, even though they were driven to annex more often. British policy followed the principle of extending control informally if possible and formally if necessary. To label the one method 'anti-imperialist' and the other 'imperialist', is to ignore the fact that whatever the method British interests were steadily safeguarded and extended. The usual summing up of the policy of the free trade empire as 'trade not rule' should read 'trade with informal control if possible; trade with rule when necessary'. This statement of the continuity of policy disposes of the over-simplified explanation of involuntary expansion inherent in the orthodox interpretation based on the discontinuity between the two periods.

Thus Salisbury as well as Gladstone, Knutsford as well as Derby and Ripon, in the so-called age of 'imperialism', exhausted all informal expedients to secure regions of British trade in Africa before admitting that further annexations were unavoidable. One device was to obtain guarantees of free trade and access as a reward for recognizing foreign territorial claims, a device which had the advantage of saddling foreign governments with the liability of rule whilst allowing Britons the commercial advantage. This was done in the Anglo-Portuguese Treaty of 1884, the Congo Arrangement of 1885, and the Anglo-German Agreement over East Africa in 1886. Another device for evading the extension of rule was the exclusive sphere of influence or protectorate recognized by foreign powers. Although originally these imposed no liability for pacifying or administering such regions, with changes in international law they did so after 1885. The granting of charters to private companies between 1881 and 1889, authorizing them to administer and finance new regions under imperial licence, marked the transition from informal to formal methods of backing British commercial expansion. Despite these attempts at 'imperialism on the cheap', the foreign challenge to British paramountcy in tropical Africa and the comparative absence there of large-scale, strong, indigenous political organizations which had served informal expansion so well elsewhere, eventually dictated the switch to formal rule.

One principle then emerges plainly: it is only when and where informal political means failed to provide the framework of security for British enterprise (whether commercial, or philanthropic or simply strategic) that the question of establishing formal empire arose. In satellite regions peopled by European stock, in Latin America or Canada, for instance, strong governmental structures grew up; in totally non-European areas, on the other hand, expansion unleashed such disruptive forces upon the indigenous structures that they tended to wear out and even collapse with use. This tendency in many cases accounts for the extension of informal British responsibility and eventually for the change from indirect to direct control.

It was in Africa that this process of transition manifested itself most strikingly during the period after 1880. Foreign loans and predatory bankers by the 1870's had wrecked Egyptian finances and were tearing holes in the Egyptian political fabric. The Anglo-French dual financial control, designed to safeguard the foreign bondholders and to restore Egypt as a good risk, provoked anti-European feeling. With the revolt of Arabi Pasha in 1881, the Khedive's government could serve no longer to secure either the all-important Canal or the foreign investors' pound of flesh.

The motives for the British occupation of 1882 were confused and varied; the desire, evident long before Disraeli's purchase of shares, to dominate the Canal; the interests of the bondholders; and the over-anxiety to forestall any foreign power, especially France, from taking advantage of the prevailing anarchy in Egypt to interpose its power across the British road to India. Nearly all Gladstone's Cabinet admitted the necessity of British intervention, although for different reasons, and, in order to hold together his distracted ministry, the Prime Minister agreed.

The British expedition was intended to restore a stable Egyptian government under the ostensible rule of the Khedive and inside the orbit of informal British influence. When this was achieved, the army, it was intended, should be withdrawn. But the expedition had so crushed the structure of Egyptian rule that no power short of direct British force could make it a viable and trustworthy instrument of informal hegemony and development. Thus the Liberal Government following its plan, which had been hastily evolved out of little more than ministerial disagreements, drifted into the prolonged occupation of Egypt it was intent on avoiding. In fact, the occupying power became directly responsible for the defence, the debts and development of the country. The perverse effect of British policy was gloomily summed up by Gladstone: 'We have done our Egyptian business and we are an Egyptian government.'[24] Egypt, then, is a striking example of an informal strategy misfiring due to the undermining of the satellite state by investment and by pseudo-nationalist reaction against foreign influence.

The Egyptian question, insofar as it was closely bound with the routes to India and the defence of the Indian empire itself, was given the highest priority by British policy in the 'eighties and 'nineties. In order to defend the spinal cord of British trade and empire, tropical African and Pacific claims were repeatedly sacrificed as pawns in the higher game. In 1884, for example, the Foreign Office decided that British vulnerability in Egypt made it unwise to compete with foreign powers in the opening scramble for West Africa; and it was therefore proposed '. . . to confine ourselves to securing the utmost possible freedom of trade on that [west] coast, yielding to others the territorial responsibilities . . . and seeking compensation on the east coast . . . where the political future of the country is of real importance to Indian and imperial interests.'[25] British policy was not one of indiscriminate land-grabbing. And, indeed, the British penetration into Uganda and their securing of the rest of the Nile Valley was a highly selective programme, insofar as it surrendered some British West African claims to France and transferred part of East Africa to Germany.

IV

Thus the mid-Victorian period now appears as an era of large-scale expansion, and the late-Victorian age does not seem to introduce any significant novelty into that process of expansion. The annexations of vast undeveloped territories, which have been taken as proof that this period alone was the great age of expansion, now pale in significance, at least if our analysis is anywhere near the truth. That the area of direct imperial rule was extended is true, but is it the most important or characteristic development of expansion during this period? The simple historical fact that Africa was the last field of European penetration is not to say that it was the most important; this would be a truism were it not that the main case of the Hobson school is founded on African examples. On the other hand, it is our main contention that the process of expansion had reached its most valuable targets long before the exploitation of so peripheral and marginal a field as tropical Africa. Consequently arguments, founded on the technique adopted in scrambling for Africa, would seem to be of secondary importance.

Therefore, the historian who is seeking to find the deepest meaning of the expansion at the end of the nineteenth century should look not at the mere pegging out of claims in African jungles and bush, but at the successful exploitation of the empire, both formal and informal, which was then coming to fruition in India, in Latin America, in Canada and elsewhere. The main work of imperialism in the so-called expansionist era was in the more intensive development of areas already linked with the world economy, rather than in the extensive annexations of the remaining marginal regions of Africa. The best finds and prizes had already been made; in tropical Africa the imperialists were merely scraping the bottom of the barrel.

NOTES

[1]The term has been given authority by Dr. C. R. Fay. See *Cambridge History of the British Empire* (Cambridge, 1940), II, 399.

[2]J. A. Hobson, *Imperialism* (1902); V. I. Lenin, *Imperialism, the Highest Stage of Capitalism* (Selected Works, (n.d.), v); P. T. Moon, *Imperialism and World Politics* (New York, 1926); L. Woolf, *Empire and Commerce in Africa* (n.d.).

[3]Lenin, *op. cit.*, v, 71.

[4]R. L. Schuyler, *The Fall of the Old Colonial System* (New York, 1945), p. 45.

[5]W. L. Langer, *The Diplomacy of Imperialism, 1890–1902* (New York, 1935), I, 75–6.

[6]C. J. Uys, *In the Era of Shepstone* (Lovedale, Cape Province, 1933); and C. W. de Kiewiet, *British Colonial Policy and the South African Republics* (1929), *passim*.

[7]De Kiewiet, *op. cit.*, p. 224.

[8]Quoted in J. M. Ward, *British Policy in the South Pacific, 1786–1893* (Sydney, 1948), p. 138.

[9]Quoted in L. H. Jenks, *The Migration of British Capital to 1875* (1938), pp. 221–2.

[10]Sir W. K. Hancock, *Survey of British Commonwealth Affairs* (1940), II, pt. I, 28.

[11]A. H. Imlah, 'British Balance of Payments and Export of Capital, 1816–1913', *Econ. Hist. Rev.* 2nd ser. v (1952), pp. 237, 239; Hancock, *op. cit.*, p. 27.

[12]V. T. Harlow, *The Founding of the Second British Empire, 1763–1793* (1952), pp. 62–145.

[13]Quoted in A. K. Manchester, *British Pre-eminence in Brazil* (Chapel Hill, 1933), p. 90.

[14]Quoted in W. W. Kaufmann, *British Policy and the Independence of Latin America, 1804–1828* (New Haven, 1951), p. 178.

[15]Quoted in J. F. Rippy, *Historical Evolution of Hispanic America* (Oxford, 1946), p. 374.

[16]M. Burgin, *Economic Aspects of Argentine Federalism* (Cambridge, Mass., 1946), pp. 55, 76–111.

[17]J. H. Williams, *Argentine International Trade under Inconvertible Paper Money, 1880–1900* (Cambridge, Mass., 1920), pp. 43, 103, 183. Cf. W. W. Rostow, *The Process of Economic Growth* (Oxford, 1953), p. 104.

[18]J. F. Rippy, 'British Investments in Latin America, end of 1913', *Inter-American Economic Affairs* (1951), v, 91.

[19]J. Chesnaux, 'La Révolution Taiping d'après quelques travaux récents', *Revue Historique,* CCIX, (1953), 39–40.

[20]Quoted in N. A. Pelcovits, *Old China Hands and the Foreign Office* (New York, 1948), p. 85.

[21]V. J. Puryear, *International Economics and Diplomacy in the Near East* (1935), pp. 216–17, 222–3.

[22]Quoted in Cromer, *Modern Egypt* (1908), I, 388.

[23]Hansard, 3rd Series, CCCXXVIII, Col. 550, 6 July 1888.

[24]Quoted in S. Gwynn and G. M. Tuckwell, *Life of Sir Charles Wentworth Dilke* (1917), II, 46.

[25]F. O. Confidential Print (East Africa), 5037.

The Partition of Africa

RONALD ROBINSON AND
JOHN GALLAGHER

Though it might be regarded as a trial balloon which inflates their theories to fullest dimensions, this essay was intended by the authors to be an elaboration of Africa and the Victorians. *It attempts to generalize the book's thesis from the British to the other European participants in the Scramble. It accentuates the non-European or African factors in the partition. Sydney Kanya-Forstner remarks in his commentary in this volume that it is "the most Afrocentric interpretation ever advanced."*

"The Partition of Africa" first appeared in 1962 in the New Cambridge Modern History, *Volume XI, "Material Progress and World-Wide Problems, 1870–1898," edited by F. H. Hinsley. It is reprinted by permission of the authors and the Cambridge University Press.*

Since the nineteenth century began, the Europeans had been strengthening their hold over those parts of the world selected during the era of mercantilism. Australasia, India, South-east Asia, above all the Americas—they were either temperate regions peopled with white immigrants or tropical countries already under white rule. Step by step the mode of white expansion had altered: liberalism and industrial growth shifted the emphasis away from colonies of formal empire to regions of informal influence. But whatever the form it had taken, the groundwork of European imperialism had been truly laid long before the cartographical exercises in partition at the end of the century. Africa was the last continent to win the interest of the strategists of expansion; it seemed to them that here they were scraping the bottom of the barrel.

Dividing Africa was easy enough for the Europeans. They did it at that moment in history when their lead over the other continents was at its longest. Economic growth and technical innovation gave them invincible assurance and force. Their culture and political organisation gave them a carrying power to match their iron ships and high-velocity guns. That Europe had the capacity to subjugate Africa was self-evident; but had her rulers any firm wish to do so?

Twenty years were enough to see the continent carved into symmetries devised by the geometers of diplomacy. By the end of the century only Morocco and Ethiopia were still independent, and their turn was coming. But the statesmen who drew the new frontier lines did not do so because they wanted to rule and develop these countries. Bismarck and Ferry, Gladstone and Salisbury, had no solid belief in African empire; indeed they sneered at the movement as something of a farce. A gamble in jungles and bush might interest a poor king such as Leopold II of the Belgians, or a politician on the make such as Crispi, but the chief partitioners of the 1880's glimpsed no grand imperial idea behind what they were doing. They felt no need of African colonies and in this they reflected the indifference of all but the lunatic fringe of European business and politics. Here their historians must follow them. For all the hindsight of social scientists, there was no comprehensive cause or purpose behind it. In all the long annals of imperialism, the partition of Africa is a remarkable freak. Few events that have thrown an entire continent into revolution have been brought about so casually.

Why then did statesmen bother to divide the continent? It used to be supposed that European society must have put out stronger urges to empire in Africa at this time; and all sorts of causes have been suggested to support the supposition. One and all, however, they suffer from a tiresome defect: of powerful new incentives there is remarkably little sign. Only after the partition was long over and done with did capital seek outlets, did industry seek markets in tropical Africa. As late as the end of the century the European economy went on by-passing these poor prospects in favour of the proven fields of America and Asia. Neither is it realistic to explain the movement by some change in the temper of the European mind. The pride and pomps of African empire did not suit the popular taste until late in the 1890's when the partition was all but completed. Only after Africa lay divided and allotted did European opinion embrace the mythology of empire. Defined as a movement of white men to transform African society, as they had transformed the societies of India or Java, imperialism was not the cause of partition. It was one of the side effects.

This is not to say that there is no rational explanation. It is only to suggest that no single, general cause underlay a movement to which so many things contributed at random. All of them must be included, for it was their concatenations that brought on the partition. And these cannot be revealed unless the view is wrenched away from the standpoint that has obscured it hitherto. Scanning Europe for the causes, the theorists of imperialism have been looking for the answers in the wrong places. The crucial changes that set all working took place in Africa itself. It was the fall of an old power in its north, the rise of a new in its south, that dragged Africa into modern history.

From these internal crises, erupting at opposite ends of the continent, there unfolded two unconnected processes of partition. That in southern Africa flowed from the rise of the Transvaal on its gold reefs, from a struggle between colonial and republican expansion that reached from Bechuanaland to Lake Nyasa. It eventually drove South Africa into the Jameson Raid and the Boer War. The second crisis was the breakdown of the Khedivate in the Egyptian revolution of 1879–82. Their misdealings with this new proto-nationalism brought the British stumbling on to the Nile and trapped them there. This was crucial. It led to bad blood between them and the French in a quarrel that was to spread over all tropical Africa before being settled at Fashoda in 1898.

Hence Europe became entangled in tropical Africa by two internal crises. Imbroglios with Egyptian proto-nationalists and thence with Islamic revivals across the whole of the Sudan drew the powers into an expansion of their own in East and West Africa. Thousands of miles to the south, English efforts to compress Afrikaner nationalists into an obsolete imperial design set off a second sequence of expansion in southern Africa. The last quarter of the century has often been called the 'Age of imperialism'. Yet much of this imperialism was no more than an involuntary reaction of Europe to the various proto-nationalisms of Islam that were already rising in Africa against the encroaching thraldom of the white men.

Muslim rebellion drew Ferry into the unplanned occupation of Tunis which was the prelude of the partition; Muslim revolution in Cairo drew Gladstone into his Egyptian bondage and set off the partition proper. The peoples of this part of North Africa had much to protest about. By 1880 consuls, money-lenders, engineers and philanthropists from over the water had organised both these countries into chaos. Since Egypt commanded a route to British India, since Tunis counted in French Mediterranean policy both the khedive and the bey had been playthings of Anglo-French expansion for three-quarters of a century. Although neither power could be indifferent to the fate of these areas, neither wished to turn them into colonies. Anxious to keep the Ottoman empire intact, the British chose to watch over Suez from Constantinople. Enjoying the fruits of unofficial hegemony in Tunis and Cairo, the French felt no desire for another Algeria. But European investment and trade had increased since the 1830's and it was from investment that the crash came in the 1870's, that golden age of Islamic insolvency when the Commander of the Faithful at Constantinople was himself hammered into bankruptcy. In Cairo and Tunis the financial advice of Europe hardened into something like dictation. Debt commissioners took charge of the revenues so blithely mortgaged by their rulers; payment of the coupon became the first charge on their governments; in the eyes of their peoples the two potentates had become mere debt collectors for the infidels. Inevitably they went from financial catastrophe to political disaster. Their armies, as the least rigid and most westernised group in these states, threatened a *putsch;* or the tribes of the marches talked of revolt. The more they squeezed money from landlord and peasant, the nearer came revolt against their rapacity. By 1881 Egypt and Tunisia were sliding into the ruin which overtook almost all the non-European polities in the nineteenth century that essayed a programme of European-style development. Islam provided neither the law nor the ethos nor the institutions for such work, and the rulers discovered that they could not modernise without loosing their authority or their independence.

In spite of the bankruptcy, the French were far from anxious to occupy Tunisia. But with Italian encouragement after 1877 the grand peculator, Mustapha ben Ismail, replaced Khérédine, the tool of France, as first minister and set about rooting up the concessions which gave Paris the option over the economic and political future of the country. Here was a new situation. Making good these options would require more than gunboats and peddlers of contracts.

Many in Algeria, but few in France, called for a punitive expedition. There were admirals and generals who looked forward to adding Tunis to their domain in Algeria, there was rubbing of hands among speculators at the prospect of the *coup de Bourse* which would come if their government ended by guaranteeing the debts of a defeated bey. But most French politicians saw more risk than gain. 'An expedition to Tunis in an election year?', the premier, Ferry, exclaimed to his Foreign Minister. 'My dear Saint-Hilaire, you cannot think of it!' But Gambetta, the President of the Chamber, was for intervention, and this was decisive. Assured of his aid, the government at last unleashed the army. On 22 April 1881 the military promenade into Tunisia began.

How large were the French intentions? They were remarkably small for the so-called age of imperialism. Gambetta, defining the expedition's aims, wrote: 'We ought to extort a large reparation from the bey . . . take a large belt of territory as a precaution for the future, sign a treaty with effective guarantees, and then retire . . . after having made a show of force sufficient to assure for ever a preponderant position there, in keeping with our power, our interests and our investments in the Mediterranean.' With Ferry also, the aim was to reassert external sway rather than to acquire a new colony and these limited aims were mirrored in the Treaty of Bardo, extorted from the bey on 12 May 1881. It merely announced a French protectorate. By itself this meant only long-range control of his external relations; and even so mild a commitment as this was ratified in the Chamber with a hundred and twenty abstentions. The French occupation of Tunisia was not a matter of forward policy-making in Paris. It came in response to the deepening crisis inside Tunisia itself. The Treaty of Bardo was merely an arrangement with a discredited Muslim ruler whose surrender to France could not bind his subjects.

Within his kingdom, as in Algeria, preachers of the *Sanusi* religious order were whipping up rage against the Christian invaders; a rebellion in Oran was followed by another in the south around the holy city of Kairouan. Holy war was proclaimed, a Khalifa was recognised, the tribes farthest from Tunis flocked to join the movement. Here in essence was the same situation as that which had produced the savage wars of Abd-el-Kader in Algeria during the 1840's and was to produce the Muslim theocracy of the Mahdi in the Egyptian Sudan—lightning explosions of fanaticism against the overlordship of the foreigner and the unbeliever.

Crushing the rising offered no difficulties to the generals, but it presented thorny problems to the politicians. One thing was now clear. The basis of the old system of informal control had gone for good, swept aside by political and religious revolt from below. By the summer of 1881 France had to make the same hard choice in Tunisia as Abd-el-Kader had presented her with in Algeria. She had either to get on or get out. Either the paper protectorate had to be made good, or it had to be torn up. Making it good would entail yet more criticism from the Chamber. In October the rebellion was broken. But the general dislike of African adventures in the Chamber meant that its endorsement would be oblique and ambiguous. Gambetta induced the new Chamber to resolve on the 'complete fulfilment' of the Treaty of Bardo. Behind this dexterously vague draftsmanship, the reality was quite different. The invaders of Tunisia were now compelled to conquer and rule a people whom they could no longer dominate from outside.

So devious an occupation was far from marking the start of a new imperialism. It was not the result of a profound impulse in French society to enlarge the empire in Africa. It was electorally risky. It brought obloquy upon its sponsors. It struck no spark of that Gallic love of *gloire* so often brought in by historians when the problems surrounding French expansion become too puzzling. The protectorate was no more than a continuation of the old move into Algeria, a conclusion of the old informal expansion into Tunisia.

The partition of the African tropics which began two years later was not the result of the Tunisian mishap, or of Leopold's schemes and Bismarck's wiles, or of the squabbles of white merchants and explorers on the spot. What drove it on was the Suez crisis and the repercussions of that crisis.

A recognisably modern nationalist revolution was sweeping the Nile Delta by 1882; its leaders are much more familiar figures today than the pro-consuls who put them down. The Egyptians were reacting against increasing interference over the past six years by Britain and France. Anxious to renovate the crumbling state on which their amicable dual paramountcy and their security in India and the Mediterranean in large part depended, they had acted with a high hand. At their behest, the Khedivate had been clothed in the decencies of constitutional monarchy, the army cut, and the landlords obliged to pay their dues; the khedive Ismail had been sent packing, Tewfik raised in his place and two-thirds of the revenue sequestrated to satisfy the bondholders. Small wonder that the Notables were using the constitution to break their foreign fetters. The mulcted peasantry was at the point of revolt. Muslim gorges were rising against Christians; the army had mutinied to recall dismissed comrades, and the pashas were defending their fiscal privileges in the guise of patriots ridding the country of the foreigner. By January 1882 all were uniting against the Anglo-French Financial Controllers and the khedive who did their will. The French consul reported that Tewfik had lost all prestige; the British that Arabi and his colonels had practically taken over the country.

What was afoot in Egypt was far more serious than the collapse of the bey had been. Here also was 'an anti-European movement . . . destined to turn into fanaticism';[1] but this time it had the professional army at its head. Gladstone, then prime minister, anticipated 'with the utmost apprehension a conflict between the "Control" and any sentiment truly national, with a persuasion that one way or the other we should come to grief.' 'Egypt for the Egyptians [was] the best, the only good solution to the Egyptian question.' This was true. But as the 'union between [Britain and France] on that . . . question was the principal symbol' of their overall *entente,* both gave priority in the crisis to keeping in step. Each might grumble at going it together, neither desired to go it alone. The unpopularity of the Tunisian adventure was enough to deter Freycinet's ministry from another promenade in North Africa. Gladstone's Liberals, who had just retired from the Transvaal and Afghanistan and washed their hands of Tunis and Morocco, still had their scruples about meddling abroad. Yet something had to be done. Clearly the ideal solution, the only one as Gladstone had said, was to come to terms with Arabi. This was tried. Paris offered him a paid holiday to study European armies; London tried to reconcile him to the khedive. But Egyptian feelings were too heated for Arabi to agree to the one condition that seemed indispensable: abiding by the Financial Control. So long as he refused this, the British feared a foreign thrust at the jugular vein of Suez, and the French feared Turkish intervention which would bring the aid of Islam nearer to their dissident subjects in Tunis and Algeria. On 6 January 1882 the joint note announced the conclusion of Gambetta, unwillingly subscribed to by Gladstone. The khedive must be supported and the Control upheld. What was not announced was the equally emphatic conviction of the two governments that landing an army in Egypt for this purpose would defeat its own object. Freycinet could not move because the Chamber was opposed, and so an invasion would hand Egypt to the British on a plate. Gladstone's cabinet too was in a dilemma. Intervening single-handed would mean a breach with France. A joint intervention would give France a half-share in the route to the East. Granville at the Foreign Office listed the objections: 'Opposition of Egyptians; of Turkey; jealousy of Europe; responsibility of governing a country of Orientals without adequate means and under adverse circumstances; presumption that France would object as much to our sole occupation as we should object to theirs.' The official case against going into Egypt was overwhelming. As Disraeli had said, 'Constantinople [was still] the key to India, not Cairo and the Canal'. At few times in the century had Anglo-French rivalry in the Mediterranean been so composed. Added to that, the late-Victorian pessimism about the possibilities of making English gentlemen of 'Orientals' made another strong argument against conquering new Indias. All the plans therefore were for staying out and solving the problem from outside.

But effective as the arts of 'moral influence' had been hitherto in bending pashas and mandarins to European whims, they were to prove worse than useless against Arabists, Mahdists and Boxers whose mass defiance signalled the political awakenings of Islam and the Orient. Instead of sobering the colonels and saving the Control, the pressures of gunboat diplomacy and the European Concert only added to the charismatic appeal of Arabi, *el Misr,* the 'Egyptian'. The Anglo-French naval demonstration of June provoked a massacre of Europeans at Alexandria. This destroyed Arabi's credit with the English Liberals, and although the French squadron sailed away, Beauchamp Seymour was allowed to bombard the Alexandrian forts to show that Britain at least was in earnest. This old-fashioned device proved the critical blunder, the point of no return. Arabi proclaimed a *jihad* against the British, rioting spread to the interior. According to the dogmas of strategy, if Suez was in jeopardy, it must be protected at any cost. According to Anglo-Indian orthodoxy, the *jihad* challenged imperial prestige throughout the Muslim East. Hence for Gladstone's ministers, 'the question [was] no longer what form of intervention is . . . most unobjectionable, but in what form it can be most promptly applied'. No chance of French or international co-operation was left. But in applying their conventional routine of threat and bluff to cow the Egyptians, the British had raised the stakes so high that now they had to win by any means. On 16 August Sir Garnet Wolseley and the redcoats landed on the Canal for another small colonial war. They routed the Egyptian army at Tel el Kebir, imprisoned Arabi and reinstated Tewfik. Gladstone's government pledged its word that as soon as the Canal was safe and Tewfik strong, it would bring the troops home and leave the Egyptians 'to manage their own affairs'.

There is no doubt that this is what the Liberals meant to do. Like the French in Tunisia, they simply intended to restore the old security through influence without extending their rule. The expedition was to be a Palmerstonian stroke of the kind that had brought the Turk to reason in 1839–41, had chastened the Chinese in two Opium wars, the Ethiopians in 1869 and the Ashanti in 1874. Many months passed before they realized that, having rushed in, they could not rush out again; that they had achieved the occupation which above all they had wanted to avoid. By 1884 they had to confess privately that 'the theory on which we originally undertook [to go in] . . . however plausible, has completely broken down'. The models for intervention proved as outdated as the Crystal Palace. From start to finish the British had miscalculated. They had gone to restore the *status quo ante Arabi,* and discovered that it no longer existed. They had come to restore a khedive and found him a cypher without the authority of British bayonets. And so they had gone in and they could not get out.

What first opened their eyes was another crisis in Africa. After Mehemet Ali had conquered the eastern Sudan for Egypt, the khedive Ismail had laid heavy tribute upon its people. At the same time, he had put down the slave trade, thus depriving them of their chief means of staving off the tax-collector or his bastinado. He had employed white governors to impose Christian ethics on his Muslim subjects. Detesting the imperialism of Cairo, the Sudanese struck back at the Egyptians once they had been disarmed by revolution and invasion. As so often in Muslim Africa, the liberation movement took the form of a puritan revolution against the religious latitudinarianism of the foreign ruling class. In 1881 the Mahdi, Mohammed Ahmad, began his preaching and the revivalist Dervish orders forged the politically discontented sheikhs and deposed sultans, slave traders and tribes, into an army and a state. At first the implications of the *Mahdia* were hidden from the British in Egypt behind a curtain of sands, until news came in November 1883 that the Mahdists had cut the Egyptian troops in the Sudan to pieces. Without soldiers or money, Tewfik could not hold Khartoum. There was no resistance left between the Mahdi and Wadi Halfa. Just as the British were handing back Tewfik a much qualified independence and withdrawing their troops from Cairo, the Mahdi's advance compelled them to stand in defense of the frontiers of Lower Egypt. At last the sinister truth dawned in London. As ministers complained: 'we have now been forced into the position of being the protectors of Egypt'. As with Arabi, so with the Mahdi, there was no chance of striking a bargain of the old mid-Victorian sort. Against fierce Egyptian opposition Gladstone ordered Tewfik to abandon the Sudan and stop the drain on his exchequer, while Gordon was sent to his death at Khartoum attempting the impossible. In enforcing the abandonment, Baring practically had to take control of the khedivial government and, the tighter he gripped it, the deeper the British became involved in its financial difficulties. By this time the unpopularity of the Egyptian fiasco matched that of the Tunisian affair in France. It was increasingly clear that Gladstone's ministry had made fools of themselves. They had hoped to set up an independent Egyptian government; but hampered by the *Mahdia,* the loss of the Sudan, the bankruptcy and the Control's unpopularity with the proto-nationalists, they found no Egyptian collaborators to whom they could transfer power with safety. Nor could they retire so long as the infuriated French refused to admit the exclusive paramountcy in Cairo which they claimed as their due reward. For if they left, the French would upset their influence, or the Egyptian nationalists or Sudanese invaders might upset the financial settlement, and all the dangers of the Suez crisis would arise again.

In the event, the *Mahdia* had trapped the British in Egypt in much the same way as the southern rising had caught the French in Tunisia. No sooner did a European power set its foot upon the neck of the Ottoman rulers of the coastal cities than the nomads of the inland steppes and deserts seized their chance of throwing off the pashas' yoke. Hence the Europeans found the regimes which they had come to discipline or restore falling about their ears and they had to stay and pick up the pieces. Gladstone wearily summed up the result of dealing as if they were politically uninhabited with an Egypt in revolution and a Sudan in religious revival: 'we have done our Egyptian business; we are an Egyptian government.'

The longer the British garrisons remained, the stronger grew the arguments for staying. By 1889 the 'veiled protectorate' had become a necessity for imperial security in the world. As Salisbury said, 'the appetite had grown with the eating'. Sir Evelyn Baring and the Anglo-Indian officials who governed in the name of the khedive, brought from Calcutta to the Nile their professional distrust of nationalists. It became inconceivable that the Egyptians could be trusted to govern themselves. Arabist sentiment still smouldered. In taking over the country, the English had stopped its politics in a state of betwixt and between. Its obsolete Turkish rulers had fallen, but its rising liberal leaders had been put down. So Baring had to rule until native authority revived, but native authority could hardly revive while Baring ruled. If evacuation was impossible for internal reasons, it soon became impracticable on external grounds. Eventually the occupation drove France into the arms of Russia; and this combined menace in the Mediterranean, together with the further crumbling of Turkish power, enhanced Egypt's importance to Britain. After 1889 therefore, the resolution was to stay and keep the lid on the simmering revolution, rather than withdraw and invite another power to straddle the road to India. Henceforth England's statesmen were to be bewitched with the far-fetched fancies of the Nile-valley strategy. To be sure of the canal and lower Egypt, they were to push their territorial claims up the Nile to Fashoda and from the Indian Ocean to Uganda and the Bahr-al-Ghazal.

On an Olympian view, the taking of Egypt might seem to have been the logical outcome of two great movements of European expansion since the end of the eighteenth century. One was the long build-up of British trade and power in the East; the other was the extension of Anglo-French influence which had so thoroughly disrupted Ottoman rule in Egypt and the Levant that the routes to the East were no longer safe. Certainly this long-term logic set limits to the problem. But what determined the occupation of Egypt in concrete terms was not so much the secular processes of European expansion as the Arabist and Mahdist revolutions against its encroaching mastery. When they baffled the customary informal techniques of France and Britain, it was too late to find any other solution but conquest and rule.

The shots of Seymour at Alexandria and Wolseley at Tel el Kebir were to echo round the world. It transpired in the end that their *ricochets* had blown Africa into the modern age. The onslaught on Arabi opened the long Anglo-French conflict over Egypt which more than anything brought on the division of East and West Africa. Up to the 1890's it was merely a partition on paper. The politicians in the European capitals at least intended it to go no farther than that. Hitherto they had ignored the clamour of their merchants, missionaries and explorers for advances in tropical Africa. They had done so with good reason. Communications were difficult; the tribes of the hinterlands seemed lost in chaos; there were grave doubts whether the African could be persuaded to work, or whether he could work at anything worth producing; prospects of trade or revenue seemed gloomy indeed. If governments had sometimes bestirred themselves to help private traders and sent frigates along the coasts to atone for the sins of the slave trade, such acts were not intended as commitments. Since large or stable authorities were few and far between, even the simplest methods of informal expansion worked badly in tropical Africa. Clearly then, this was no place for colonies. For decades before 1882, therefore, a gentlemen's agreement between the powers saw to it that the petty quarrels of their merchants and officials on the coasts did not become pretexts for empire.

But when Gladstone stumbled into Egypt that era ended. To the French, the veiled protectorate was the worst humiliation since Sedan. Their canal and the country which they had nursed since Napoleon's landing had been snatched away under their very noses. This broke the Liberal *entente* and kept Britain and France at odds for twenty years. Once in Egypt, moreover, Britain became highly vulnerable to continental diplomacy. To set Egyptian finances in order, she needed German support against French vetoes in the Debt Commission, if her ministers were to avoid asking their critical Parliament to subsidise the khedive. By altering European alignments thus, the Egyptian occupation for the rest of the century gave the powers both incentive and opportunity to break the traditional understandings about tropical Africa. While Baring played the puppet-master in Cairo, the French sought to force him out by loosing their pro-consuls against exposed British interests in unclaimed Africa; while the Germans did likewise to extort more British aid in their European affairs. Once the powers began to back their nationals' private enterprises for diplomatic purposes, commerce south of the Sahara ceased to be a matter of restricted influence over coasts; it became a business of unlimited territorial claims over vast hinterlands. In this roundabout fashion, Arabi's revolution and Gladstone's blunder exaggerated the importance of intrinsically tiny disputes in tropical Africa and brought the diplomatists to the auction rooms.

On the western coasts before October 1882 there were few signs that the *modus vivendi* was to end so abruptly. Wars between producers and middlemen chiefs along the unpacified lines of supply were strangling the British and French trading stations on the Bight of Benin. For twenty years past, the Colonial Office had been thinking of giving up the Gambia, the Gold Coast, Lagos and Sierra Leone. The French government had left the Ivory Coast and in 1880 it was thinking of moving out of Dahomey and Gabon 'because of the trivial scale of French interests there.'[2] With the turmoil in the hinterlands, the unofficial *pax* rigged up by the palm-oil traders was ceasing to work; but London and Paris refused to replace it with the extravagant order of colonial rule.

The only regions where Europeans had broken through the middlemen chiefs who closed all ways inland, had been along the three great rivers. On the Senegal by 1865 General Faidherbe had carried French influence up-river to Kayes. Sixteen years later their men in the field had visions of going on to bring the formidable Muslim states of the western Sudan under their sway and of building a trans-Saharan railway between Senegal and Algeria. This scheme went back into a pigeon-hole. In 1881, however, an Upper Senegal Command was formed and Colonel Borgnis-Desbordes was instructed to throw a chain of posts from Bafoulabe to Bamako on the Upper Niger. But as soon as the soldiers ran into trouble, the politicians of Paris cut their credits and talked of scrapping the command. The statesmen in London and Paris refused to quarrel about this expansion of Senegal which pointed no threat to the chief centre of British trade three thousand kilometres away on the Lower Niger.

Nor were there the makings of a West African 'scramble' here, where Liverpool merchants throve without the aid of colonial government. By 1881 George Goldie had amalgamated the most enterprising of the Niger firms into the National Africa Company, the better to monopolise the up-river traffic and drive out French competitors. This was Anglo-French rivalry of a sort, but only at the level of private traders cutting each others' throats in the ordinary way of business. So long as the Anglo-French *entente* lasted, their governments had no wish to become involved, as Goldie discovered when he was refused a royal charter for his company. They were as uninterested in the merchants and explorers jostling in the no-man's-land along the Congo river. Disraeli's ministers had rejected the Cameroon treaties which offered them a political option on the inner basin. Leopold II of the Belgians was to be more reckless. Under cover of the International African Association which he floated in 1876, this inveterate projector was plotting a private Congo empire under the innocent device of a free state. In 1879 Stanley went out to establish its claims. To preserve a hinterland for its poverty-stricken posts on the Gabon, the French government asked Brazza to pick up counter-treaties that would 'reserve our rights without engaging the future'. All this was but the small change of local rivalry that had gone for decades. Brazza's was a private venture of passing interest to his government. Leopold's Congo scheme had as little chance of being realised as a dozen others he had hatched for concessions in China, the Philippines, Borneo and the Transvaal. The Belgian government would have nothing to do with it. Nor, as the king admitted, would investors subscribe a centime until the powers recognised his rights in the Congo. But what was the chance that they would then be so generous as to endow his house with a great estate which he was too puny to seize for himself? As long as France and Britain could agree, his hopes of becoming an African emperor were exceedingly thin.

But immediately the British ejected the French from the Dual Control in October 1882, these minor intrigues in West Africa were drawn into their quarrel over Egypt. In Paris there was less talk of jettisoning outposts and more speculation about extending claims to strengthen the diplomatic hand against the English. Treich Laplène was allowed to expand French influence on the Ivory Coast. More important, the French consul on the Lower Niger started a flurry of treaty-making, menacing the chief British trade on the coast. Early in 1883 Granville tried to renew the old self-denial arrangements by offering the French exclusive influence on the Upper Niger if they would respect the *status quo* on the lower river. But the time for such happy understandings had gone. As the ambassador reported, the breaking of the Egyptian gentlemen's-agreement had so outraged the French that a West African standstill was now out of the question. So by November the Foreign Office could see nothing for it but to send out consul Hewett to bring the Niger districts under treaties of protection and 'prevent the possibility of our trade there being interfered with'. His sailing was delayed for six months. Neither the Treasury nor the Liverpool traders could be persuaded to pay his fare!

At the same time, the Anglo-French estrangement overturned the hands-off arrangements on the Congo. Paris scorned Granville's efforts to renew them. In November 1882 the Chamber ratified Brazza's treaty of claim to the right bank of the river instead. A month later, Granville countered by accepting Portugal's ancient claims to the Congo in return for guarantees of free trade. To the French this treaty seemed West African insult added to Egyptian injury; 'a security taken by Britain to prevent France . . . from setting foot in the Congo Delta'; a violation of an undertaking that went back to 1786. In riposte, Ferry mounted a diplomatic onslaught against the Anglo-Portuguese agreement. Once she had obtained a pre-emptive right over Leopold's holdings, France pressed the counterclaims of the Congo Free State as if they were already her own. At the end of March 1884 the most powerful statesman in Europe took a hand. His own metaphor for it was much more revealing: he would take up his 'Egyptian baton'.

With Egypt dividing them, France and Britain both courted German favour; Granville needed Bismarck's help to extricate his government from their financial troubles in Cairo; while Ferry solicited it in resisting the Anglo-Portuguese Treaty and English ambitions in Egypt—'a consideration which dominated all others' in Paris. The Chancellor could sell his support to the highest bidder; or if need be, he could encourage the weaker contender against the stronger, and so keep the Egyptian issue from being settled. In any case there would be something for Germany; Heligoland might be recovered from England; a number of colonial trifles could certainly be picked up; better still, an isolated France might be diverted from allying with

Russia or rejoining Britain into a healing *rapprochement* with the conquerors of Alsace-Lorraine. In March Bismarck began to try out these ideas. He hinted at German help for France if she pressed her rights in Egypt. But Ferry, suspecting that Bismarck did 'not want to do anything to annoy England, but . . . [would] be delighted to see her opposed by others, especially by [France]', negotiated an Egyptian agreement with Britain. In June the English were promising to evacuate the country in 1888, if the French would agree to neutralise it on Belgian lines thereafter.

With the Egyptian baton falling from his grasp, it was time for Bismarck to stiffen the French with offers of German support, if they would raise their terms to Granville. Time also to remove Ferry's suspicions by proving that Germany had serious reasons of her own to act with France against Britain. There were none in Egypt, as the Chancellor had often declared. So for verisimilitude, he blew the petty Anglo-German trade disputes around the African coasts into a noisy anti-British demonstration. In May he pressed the German government's protection over Lüderitz's concession at Angra Pequena, on the barren south-west coast of Africa. A month later, he denounced the Anglo-Portuguese Treaty and demanded an international conference to decide the Congo's future. At the beginning of July he proclaimed Togoland and the Cameroons to be German protectorates. There was no popular cry for African colonies inside the Reich; and as Bismarck always insisted, he himself was 'against colonies . . . which install officials and erect garrisons'. But paper claims to protectorates cost nothing, and they were good bait to draw France away from Britain into an *entente* with Germany. Surprisingly, this devious diplomacy succeeded. At the London Conference of July, Bismarck, together with the French Chamber and bondholders, contrived to wreck the Anglo-French agreement over Egypt. To drive the wedge home, he proposed a Franco-German *entente* on West African questions. In August the French accepted. 'After the bad treatment inflicted on us by England', wrote de Courcel, 'this *rapprochement* is essential to us under penalty of utter and most dangerous isolation.' To show good faith, the Germans joined France in backing Leopold's Congo Free State. By October 1884 the two powers had agreed to settle the fate of the Niger as well as the Congo at an international conference in Berlin; and the British, who had conceded all Bismarck's African claims and dropped the Portuguese treaty lest 'a breach with Germany . . . make our chances of honourable extrication from the Egyptian difficulty even less than they are', were compelled to attend.

To strengthen their governments' hands in the coming negotiations, consuls and merchants were now treaty-making wherever they hoped to trade on the west coast. Astonished ministers in London observed that 'the attention of European Powers is directed to an unprecedented extent to . . . the formation of Settlements on the African coast'. Forestalled by Nachtigal in the Cameroons, Hewett rushed around the Niger Delta bringing the chiefs under British protection to block the Germans and French there. On the Lower Niger, Goldie bought out the *Compagnie du Sénégal* and the *Société française de l'Afrique Equatoriale,* and sent Joseph Thomson to outrun a German expedition for treaties with the northern Nigerian emirates of Sokoto and Gandu. Meanwhile, the French, who had no great hopes of the Lower Niger, were advancing down the upper river from Bamako, occupied by Galliéni in 1883, and were extending their treaties along the Ivory and Slave Coasts. Governments had let the local expansionists off their leashes, now that the Egyptian occupation had merged territorial claims in Africa with power-politics in Europe. How high the symbolic importance of these trivial African clashes had risen was shown when the French and English went meekly to their little Canossa at Berlin. The two leading naval and colonial powers in the world were bidding for West African commerce under the hammer of a third-rate naval person who hitherto had had no colonies at all.

In strange contrast to the zealots on the coasts, the statesmen who met in Berlin at the end of 1884 found each other reasonably accommodating. The conference in fact was something of an anti-climax. Before it had ever met, it had served its main purposes. The Egyptian baton had thwacked Gladstone back into line. The Franco-German *entente* had been formed; and it had kept Granville from declaring a protectorate in Egypt and from taking exclusive charge of its finances. Toward the end of the meeting, indeed, Ferry and Granville were agreeing in the London Convention to pump an international loan into the Khedivate and to continue international control of its revenues. Though they were left pining for the British to leave Cairo, the French had at least prevented them from digging-in any deeper. Hence the West African disputes which had served as outer markers for these evolutions of grand diplomacy were easily dismissed in Berlin. And public opinion in Europe took scant notice of the manner of their going.

The diplomats dealt briskly enough with the outstanding trivia. Who should be saddled with the responsibility for free trade and navigation on the Niger; and on the Congo? How little the powers cared, they showed by recognising the legal personality of the Congo Free State. It was Leopold's year for a miracle. The lions agreed to toss him the lion's share of the Congo basin, while contenting themselves with the scraps. Ferry took for France a much more modest sphere; the region around Brazzaville on the north bank was to be the Gabon's hinterland. For the rest, the Congo river was placed under an international regime and its conventional basin, covering most of Central Africa, became a free-trade area. Having conceded the Congo, Granville was able to keep international authority out of the Niger. Control of the lower river went to Britain, that of the upper river to France, arrangements which merely preserved the *status quo*. Though the Berlin Act laid it down that territorial claims on African coasts should depend on effective occupation, this magical phrase was left so vague that it meant almost nothing.

Far from laying down ground rules for the occupation of Africa, the statesmen at Berlin had no intention of playing that game. Despising colonial ventures in tropical Africa, they had extended their hands-off arrangements largely in order to avoid it. The last thing they wanted was to commit themselves to administering such comparatively unimportant places. Once these countries had been saved from foreign clutches by adjusting their international status, the diplomats planned to wash their hands of them. Except in the Cameroons and Togoland, where the traders refused such gifts, Bismarck gave over his paper protectorates to the Germans trafficking in them. The British hastened to do the same with the Lower Niger. In June 1886 Goldie at last got his monopoly chartered under the title of the Royal Niger Company; this was 'the cheapest . . . way of meeting' the obligations accepted at the Berlin Conference. Until 1891 the Foreign Office hoped to saddle the Liverpool firms with the governance of the Niger Delta, just as it had fobbed on to Goldie the costs of administering the lower river. But these merchants refused the privilege. There was nothing for it but to put the Niger Coast protectorate squarely under the rule of London. Throughout the British attitude to the Niger had been negative: 'so long as we keep other European nations out, we need not be in a hurry to go in.' Whatever this dictum rings of, it does not sound like imperialism.

The politicians of Paris were equally averse to colonising their new spheres. True, Ferry was saying by 1885 that France must have colonies for all the usual reasons—investment, markets, prestige, the civilising mission—but he had been swept out of office in March by the critics of his colonial adventures: the Freycinet who had followed him in office did not wish to follow him out again. Plainly, the French Congo was a new white elephant. The Gabon was an old one. The

French government treated both of them with scorn. In 1887 it stopped its annual subsidy to the Gabon[3] and loftily warned Brazza, the administrator of the Congo, that 'we cannot stay indefinitely in a period of costly exploration'.[4] Until the 1890's there were only fifteen French officials in the region. Its annual export was only worth £1500.[5] Paris was no less sceptical about its possessions in the Gulf of Benin. All the Quai d'Orsay could find to say in their favour was that 'even if we admit that they are of small value . . . [they] are bargaining counters which . . . may be useful for our interests elsewhere'. The heads of the Ministry of Marine 'show[ed] themselves very lukewarm, not merely to the development, but to the maintenance pure and simple of the French holdings in West Africa'.[6] On the Upper Niger too, they felt no enthusiasm for turning their sphere into a full-blown colony. At the Berlin Conference, neutralisation of the river and free trade along its entire course had been the most they had wanted.[7] But when the British made the Niger Company the monopolists of free trade on the lower river, they may have fooled themselves, but they did not fool the French. The glaring paradox behind this goaded Freycinet into declaring a protectorate over the Upper Niger in 1887 to forestall an extension of so bizarre a theory of free trade.[8] Politically, he meant to go no farther than a vague network of alliances with the Muslim rulers of the area, and early in 1887 Galliéni signed treaties with Amadu Shehu and Samori, by far the most powerful of them. His agreements did not commit France, he explained, neither would they cost her anything. They were simply meant 'to enlarge the limits of our future commercial empire and to close these regions to foreign designs'. Trade was supposed to bind these Muslim states to France:[9] but there was not enough of it. 'It is only retail business,' Galliéni's successor reported, 'the means of transport are lacking for anything larger.'[10] All that Paris had envisaged on the Upper Niger was a small, cheap and conditional option on the region.

If the diplomats and commercial travellers after the Berlin Conference had been deciding these West African affairs on their merits, things would have gone no farther than that. But as usual they had reckoned with an Africa without the Africans. So their intentions were one thing; the outcome on the spot was another. Driven on by the Egyptian crisis, the West African 'scramble' could no longer be halted at will. The old stand-still arrangements could no longer stand. In the end, even paper protectorates were to perform that special alchemy which makes one people regard the remote lands of others as 'possessions' and itself as responsible for their well-being.

But it was not working strongly yet; imperial sentiment in Europe was the least of the reasons for the scramble. They are rather to be found in West Africa itself. The diplomatic flurry had compelled governments to back their traders' efforts to break through the middlemen chiefs and trade up-country. So a rivalry for commercial options was spreading as a result from the coast to the interior, with every port competing against its neighbours for a hinterland and its officials plunging deeper into the politics of the African bush. Even so, most of the powers held these local tendencies in check. Germany ceased to extend her claims once the diplomatic manoeuvres of 1884 and 1885 had been completed, content to take diplomatic advantage of the Anglo-French dissension to improve her position in Europe. No more ambitious were the British, on the west coast at least. Not only were they wary of going too far in their dealings with powerful Muslims in the backlands, they parsimoniously reined back all advances until local trade and colonial revenue had developed sufficiently to pay for them. What they had on the Niger, they held; but elsewhere the English usually let West Africa go.

It was to the French that it went. For the next fifteen years they made all the running in the western parts of the continent; but not altogether by choice. It would be puerile to argue that they were driven on by a search for glory—most Frenchmen had no idea of the whereabouts of Bafoulabe. Admittedly, the established influence of the military in their colonial affairs made the politicians prone to give their army in Africa its head. But what necessitated their headlong conquest of the middle Niger, the northern Ivory Coast and the western Sudan after 1887 was a series of involuntary imbroglios with the fighting Muslim theocracies of these regions. The hapless policymakers of Paris had designed no more than a vague paramountcy over them. It was bad luck that, like the Egyptians, the Mahdists and southern Tunisians, the theocrats preferred the *jihad* to working with the French and so dragged them into vast imperial conquests instead. The paper partition had set the French army to grips with a reviving and recalcitrant Islam. In subjugating it, the paper empire had to be occupied.

In the history of Africa, the long expansion of Islam since the eighth century dwarfs the brief influence of Europe. From this western Sudan between the Senegal and Lake Tchad, between the coastal forests and the Sahara, the puritanic Almoravides had set forth to rule over Spain and the Maghreb. Here the golden empires of Mali and Ghana had risen and fallen; here Muslims and animists had struggled for centuries. Yet the difficulty of assimilating tribes into nations had foiled the making of enduring states. By the seventeenth century, Islam here was at best the cult of aristocracies lording it over a mass of pagan subjects. But from the later eighteenth century, the creed was on the march once more. United by the spread of Muslim brotherhoods with their calls for religious reform, the Tokolor and Fulani peoples rose in holy war upon their decadent Muslim rulers, riveting new empires upon the animists. At the end of the nineteenth century, when the British bumped into them in what is now northern Nigeria, their force was spent, and the Fulani emirs who had inherited the disunited provinces of the Sokoto empire were unable to resist British suzerainty. But the French had no such luck with the Tokolor and Manding empires to the west. By 1864 El Hadj Omar at the head of the *Tijani* order had brought the western Sudan from Futa to Timbuktu under his sway. When the French confronted this empire, Amadu Shehu, his successor, was imposing conformity to his version of Islam, and so overcoming the cleavage between rulers and ruled to forge a unified power. It was in the nature of such empires, founded in holy war, bound together by theocracy and the brotherhood of all believers, that their commanders could no longer command if they co-operated with a Christian power. Amadu and Samori were the prisoners of their own systems of leadership, unable to work their treaties with France without destroying their own authority. Both chose to fight rather than to abdicate. By 1889 Paris found out that Galliéni's loose protectorate meant a far-reaching military conquest.

All the traditions of the Ministry of Marine were against it. 'It is the negation of all our policy', the governor protested, '. . . it means starting a holy war . . . poor Senegal.'[11] But covered by Étienne, the Algerian Under-Secretary for Colonies, the local army commanders seized their chance.[12] In 1890 Colonel Archinard broke the power of Amadu. Thenceforward protests from Paris could not stop the sand-table thinkers of the Upper Senegal Command from encompassing and crushing the embattled Muslim aristocracies one by one. In 'absolute violation of orders',[13] Archinard next invaded Samori's empire. For the next eight years that potentate and his mobile, Sofa hordes kept the French army in hot pursuit from the Upper Niger to the Ivory Coast. Grappling with him and other disaffected Muslim leaders, the French were to end by occupying the entire western Sudan. Having gone so far against their will in the 1880's logic brought them to rationalise these haphazard conquests in the 1890's. French Africa was to be all of a piece; Senegal and Algeria to be joined with the hinterlands of the Guinea, Ivory and Dahoman coasts; these in their turn to be linked with the French Congo at the shores of Lake Tchad.

For the most part, the British looked on and acquiesced. As Salisbury put it ironically, 'Great Britain has adopted the policy of advance by commercial enterprise. She has not attempted to compete with the military operations of her neighbour.' Her priority in Africa lay in protecting the position in Egypt and, from 1889, in closing off the Nile valley for this purpose. In hope of damping down the Egyptian quarrel, Salisbury saw no harm in offering another round of West African compensations to France between 1889 and 1891. This vicarious generosity cost nothing either to give or to take, so Paris accepted it. The Gambian hinterland was signed away to French Senegal; that of Sierra Leone to French Guinea. But it was the Convention of August 1890 that gave the French their largest windfall; and once again the Egyptian priorities of the British shook the tree. To compensate Paris for the Heligoland-Zanzibar Treaty of 1890, in which the Germans gave him a free hand at Zanzibar and over the Nile, Salisbury cheerfully consigned to France the 'light soils' of the Sahara and the western Sudan between Algeria, Senegal and the Say-Barruwa line resting on Lake Tchad. This enormous paper concession of other people's countries the Quai d'Orsay accepted with the same irony with which it was given: 'Without any appreciable effort, without any large sacrifice, without the expense of exploration . . . , without having made a single treaty . . . we have induced Britain to recognise . . . that Algeria and Senegal shall form a continuous belt of territory. . . . Political access to Lake Tchad *seems* important. . . . It may become the nodal point for trade routes. . . . But in striving to extend our activity towards central Africa, there is a more important consideration, bound up with more pressing and concrete interests. We want to get it recognised once and for all that no European nation can ever resist our influence in the Sahara and that we shall never be taken in the rear in Algeria.'[14] For the colonial zealots, there may have been enchantment in such a view. But for the technicians of national security these large but unconsidered trifles were worth picking up only so far as they improved French security in North Africa, and so in the Mediterranean. Like their counterparts in London, it was not so much a new empire as the future of their old interests in Europe and the East that they were seeking in Africa. For the French this meant security in Algeria's hinterland. But it also meant security in Egypt. So Salisbury's bargains could not end the scramble for Africa. France would take all she could get in the west. But she could not afford thereby to be appeased along the Nile.

On the east coast, the Egyptian occupation had also shattered the old *modus vivendi*. Up to 1884 naval power had given Britain the leading influence from Port Natal to Cape Guardafui—an influence exerted through the puppet sultan of Zanzibar, partly to keep other powers off the flank of the route to India, chiefly to put down the Arab slave trade. Unlike West Africa, the east coast had no large states on the mainland. Neither was there any large trade. Ivory was hauled by slaves, cloves were grown by slaves, caravans were stocked with slaves; commerce of this sort had fallen foul of European prejudices and it was being snuffed out. In doing this the powers kept on good terms with each other. In 1862 the British and French had made one of their gentlemen's agreements to respect the sultan's independence. True, his regime was failing. Europe had used him to impose the anti-slavery ethics of Christendom upon his Muslim subjects, and this was over-stretching his authority as their religious head. Yet no government wanted a colony where there was so little to colonise. In 1878 the Foreign Office had refused to back the shipowner William Mackinnon in developing a concession of Zanzibar's mainland possessions. Four years later it turned a deaf ear to the sultan's pleas for what amounted to a British protectorate. London and Bombay considered that this would call for expenditure 'out of all proportion to the advantages to be gained'. Towards the end of 1884 Karl Peters could tout his blank treaty forms around Tanganyika acting as commercial traveller for the struggling *Kolonialverein;* yet Gladstone's ministry would not hear of a Kilimanjaro protectorate.

But in February 1885 a new factor upset this equilibrium. Bismarck recognised the agreements of Peters—the man he had previously called a mountebank. As the Berlin West African Conference was disbanding, the Chancellor rigged up a paper protectorate for the German East Africa Company. Britain and France were reaching agreement on Egypt's finances. The time had come to pick another small African quarrel with Granville and to give another boost to the *entente* with France. Once again the Egyptian baton did its work. London accepted Bismarck's claims and bade the sultan of Zanzibar do the same. As Gladstone put it: 'It is really impossible to exaggerate the importance of *getting out of the way the bar to the Egyptian settlement* ... [and] wind[ing] up at once these small colonial controversies.' Just the same, the Indian and Foreign Offices did not wish to be ousted from the entire coast, for the harbours at Mombasa and Zanzibar had some bearing on the security of India. The upshot was another paper partition. In their East African agreement of October 1886, Salisbury and Bismarck divided the mainland, giving the northern sphere to Britain, the southern to Germany. But the governments meant to keep out of the lands they had earmarked. Here at last was Mackinnon's chance. London chartered his British East Africa Company, so as to put a sentry on its claim; to the south Berlin placed the German company in possession.

These paper insurances, casually fobbed off on traders, left the old political hands elegantly bored. Granville and Derby agreed that 'there [was] something absurd in the scramble for colonies'. They were 'little disposed to join in it'. Gladstone welcomed Germany's protectorates. Salisbury did not mind either, so long as they guaranteed free trade. German support in Cairo and Constantinople was cheap at the price. In Berlin and Paris the statesmen were taking their new possessions just as lightly. But here, as in West Africa, they were committing themselves to more than they bargained for. By 1889 the German company was at war with Bushiri and the Swahili slaving chiefs; and the Berlin government had to rescue and replace its penniless caretaker so as to save face. Mackinnon's company was heading for ruin as well, so little did British investors value the attractions of East Africa. This was far more serious. By this time, the hinterland of the British sphere had become entangled with the security of the Nile valley and Salisbury's plans for the safety of India in Egypt.

Baring's failure to come to terms with Egyptian nationalists was partly responsible for this far-fetched design. The continuing occupation had directly shifted the Mediterranean balance. In 1887 Salisbury had sent Drummond Wolff to Constantinople to make what was probably his last serious offer to evacuate the Nile Delta. The troops would sail away within three years if the powers would agree that they could sail back again in case of need. The Porte accepted. But French and Russian diplomacy combined to wreck the agreement. Salisbury pondered the meaning of this debacle. British influence at Constantinople was not what it had been. Plainly the chances of patching up and packing up in Egypt had dwindled since 1885. Despite Bismarck's manoeuvres, France was now moving out of isolation and into the *Franco-Russe* toward the end of the 1880's. Worse still, Salisbury found that there were not enough ironclads to fight their way through the Mediterranean against such a combination.

How then could the Turk be propped up against Russia? As the margin of security shrank at Constantinople, Salisbury saw the need of broadening it at Cairo. To be safe in Egypt he adopted the policy of keeping other powers out of the Nile basin. Fear lay behind this policy, the alarmist calculation that 'a civilised, European power . . . in the Nile valley . . . could so reduce the water supply as to ruin [Egypt]'. So from 1890 the British ran up their bids, claiming a sphere along the whole river and its approaches, from Mombasa and Wadi Halfa to Lake Victoria Nyanza. To gain as much as this, they were ready to tout compensations over most of the continent. As the British pivot began to swing from the Asiatic to the African shores of the eastern Mediterranean, the second phase of partition spread from Uganda and Ethiopia to the Zambezi river, from the Red Sea to the Upper Niger. By 1891 there was little more of Africa left to divide. The partition was all over, bar the ultimatums.

Without much cavil, Berlin agreed to stay out of the Nile basin. Haunted by her nightmare of coalitions, Germany was more trapped by European circumstances than any other of the partitioners. In March 1890 William II and Caprivi had decided to abandon the Reinsurance Treaty with Russia. They made no difficulty about scrapping many of their options in East Africa in return for a visible *rapprochement* with Britain in Europe. Gaining Heligoland and the extension of their sphere from Dar-es-Salaam westward to Lake Tanganyika and the northern end of Lake Nyasa, they agreed to a formal British protectorate over Zanzibar; they gave up their claims to Witu, which would otherwise have blocked British access to Lake Victoria from Mombasa; and they cut back their claims in the north, so conceding Uganda to the British and shutting themselves out of the Upper Nile valley. For Salisbury, things could not have been better. 'The effect of this [Heligoland-Zanzibar] arrangement', he congratulated himself, 'will be that . . . there will be no European competitor to British influence between the 1st degree of S[outh] latitude [running through the middle of Lake Victoria] and the borders of Egypt.' On paper, at least, his chief purpose had been achieved. This entailed scrapping Rhodes's romantic idea of a Cape-to-Cairo corridor between the Congo Free State and German East Africa. But Salisbury was no romantic. And in any case he had also cleared all German obstacles out of the way of the British South Africa Company's advance into what is now Rhodesia. After Berlin, he dealt with Lisbon. By the Anglo-Portuguese Treaty of 1891, Salisbury threw back the musty claims of Moçambique in Matabeleland to secure the company's claim there. This was partition with a vengeance. But Salisbury had not finished yet. Next it was the turn of the Italians.

No European nation had moved into Africa with less authority or less enthusiasm than they. In 1882 their government had bought the Bay of Assab from an Italian firm; three years later it had occupied the Red Sea port of Massawa with British encouragement. Better the Italians than the French or the Mahdists. This brought the new Romans into contact with the Ethiopians. Questioned about the possibilities of the new sphere two years later, di Robilant, the Foreign Minister, refused 'to attach much importance to a few robbers who happen to be raising dust around our feet in Africa'. But things were to be different. The old system of ministries living on the freedom-fighting of the *Risorgimento* gave way to a confusion that Francesco Crispi contrived to dominate from 1887 to 1896. Before he came to office he had opposed imperialism. After the old Redshirt had reached the head of the regime of which he had once been the critic, he had to find a new field for his extremism. He found it in African expansion. For successful radicals this was not unusual at the end of the century. The new brand of full-blooded imperialism was occasionally the resort of *arrivistes* moving from left to right; for in joining the old oligarchs, they gave up much of their former domestic stock-in-trade. Chamberlain forgot about his unauthorised programme; Gambetta's heirs turned their backs on the *nouvelles couches:* Crispi passed laws against the socialists. As the least disturbing issue for the transitional ministries to which they belonged, they were all permitted to express overseas the nonconformism they had to muffle at home.

The empty wharves of Massawa gave Crispi his chance for originality. Without a hinterland they would continue to crumble. To avenge the Italian defeat at Dogali at the hands of the Ethiopian Ras Alula, Crispi launched a punitive expedition whose gains were organised into the colony of Eritrea in 1890. More than that, he embarked upon a design for informal paramountcy over Ethiopia. It was full of conundrums, but when the negus Yohannes was killed in battle with the Mahdists in 1889, the Italians imagined that their erstwhile protégé, Menilek, Ras of Shoa, would continue to be their man as negus. He seemed to be a westerniser. He looked like a client. By the treaty of Ucciali, signed on 2 May, Rome claimed that he had accepted its protection; Menilek denied it—after taking delivery of the four million lire and thousands of rifles with which the Italians had endowed him. For the moment, Eritrea seemed to have a bright future of trade with Ethiopia. A year later the di Rudini ministry in pursuit of more trade pushed their colony's frontier westwards to Kassala, which lies on a tributary of the Nile, flush inside the Dervish country.

Fecklessly, the Italians were being drawn into the dangerous vortices of Dervish and Ethiopian politics, as the British had been drawn into those of Egypt, and the French into those of Tunis and the western Sudan. They were rushing in to meddle with two African societies ferociously united through a species of proto-nationalism against the unbelievers; but their catastrophe was yet to come. What concerned Salisbury and Baring in 1890 was that these Roman inroads into Ethiopia and the Eastern Sudan had brought them closest to the sacred serpent of the Nile. Italian expansion into the realms of the King of Kings was not unwelcome in London. It had the merit of blocking any French advance on the Nile valley from the Red Sea ports of Djibouti and Obok. But the thrust on Kassala was a different story. Salisbury was not shutting the French and Germans out of the valley to let the Italians in. Early in 1891 therefore, he brought them to sign a treaty in which they agreed 'to keep their hands off the affluents of the Nile'; and rewarded them by recognising their claim to preponderance over much of the Horn of Africa.

By edging towards the Triple Alliance and signing away huge stretches of unoccupied Africa, Salisbury had bought safety in Egypt from the Germans and Italians. But it was not to be bought from the French. All the donations of 'light soils' in West Africa would not soothe them into letting bygones be bygones in Egypt. Instead of consenting to leave the Nile alone, Paris, with increasing support from St. Petersburg, demanded evacuation. More and more firmly, London refused. Egypt was still the deep rift between France and Britain. The way to the Nile still lay open from the west. Hence the partition of Africa went furiously on into the 1890's.

It is familiar enough, the diplomacy which contrived the astonishing partitions of the 1880's; but the motives behind them are stranger than fiction. As they drew their new map of Africa by treaty, the statesmen of the great powers intended nothing so simple or so serious as the making of colonies there. There were traders and missionaries who clamoured for imperial aid for their enterprises; but it was not they, it was the politicians who decided: and the politicians had no time for the notion that state action should develop the tropics in the interest of national prosperity. Trade, and the political influence that went with it, might expand in Africa; or again it might not. In either case the statesmen were happy to leave the matter to private energies. For tropical Africa at the end of the nineteenth century this meant that next to nothing would be done, for private business was as yet utterly unready to do it. Then were 'claims for posterity' the objects? There is a grain of truth in this old view, but it was more a rationalisation after the event. As they sliced up more and more of the continent, the politicians found it easier to explain their actions in terms of new markets and civilising missions than in terms of the more sophisticated and less high-minded concepts on which their minds were privately running.

Those who presided over the partition saw it with a cold and detached view. It was not Africa itself which they saw; it was its bearing on their great concerns in Europe, the Mediterranean and the East. Their preoccupations were tangential to the continent to a degree possible only in the official mind. They acted upon their traditional concepts of national interests and dangers. They advanced, not the frontiers of trade or empire, but the frontiers of fear.

From a European point of view, the partition treaties are monuments to the flights of imagination of which official minds are capable, when dealing with a blank map of two-thirds of a continent. The strategists anticipated every contingency: the diplomats bargained for every farthing of advantage; while the geographers showed them the whereabouts of the places they were haggling over. From an African standpoint, the main result of their efforts was to change the international status of territory on paper. Turning *res nullius* into *res publica* made work for lawyers. It was to be a long time before it made work for Africans.

This perpetual fumbling for safety in the world at large drove the powers to claim spheres, to proclaim protectorates, to charter companies; but in almost all cases this was done with no purpose more positive than to keep out others whose presence could conceivably inconvenience a national interest, no matter how speculative or unlikely. So Bismarck had laid out a paper empire in 1884–5 mainly to make a Franco-German *entente* look plausible. Caprivi had added to it in 1890 to make an Anglo-German *rapprochement* feasible. So Gladstone had moved into Egypt to protect Suez; Salisbury had laid out the ground-plan of British East Africa to be safe in Egypt and Asia. In the main, British Africa was a gigantic footnote to the Indian empire; and much of the long struggle between France and the Muslims was an expensive pendant to her search for security in the Mediterranean. Perhaps the only serious empire-builders of the 1880's were Crispi and Leopold, and they merely snatched at the crumbs from the rich men's tables. For the rest, there was indeed a 'scramble in Africa'. But it was anything but a 'scramble for Africa'.

Yet if the procedures of the partition were diplomatic and European rivalries affected it, this is far from saying that it was caused chiefly by the workings of the European power balance. Had this been so, these new empires would have ended as they began—on paper. Anglo-French competition, which had given the Germans their chance in Africa, had sprung from the English fiascos with Egyptian revolutionaries and Mahdists; it was to quicken as these imbroglios merged into those of the French with the Muslims of the western Sudan and into those of the Italians with the Christian nationalists of Ethiopia. The European pretensions provoked new African resistances, and these compelled further European exertions. So the partition gained a new momentum. The quickening occupation of tropical Africa in the 1890's, as distinct from the paper partitions of the 1880's, was the double climax of two closely connected conflicts: on the one hand, the struggle between France and Britain for control of the Nile; on the other, the struggle between European, African, Christian and Muslim expansions for control of north and Central Africa. Having embarked so lightly on the African game, the rulers of Europe had now to take it seriously.

What was the nature of this continent into which Europe was spreading? If 'Africa' is merely a geographical expression, it is also a sociological shorthand for the bewildering variety of languages, religions and societies that occupy it. At one end of the scale in aptitude and achievement, the white men found peoples organised in minute segmentary groups, lacking any political authority at the centre, and finding their social cohesion in the unity of equals, not in the unity imposed by a hierarchy. These merged into a second type, the segmentary states where kinship had made little lasting impression upon the particularism of tribal kinships, where the forces of assimilation had been baffled. At the other end of this range came the sophisticated Muslim states and the military confederacies of the most dynamic Negro and Bantu nations. As the Europeans began to deal with Africa, they met trouble from societies of all these types. But their scuffles with the warriors of the segmentary systems have no great significance from the standpoint of the partition: for the rivalries of the kinships and tribes within them almost always provided collaborators, as well as rebels against alien control. But in the case of the organised African states things were very different. Their reception of the white man had a profound effect on the partition of the nineteenth century, just as it left a fiery legacy for the African nationalism of the twentieth.

They reacted in different ways. Some began by resisting, but went down before the first whiff of grape-shot, and have remained passive until only yesterday. Others accepted their new overlords only to rebel within a decade. Others again were flatly opposed to white influence in any shape or form, and were beaten down only after years of savage guerrillas. Yet there were other peoples who came easily to terms with the European, signing his treaty forms, reading his Bibles, trading with his storekeepers. How are these differences to be explained? What led Africans to bare the teeth or to smile a welcome, to come to school or to fight a war to the death? It depended perhaps upon the kind of unity they possessed and on the state of its repair.

From what little is known about it, African political history has shown an extremely high turn-over of regimes. Like the kingdoms of Europe in the Middle Ages, they were chronically short of reserve power at the centre against the overmighty subject and the turbulent priest. Much more than the medieval governments of Europe, they lacked the binding principles of political association which could assimilate conquered neighbours into loyal subjects. This seems to have been particularly true of animist Africa. An animist people, bound together by the web of kinship and by an ancestral religion, could hardly extrapolate these points of union to those it had conquered. In the states which they created, rulers and ruled tended to remain divided. In organisation, the empires which they founded were but tribes writ large; and as kinship loyalties loosened down the generations, their provinces split off and their centres fell into disorders. So much of the history of African policies runs through very-short-term cycles of expansion and contraction, like the heavings of a diaphragm. Hunting for gold or salt or slaves, they might enlarge their territories, but this geographical expansion usually led in the end to political crack-up. How they reacted to the inroads of Europe, therefore, was partly determined by the point they had reached in their cycle of growth and decay. At a time of down-turn, their rulers would have strong reasons for striking a bargain with the new invaders. But challenged during a period of upswing, they might choose to fight it out to the end. Yet again, the more urbanised, commercial and bureaucratic the polity, the more its rulers would be tempted to come to terms before their towns were destroyed. On the other hand, the more its unity hung together on the luxuries of slave-raiding, plunder and migration, the less its aristocracy had to lose by struggling against the Europeans.

Here then were two of the many variables in settling the issue of co-operation or resistance. Not a few animist states whose economy was predatory and whose expansion was in progress fought for their independence. Both the Matabele and the Dahomians did so; but once they were beaten they stayed beaten. Perhaps the low generality of their creeds made them highly vulnerable to the culture of their conquerors. The work started with powder and shot could be completed with the New Testament, and many who came to fight remained to pray. Within a decade of the running up of the Union Jack, the Baganda and Nyasa had taken avidly to the new learning and were staffing the government offices of East and Central Africa. In French Equatorial Africa the Bacongo became the agents of white administration, just as the Baluba were to do in the Katanga.

Such docility was possible among the Muslims, too, when it was a question of dealing with settled Islamic states which had flowered into bureaucracies and passed their peak. For their staid and venerable sultans and *almamys* there was as small an attraction in calling a *jihad* as there was for the Bey of Tunis. Yet apparently religion had much to do with the issue. In many other Muslim polities the harsh imperatives of the Koran were readily obeyed. The plain fact is that the longest and bloodiest fighting against the forces of Europe was carried out by Muslims. No European blandishments could charm them into becoming good neighbours. The task was one for firepower, not philanthropy.

Robber empires, still expanding into black Africa, still mobile, still led by prophets of the faith—there were good reasons why they could not yield. They were incomparably better fitted to defy and resist than the animists. Islam's insistence on the equality of all believers under one law, together with its extensive brotherhoods and orders, provided firmer strands of unity which transcended the bonds of mere kinship and ancestral religions. Moreover, it postulated a principle of universal Godhead above any of the local deities and fetishes which divided black Africa. Supratribal Muslim institutions and discipline sometimes presented a coherent and continuous resistance. They also made surrender to Christian powers impossible without dissolving the forces of Muslim authority and empire. For many of these fierce foes had fashioned their power out of a sort of Muslim protestantism—attempts to purge Islam of scholiast accretions by moving back to the pristine purity of the Koran of the desert and rejecting the authority of the corrupted Caliphate at Constantinople. On the frontiers of the faith, it was new prophets who combined this stern, unbending fundamentalism with the thirst of tribes for independence and conquest. Muhammad al-Mahdi in the Sudan, Sayyid al-Mahdi among his Sanusi, Amadu Shehu and

Samori of the Sofas, Rabih—all of these were prophets or caliphs of prophets and local theocrats. They were no less leaders of independence movements. Independence in African terms meant expansion and the dependence of others upon them, so they became conquerors of infidels for the true faith. After all, it is only armed prophets who have not been destroyed.

To survive, embattled theocrats of this sort had to be proof against the politics of influence practised by invading Christendom. The new dispensations which they preached had made obsolete all the cities and kingdoms of this world. They called upon all to return to God according to their revelation or be destroyed by him. If they compromised with the enemy after such preachings, they would be digging their own graves. Something of this adamantine attitude to unbelievers still rings in the Mahdi's message to the Christian emperor, Yohannes of Ethiopia: 'Become a Muslim and peace will be unto you. . . . If on the other hand you choose disobedience and prefer blindness . . . [have] no doubt about your falling into our hands as we are promised the possession of all the earth. God fulfils His promises. . . . Let not the Devil hinder you.'[15] African Christianity, at least in Ethiopia, produced the same unyielding toughness. Shadowy and bizarre though the monophysite creeds of the Coptic church might be, they helped to rally national solidarity behind the emperor when the Italians brought the time of troubles.

The deadliest enemies of European expansion into Africa were those states suffused by Islam or Christianity, both of them supratribal religious organisations capable of forging tribes into national unities. Believing that the white man was an infidel as well as an invader, these Copts and Muslims faced him, strong in the knowledge of a righteous cause. Meeting with so complete a self-confidence, the white men were pushed into choices they would have preferred—indeed, that they expected—to burke. There was no sensible negotiating to be done with theocrats, still less any converting. Their opposition raised local crises which could not be glossed over. Once the theocracies had been aroused by the challenge of Europe, it become a matter of everything or nothing. Dragged ever deeper into reactions which their own coming had provoked, the powers were forced in the 1890's to occupy the claims which they had papered on to the African map in the 1880's. The spectacular expansion that resulted has often been called imperialism. But at a deeper level it was a reflex to the stirrings of African proto-nationalism.

Whether they liked it or not, the white men were now committed to making sense out of the abstract dispositions of the 1880's. The harsh facts of Africa compelled it. For the French, lured on by British acquiescence and the dashing strategies of their colonial soldiers, there was no escape. In pursuit of Amadu the army had been drawn westward to Timbuktu. It was soon to go on to Gao, and the Upper Niger Command modulated into *Soudan Français.* In Paris the politicians had had enough. In 1891 and 1893 they called a halt to the soldiers, announcing that 'the period of conquest and territorial expansion must be considered as definitely over'.[16] Already the problem was how to make their new acquisitions pay; but the colonels, with one hand on their Maxims and the other on their next set of proofs, were bent on routing out Muslim resistance yet farther afield, in Futa Jalon and the Upper Volta. Paris turned up its nose at the new provinces. But the very fact of pacification gave them a fictitious value—since hard-won territory could hardly be given up. So step by step the army eventually involved Paris in the economics of development. When Trentinian took over the Sudan in 1895 the era of the sabre had ended. With the coming of government investment to push the railway up to the Niger, closer administration became possible and the battlefield was turned into a colony.

Gradually, the French grew more entangled in Dahomey and the Congo. In 1890 General Dodds, covered by Étienne in Paris,[17] slipped the leash and crushed the pagan slave-raiding confederacy of Dahomey, which had proved an impossible neighbour to the French on the coast. The way was open for a thrust inland. By 1894 French agents were reconnoitring Nikki; they were poised to invade the undefined western flanks of Goldie's monopoly on the lower Niger; what was more, they had seen a chance of uniting Dahomey with their fields of influence on the Senegal, Ivory Coast, Upper Volta and Upper Niger. Since 1889 the colonial zealots had been pressing the government to go one better still. Belatedly they would rationalise all the incongruous advances of the past decade by joining these territories to the starveling French Congo. The junction and symbol of this geographical romanticism was to be Lake Tchad.

After ten years in which their diplomats and soldiers had played ducks and drakes with West Africa, there emerged a group in Paris who demanded that the French empire should be taken seriously for its own sake. In 1890 their private subscriptions sent Crampel from Brazzaville to establish French sway in the regions of Lake Tchad and so ensure 'the continuity of our possessions between Algeria, Senegal and the Congo'.[18] So little did this pipe-dream charm the Quai d'Orsay that in August they signed away the Tchad corridor to

Britain. In protest Crampel's supporters toward the end of 1890 organised the *Comité de l'Afrique française*—the first serious pressure group in favour of a tropical African empire; but at no time did it attract any powerful business interests; and though it had the blessing of Étienne, its direct political influence was not spectacular. There was a certain grandiloquent appeal in the *Comité's* idea of turning Tchad into the linch-pin of French Africa, but it was the risks, not the rhetoric, which moved the politicians. Coming down to the lake from the north meant striking across the Sahara, but this was clean contrary to the policy of the Government-General at Algiers. Since the slaughter of the Flatters expedition by the Touareg in 1880, Algiers had turned down project after project for Saharan penetration on the ground that it would be 'too dangerous'.[19] There were equally sharp objections against moving on Tchad from the west. If the thrust went along the Upper Niger, it would have to fight its way through Muslim opposition, which might have awkward repercussions in the newly organised French Sudan; as late as 1898 the Government-General in Saint-Louis was against such an advance.[20] The only practicable route seemed to be from the south. In 1891 the *Comité* sent Dybowski, and Brazza sent Foureau, on missions towards the lake from the Congo. Both were hurled back. Once more, French expansion had contrived to entangle itself with Muslim resistance. The wreckage of the Arab slaving state in the Bahr al-Ghazal had driven its survivors into the Wadai country. Here they were reorganised by Rabih into a strong, predatory state, which saw the Europeans as dangerous rivals. Another theocracy was in the making. Rabih 'found in religion more support and strength than a mere desire for loot would have given to a band of adventurers';[21] and after he had moved on to the Bagirmi country by the shores of Tchad, the support of the Sanusi, coupled with the military skills he brought from Egypt, made him a formidable opponent.

For Brazza, the Commissioner-General of the Republic in the Congo, the *Comité's* drive on Tchad was doubly welcome. It pushed out his frontiers, and it attracted the interest of Paris towards his neglected colony; it remained for him to associate the minority enthusiasm of the Lake Tchad school with a serious national interest that would appeal to the cynics of the Quai d'Orsay. In 1891 he was suggesting to Paris that the expeditions towards Tchad 'can . . . produce a situation for us which . . . will allow us to start negotiations with Britain about reciprocal concessions over the Egyptian question . . .' .[22] This was the germ of the French Fashoda strategy. In August 1891 Liotard was sent to the Ubanghi-Shari country, the western gateway to the Nile valley, with instructions to use the well-tried Brazza methods of influence on the small sultans there. If Paris were to take the plunge into reopening the Nile question, here was a possible method of doing so, and here were the means to hand.

Paris was to take the plunge. Like all the crucial moves in the struggle for tropical Africa, this was decided by a turn in the chronic Egyptian crisis. Salisbury had taken some of the heat out of it by simply refusing to discuss it. The French had hoped for better times when the Liberals came back in 1892, but Rosebery, the new Foreign Secretary, told Paris point-blank that the Egyptian issue was closed. In January 1893 the khedive timidly tried an anti-British *coup*. Cromer shouldered him back into subservience; but the crisis had its bright side for Paris. It showed that the revolutionary situation in Egypt was far from played out. It suggested that the nationalists inside the country might be usefully allied with pressure from outside to turn the British out of their citadel. The chances of external action were brightening as well. By 1893, with the *Franco-Russe* all but consummated, the strategic position in the eastern Mediterranean looked much more secure to the Ministry of Marine, once the tsar's warships had visited Toulon. The politics of deference were over.

Paris therefore had good reason to take a higher line in the Egyptian affair. From the diplomats' viewpoint, the partition of Africa was a large-scale example of game-theory. One of the rules of the game was that control of a river's course amounted to a forcing bid for territory. So it had been on the Niger. So it had been on the Congo. Why not install a French force on the Upper Nile? The Nile was Egypt, as everyone knew. Once the *infanterie de Marine* had straddled the river, the famous Egyptian question could be reopened with a vengeance. In May 1893, Carnot, President of the Republic, revived the Brazza scheme. A task-force could follow the old route towards Tchad, filter north-west through Liotard's empire of influence in Ubanghi-Shari, and then strike hard for the Nile. They would have to join it south of the Mahdists' country, since the Dervishes did not welcome visitors. But one theocracy was as good as another. Striking the river south of Khartoum would allow the French to work with Menilek, who was hunting for European rifles and sympathy. A handful of Frenchmen on the Nile would be picturesque; but joined by an Ethiopian army they would be portentous.

The contest for Egypt and the Mediterranean was speeding up again. As it did so, one remote African polity after another was enmeshed into its toils: the starveling colony of the Congo, the theocracies around Tchad, the petty Muslim oligarchies of Ubanghi-Shari, the wanderers in the marshes of the Bahr al-Ghazal, the Coptic state of Ethiopia, the stone-age men living around the sand-bank at Fashoda. As for the two European powers whose rivalry had provoked this uproar, they each strained every nerve to race the other to the dingy charms of the Upper Nile. There had been a time when light soils were booby prizes. Only the remarkable insights of late nineteenth-century imperialism could have seen them as pearls beyond price.

But the Fashoda scheme was risky. The Quai d'Orsay could not assume that the British would sit smoking their pipes in Cairo while the French were pitching camp by the banks of the Nile; and so the policy-makers in Paris held back the colonial *enragés*. To their minds, the scheme of planting the tricolour on the Nile was not a colonial scheme but a diplomatic weapon; they hoped to use it as a *bâton Soudanais* to thwack the British into an Egyptian negotiation. Hence the Fashoda plan went in stops and starts, to be dragged out of the pigeon-holes whenever London grew refractory. Before Paris had summoned up the nerve to carry it out, London was taking precautions against it. On their side, the British were hard at work building up positions of strength in the valley of the Nile. It was in Uganda that they were building. Goaded by the Foreign Office, Mackinnon's company had sent Lugard inland to Buganda, to tighten Britain's hold on the headwaters of the river. The country was in uproar, through the struggles of rival factions, goaded on by British Protestant, French Catholic and African Muslim missionaries. Early in 1892 Lugard managed to set the Protestants into precarious authority: but vindicating the principles of the Reformation had exhausted Mackinnon's finances, and he ordered Lugard to withdraw from Uganda. This alarmed the government. Already, military intelligence in Egypt was predicting that once the company moved out of Uganda, the French forces in Ubanghi would move in; and the Africanists in the Foreign Office conjured up French threats on all sides. To them, and to Lord Rosebery, the best defence lay in going forward. Formally occupying the country would shut out the French from the sources of the Nile; linking it by rail with Mombasa would make it a base for shutting them out of the upper valley as well. But the Gladstonians in the Cabinet would not go so far as Rosebery. The best he could do was to send Portal to Uganda to report on the pros and cons of holding it.

Both London and Paris were to find that their insurance premiums were too low, for now another partitioner, and one much suppler and subtler than Carnot or Rosebery, declared an interest in the Nile. To a remarkable extent, Leopold II of the Belgians combined the unction of a monarch with the energy of a businessman. For all their modest beginnings, it is Rockefeller, Carnegie and Sanford who offer the closest parallels with this royal entrepreneur. Like them, he gambled on futures; like them, he formed cartels out of chaos; like them again, he was careless of the consequences. Leopold had been given the Congo since his Independent State was the regime which divided the powers least. It was his own money and not the taxpayers' which was used for embellishing the new royal demesne. But since Leopold's African flutter was not an act of state but a private venture, it had to show a cash return—no easy matter this, in the Congo, where there seemed to be no minerals and where the population showed no great zest in working for the market. To keep his private empire going, Leopold badly needed something to export. There was ivory; there was ebony; but these trades were in the hands of the Arabs, especially those of the eastern regions of the Congo. Leopold would have come to terms with them if he could, but his treaties of trade and friendship had no attraction for these oligarchs and oligopolists lording it over the Negro. So it came to war, and this drove the Congo Free State deep into the Arab territories which lay between it and the Nile. In 1891 its missions were setting up posts in Ubanghi, in 1893 in the Bahr al-Ghazal, and in the same year the forces of Van Kerckhoven struck as far as Lado on the Upper Nile itself.

Such spirited advances were welcome neither in Paris nor in London. They were especially awkward for the French. Leopold's men were undoubtedly spilling north of the rough frontier proposed in 1887 between his sphere and theirs on the Congo; but when they tried to draw the frontier with some precision in 1892–4 the negotiations showed that none of the diplomats had the faintest idea of the lie of the land. What was more, these probings by the Free State showed how weak French authority was on the ground in the Ubanghi-Shari, scheduled as the launching-site for a move on Fashoda. Rosebery too had his troubles. He could order Portal to extend the British sphere from Buganda to the north; after the Liberals had succeeded at last in dropping their pilot, Gladstone, he could bring Uganda proper under a formal protectorate. But in the unreal game the powers were playing for the Upper Nile, the paper bargains of diplomacy still seemed the best insurances. In May 1894 Rosebery clinched two agreements. In the first place, the Italians became a holding company for British interests in Ethiopia. By recognising a Roman hegemony over Ogaden and Harar, Rosebery could take it for granted that the negus would not be of much use to French plans, so long as the Italians were sitting on his border. Secondly, the British tried to neutralise Leopold. By the Anglo-Congolese agreement he was assigned Equatoria and much of the Bahr al-Ghazal, so as 'to prevent the French who are about to send an expedition to [the Bahr al-Ghazal] from establishing themselves there, and to settle with the Belgians who are there already. . . . The presence of the French there would be a serious danger to Egypt.'

Elegant as this paper-work might be, it was all in vain. Rosebery's ill-judged attempt to settle the Egyptian issue on the Upper Nile only provoked the French to greater exertions. In Paris the Colonial Minister thought that the Anglo-Congolese Treaty 'seems to call for new measures on our part'.[23] One of these was to revive, with £70,000 worth of credits, the scheme of going to Fashoda by way of Ubanghi-Shari. But even now Hanotaux at the Quai d'Orsay managed to pour water into the Colonial ministry's wine. The expedition was to advance along the Ubanghi; but it was ordered 'to avoid breaking into the Nile valley'.[24] By August the second counter-measure was complete. The Anglo-Congolese treaty had been broken by the classic method of a joint Franco-German denunciation. Much to Hanotaux's relief, the Ubanghi striking-force could now be side-tracked out of harm's way, to try conclusions with Samori on the Ivory Coast.[25]

Rosebery was forced into direct negotiations with Paris. He was reported as saying 'Take all you want in Africa, provided that you keep off the valley of the Nile',[26] and like Salisbury before him it was in West Africa that he hoped to give his generosity full play. The hinterlands of the Gold Coast and the borderlands between the French and British spheres on the Lower Niger might all go in return for safety in Egypt. But since the French no less than the British thought much more highly of Egypt than they did of the west coast, there was no basis for a bargain. So the exchanges over the Nile and the Niger grew angrier, until in March 1895 Grey publicly warned the French that any advance into the Nile valley would be taken as an 'unfriendly act'. Sabres were beginning to rattle.

If the contention for Egypt and the Nile had been kept on the diplomatic level hitherto, it was now to burst into active conquest and occupation. As it neared its climax, the partition, which had begun almost frivolously, became hectic. It had been going on for so long that some of the new generation of politicians—the Delcassés and Chamberlains, had come to take it seriously, not only as a matter of old-fashioned power-politics but as a question of African colonies. The partition had brought them to a kind of geopolitical claustrophobia, a feeling that national expansion was running out of world space, and that the great powers of the twentieth century would be those who had filched every nook and cranny of territory left. Yet it was not ambitions or rivalries of this sort which drove France and Britain into carrying out their Nile strategies. It was the defeat of the Italians by the resurgent proto-nationalists of Ethiopia.

How this quasi-feudal, monophysite realm of the Lions of Judah survived the onslaughts of Islam and the Galla nomads through the centuries is a question. From the mid-eighteenth century, the emperors had been shadows, the king-makers all powerful. But after the accession of Teodros II in 1855 the emperor and his feudatories slowly reunited to meet the growing menace of foreign invasion. Their disunity had prevented any effective resistance when Napier's columns marched to Magdala in 1867 to release the imprisoned British consul. When Crispi, hoping to buttress his divided ministry with colonial success, occupied Tigré and ordered the Italian army forward into the Ethiopian highlands in 1896, he relied on the same weakness. His General, Baratieri, knew better. Italian expansion, he observed, was provoking among the Ethiopians 'a kind of negative patriotism'.[27] The negus Menilek was not only equipped with modern fire-power through the courtesies of white-man's diplomacy, he also had the great Rases of Tigré, Gojam, Harar and Wollo behind him. At Adowa on 1 March 1896 these Ethiopian proto-nationalists crushed the Italians. It meant the freedom of Ethiopia and the fall of Crispi. It also meant the first victory of African proto-nationalism. The Mahdists as well as the Ethiopians were moving against Italian Eritrea. The Italian outposts of Kassala on the Atbara tributary of the Nile looked like being cut off altogether.

Adowa so sharply transformed the politics of the Nile basin that twelve days later Salisbury ordered the Egyptian army under Kitchener to invade the eastern Sudan. This decision, so he informed Cromer, 'was inspired specially by a desire to help the Italians at Kassala; . . . to prevent the Dervishes from winning a conspicuous success which might have far-reaching results; and to plant the foot of Egypt rather farther up the Nile'. It is true that the plight of the Italians seemed fortunate to the British. The Kaiser urged Salisbury to do something to help his unhappy partner in the Triple Alliance; and this meant German help in unlocking the Egyptian treasury to pay for the invasion. But if the Italian defeat gave the opportunity of attacking the Mahdists, the Ethiopian victory made it necessary to do so. Hitherto the English had done everything possible to keep out of the Egyptian Sudan. 'If the Dervishes have occupied the valley of the Nile', Salisbury had told Cromer in 1890, 'they do not pledge the future in any way . . . they can destroy nothing, for there is nothing to destroy.' Without engineering skills, they could not tamper with the Nile flow. 'Surely . . . this people were [sic] created for the purpose of keeping the bed warm for you till you can occupy it.' Even in 1897 Cromer was opposing the advance on Khartoum, as it would only lead to the acquisition of 'large tracts of useless territory which it would be difficult and costly to administer properly'. Plainly then they were not hastening to conquer another colony. They cautiously ordered the invasion, to forestall the French *coup* on the Upper Nile which Menilek's victory seemed to have made practicable.

This calculation was wrong but reasonable. English complacency about such a *coup* had rested hitherto on the hope that a French force from the west would be unable to fight its way through to the Nile; or if it did, that it would get no help from Menilek under the Italian heel; or if it did get such help, that the Egyptian army could conquer the declining Dervish state before any dangerous Franco-Abyssinian combination could take place. Adowa transformed Salisbury's view of these possibilities. Rid of the Italians, the Ethiopians were much more formidable than had been supposed; and if, as Salisbury suspected mistakenly, they were prepared to act as allies of France, they would be formidable indeed.

The disappearance of the Italians seemed to have put new life into the Mahdists as well. It was known that Menilek was angling for an alliance with them. Not only did this make it less likely that Kitchener would be able to break through the Mahdists and forestall the French at Fashoda; it also raised the spectre that the French might launch a Mahdist-Ethiopian alliance against Egypt itself. Here the British stakes were too great to permit such risks. And Salisbury's government decided to take precautions in time. So opened the last great crisis in the partition of tropical Africa. Like its predecessors, it had been generated by the turn of events in Africa itself.

Predictably the invasion of the eastern Sudan provoked Paris to substantiate Salisbury's fears by invading it from the west.[28] Three months after Kitchener started for Dongola, Marchand left for Brazzaville, *en route* for Fashoda; and Lagarde went back to Addis Ababa to clinch the alliance with Menilek and arrange for the rendezvous with Marchand on the Nile. Whether the Egyptian army, dragging its railway from the north, could beat down the Khalifa and reach Fashoda ahead of the French seemed increasingly doubtful. So Salisbury was forced to try forestalling them from the south. He pressed on the building of the railway from Mombasa to supply the base in Uganda, and in June 1897 Macdonald was ordered to march from there along the Nile to Fashoda 'before the French get there from the west'. So the Anglo-French struggle for the Nile had set in motion four invasions of the Egyptian Sudan. French forces were now toiling towards it from east and west, British forces from north and south.

For long Salisbury was much more worried about the threat from Ethiopia than that from Marchand's expedition. Early in 1897 Rennell Rodd, the British envoy to Menilek, reported that he seemed very much under French influence; there seemed to be Frenchmen occupying high posts and assuming higher titles in the Ethiopian administration. In October the emperor appeared to be co-operating in sending Bonchamps's Franco-Ethiopian expedition along the river Sobat to Fashoda. In fact, Menilek merely intended to play off the French against the British who seemed a greater threat to his independence. Unknown to them, he had already made an agreement with the Mahdists. As for the joint expedition from Addis Ababa to the Nile, Bonchamps complained that 'the Ethiopians did not help the mission; they did all they could to stop it from heading towards the Nile'.[29]

If Salisbury had known all this, he need not have troubled to conquer the rest of the Sudan. But, on the evidence to hand in London, things looked gloomy indeed. Having reached Berber, Kitchener found the Mahdists much stronger than expected, and remembering Hicks Pasha's catastrophe in the desert, he asked for white troops. Ministers were most reluctant to send the redcoats. But Macdonald's force which was to have covered Fashoda from the south had not even set out, because his troops had mutinied and the Baganda had rebelled. Like the French strategy in the east, British strategy in the south had gone astray. There was nothing for it but to press the conquest of the Sudan from the north. In January 1898, perhaps as much from fear of a mythical Dervish counter-attack as from fear of the French moving on Fashoda, the British sent Kitchener his white reinforcements with orders to capture Khartoum. So at last the English army's imbroglio with the Dervishes dragged them into vast conquests of unwanted territory in the eastern Sudan, much as the French army since 1889 had been drawn into the western Sudan by their entanglements with the fighting Muslim theocracies of Amadu and Samori. In the event the fanaticisms of proto-nationalism had done far more to bring European imperialism into Africa than all the statesmen and business interests in Europe.

All these threads came together in the summer of 1898. On 2 September Kitchener's machine-guns proved stronger than the Khalifa's Mahdists at Khartoum. An Anglo-Egyptian condominium was soon riveted upon the Sudan. Six weeks earlier a sorely-tried Franco-Ethiopian expedition had struggled up to the confluence of the Sobat and the Nile near Fashoda, expecting to find Marchand. He was not there. After a Russian colonel had planted the French flag on an island in the Nile, they went away. Three weeks later Marchand himself reached Fashoda. It was deserted. But not for long. On 19 September Kitchener's regiments came up the river in their gunboats and sent him packing.

At first sight it looks as though a British steam-roller had been sent to crush a peanut at Fashoda. Salisbury had spent millions on building railways from Lower Egypt and Mombasa through desert and bush to Lake Victoria and the Upper Nile; he had launched a grand army into the sands and gone to the verge of war with France—and all to browbeat eight Frenchmen. Was the Nile *sudd* worth such exertions? No less an architect of expansion than Queen Victoria herself opposed a war 'for so miserable and small an object'. Yet this anti-climax at Fashoda brought the climax in Europe. For two months it was touch and go whether France and Britain would fight each other—not simply for Fashoda but for what that lonely place symbolised: to the British, safety in Egypt and in India; to the French, security in the Mediterranean. It was Paris that gave way. In the turmoil of the Dreyfus Affair, Brisson's ministry accepted the necessity of avoiding a naval war which they were in no state to undertake, even with Russian help. By the Anglo-French Declaration of March 1899 France was excluded from the entire Nile valley. In return she received the central Sudan from Darfur in the east to Lake Tchad in the west. This decided the Egyptian question in a way that the Anglo-French *entente* of 1904 merely ratified. With that settled, the drawing of lines on maps might have ended as it had begun, with Egypt; but it was too late. By this time there was no more of tropical Africa left to divide.

This central struggle for Egypt and the Nile had produced a series of side-effects elsewhere in Africa, collateral disputes which had twitched into a life of their own. Of these much the most virulent was the Anglo-French rivalry over the middle Niger. During the early 1890's this affair was as hollow as it had been during the first decade of the Scramble, with tempers on the Niger still blowing hot and cool according to the state of negotiations over the Nile. Until Kitchener invaded the Mahdist Sudan and Marchand struck towards Fashoda in retaliation there was little substance in the West African quarrels. But after 1896 they were more fiercely contested, as Lugard and the other filibusters scuffled around the chiefdoms in the Niger bend. From London's standpoint, this flurry of claims and expeditions was a tiresome business, for it had little bearing on the crucial question of the Nile except as a way of marking up bargaining points for the inevitable settlement there. But the struggle for the middle Niger had much more meaning for the official mind in Paris, since its connection with France's Nile strategy was direct. If the Fashoda operation were to succeed, there would have to be solid communications from the West African basis across the Bahr al-Ghazal to this new position on the Nile. As usual, such calculations decided that all roads must lead to Lake Tchad. 'Our Chief requirement', wrote the Minister for Colonies, 'must be to bind together our possessions in [French] Sudan with those in the Ubanghi, and the latter with the Nile. Between the Nile and the Ubanghi matters seem promising . . . between the Ubanghi and the Sudan we must rely on [fresh] missions if the desired result is to be won.'[30] Two ways were tried of carrying out these directives. Pushing up from the Congo, one force strove to come to terms with Rabih, still the man in possession of the eastern and southern sides of Tchad. But they found him far from placable, and in any case the French Congo was too poor to throw much weight behind the thrust. On the other axis of advance, Cazemajou was sent from French Sudan to make his way across the Niger bend to the west side of the lake. But this line of march took him into Sokoto, trampling down the paper barriers erected in 1890 between the French and British spheres. At the same time, a support group from Dahomey threatened to pull Nikki and Borgu out of Goldie's ramshackle empire in northern Nigeria.

Briefly, the long line of British surrenders in West Africa was now to be interrupted. At the Colonial Office, Chamberlain was one of the few powerful politicians anxious to build an African empire for the sake of a new imperialism. Whereas the old school approached the partition on the principle of limited liability which governed all their foreign policy, Chamberlain believed that a bankrupt rival should be hammered. To push forward on the Nile, they were ready to fall back on the Niger; but Chamberlain played for everything or nothing. Having annexed Ashanti in 1896, he jostled the French for possession of the Volta chiefdoms beyond. It was not long before this new forcefulness was warming up the quarrels on the Niger. To defend Borgu and Sokoto, he screwed up Goldie's company into a belliger-

ence as damaging to its dividends as it was distasteful to the diplomats. Cazemajou was to be thrown out of Sokoto by force—a work
of supererogation this, since the explorer was already dead. But for
all this fire-eating, there was a treaty. Both sides had their eyes
cocked elsewhere. Salisbury overruled his Colonial Secretary with
the argument that 'if we break off negotiations . . . it will add to our
difficulties in the Nile valley'. Hanotaux calculated that an agreement
would stop Britain employing 'a policy of grievances and compensations to block our claim over the Egyptian question'. So on 14 June
1898 they came to terms, France gaining the Upper Volta and Borgu,
while its neighbours, Ilorin and Sokoto, were reserved to Britain.

So far as London was concerned, this was the end of the West
African affair. Brought to life at the onset of the Egyptian crisis, it
could now be tidily buried before the consummation of that crisis.
For Paris, however, West Africa remained unfinished business, and
its consummation was a necessary part of keeping the Egyptian
issue alive. The Lake Tchad strategy had gone all awry. Settling with
the British offered a chance of securing the Timbuktu-Fashoda route
without the interference of Chamberlain's West Africa Frontier
Force. While the Anglo-French negotiation was in full swing, Paris
was already organising a force to settle the Tchad business once and
for all: with a certain felicity of timing, the group sailed for Africa the
day after the agreement had been signed. Organised on a larger
scale than the Marchand mission itself, the Voulet-Chanoine mission
was to move east from Timbuktu to Tchad, where they would at last
give Gentil and the Congo government the chance to impose their
will on Rabih. Another expedition, led by Foureau and Lamy across
the Sahara, was also converging on Tchad: it was no part of the main
scheme, but as things turned out, this group was to decide the issue.

Marchand's fiasco on the Nile knocked the heart out of these
plans. After Fashoda, French opinion was far from favourable to
more adventures in the African bush. Fearing trouble with the Chamber, the politicians were now inclined to leave Rabih to stew in his
own juice. Even less inclined to take risks, the commissioner-general in the Congo recommended that France should make a loose
agreement with him, leaving him to do 'whatever he likes on the left
bank of the Benue'.[31] The news that Voulet and Chanoine had gone
mad and shot it out with their brother officers and then wandered off
to found a private empire in the wastes of the western Sudan made
Paris even less anxious to try conclusions with their Muslim enemy.
But it was the local situation, not the calculations of Paris, which
decided the matter. There was no way of coming to terms with Ra-

bih; one by one he attacked Gentil, the Sahara mission and the remnants of the Voulet-Chanoine party. On 21 April 1900 the three groups joined forces. The following day they fought the battle which settled the Tchad issue, which overthrew Rabih, and which clinched the union of Algeria, the French Sudan and the French Congo. It was the end of a long story.

In Morocco, Libya and the Congo there were to be further adjustments; but these were part of the prelude to the first World War, not of the scramble. By 1900 the directors of the partition had done with tropical Africa. It remained for the administrators to make sense of their paperwork and to make their conquests pay. There could be no going back now. They had embroiled the nations of Europe and the peoples of Africa in such a fashion that their destinies were not to be disentangled.

In the 1880's the policy-makers had intended nothing more ambitious than building diplomatic fences around these territories and hamstringing their rulers by informal control. But such methods would not work with the proto-nationalists of Egypt and Ethiopia, the Muslim revivalists of Tunisia and the Sudan, the Arab slavers of Nyasaland and the Congo, the large animist kingdoms of Buganda and Dahomey. They would not collaborate. They had to be conquered. Once conquered, they had to be administered; once administered, they had to be developed, to pay the bills for their governance. Slowly this development was translated into the idiom of progress and trusteeship, as the new tints of blue or red or yellow or green on the African map awakened feelings of pride or shame among the European voters.

The conversion of the paper empires into working colonies came about from nothing so rational or purposive as economic planning or imperial ardours. The outcome of Salisbury's Nile-valley strategy was as strange as it had been unforeseen. To pay for the occupation of Egypt and its Sudan in the early twentieth century, government had to spend public funds in damming the river and developing Gezira cotton. To recover the money spent on the Uganda railway, government had to provide it with payable loads, and this was the sharpest spur for bringing white settlers into Kenya, as it was for turning the Baganda into cash-crop farmers. Elsewhere the sequence was the same. The development of French West Africa under Roume and Ponty did not come until the Government-General was reorganised to attract capital from France. The German colonies, acquired as by-products of Bismarck's tacking towards France, remained derelict until Dernburg after 1907 carried out a total reconstruction.

So African territories were launched into a development which had not been envisaged at the time they were occupied. What was more, government itself was forced to take the lead in this. Businessmen were still unwilling to plunge into African enterprises, and so most of the capital and the technical services had to be drawn from the public sector. By now the manoeuvres and blunders of the partition had been rationalised into apologias for African empire. But the crux of this imperialism lies in its sequence. It was not businessmen or missionaries or empire-builders who launched the partition of Africa, but rather a set of diplomats who thought of that continent merely as a function of their concerns elsewhere. But once started off, this paper partition was turned into occupation and colonisation by the clashes between the Europeans and the proto-nationalists, the religious revolutionaries of Africa. Only at the end of the process did the businessmen arrive—when Europe had to foot the bill for having dealt with Africa as though it was uninhabited. The sequence is quite the reverse of that postulated in the traditional theories. Imperialism was not the cause of the partition. It was the result.

As the Egyptian crisis was giving rise to the devious geometry of partition, an independent process of expansion reached a climax in the southern sub-continent. Unlike the rest of Africa, the temperate south was being settled by white men who since the Great Trek had pushed their homesteads northward from the Orange and the Vaal to the Zambezi and beyond, subjugating the Bantu as they went. Here, moreover, during the last quarter of the nineteenth century investors and merchants were bringing the industrial energies of Europe to develop the colonial economy on a scale unknown elsewhere in Africa. Colonisation grew dramatically deeper and wider after the gold discoveries, which brought a swift inflow of new capital and settlers. Hence the crisis in the south stemmed from the rapid growth of white colonial society and not, as in the rest of the continent, from the decay of an oriental empire and its concatenation of effects. Moreover, it arose from conflicting national aspirations among the colonists, not from rivalry between the powers. The Anglo-French quarrel over Egypt, so fateful for the rest, hardly affected this part of Africa. Occasionally the Germans made as if to intervene, but at most their contribution to the crisis was marginal. This partition was essentially an affair of Boer and Briton in South Africa—

even more than it was a matter between the imperial government in London and the colonists—with the silent Bantu looking on. Yet the South African and Egyptian emergencies were alike at least in this: neither was set off by new imperial ambitions; in both the late-Victorians, striving to uphold an old system of paramountcy against a nationalist challenge, fell almost involuntarily into conquering and occupying more territory. Between their vision and reality, between the intent and the outcome of their actions, fell the shadow of imperialism in South, as in North and Central, Africa.

Until the 1870's official London had been content to secure the Cape route to India through colonial control of the Cape and Natal, leaving the inland republics of the *Trekboers* in the Transvaal and the Orange Free State their ramshackle independence. But with the diamond discoveries at Kimberley and the beginnings of investment and railway-building, the British aim became specifically imperial, as it was not in Egypt or tropical Africa. Colonisation, which the Colonial Office had tried first to prevent and then to ignore, had gone so far that there was now nothing for it but to bring the dependencies and the republics together into a self-governing dominion. There were successful models for this kind of imperial architecture in the Australian responsible governments and the Canadian Confederation of 1867. Once united under the Union Jack and relieved of formal Downing Street control, surely the South African colonists' community of interest with Britain in trade and freedom, if not in kinship and culture, would keep them also loyal to the empire. Certainly this technique of collaborating classes worked well in the case of the Cape Dutch who, as the most anglicised and commercial of the Afrikaners, were given responsible self-government in 1872. It might have worked with the Boers of Trans-Orangia. Those of the Transvaal proved far less amenable. Their trading and cultural links with Britain were of the slightest. As they had moved farthest to escape imperial rule in the Great Trek, so were they the most anti-British and inveterately republican of the Boers; and they had a propensity for inviting foreign powers into South African affairs. Happily, or so it seemed to Disraeli's Colonial Secretary, Carnarvon, these twenty thousand Calvinist frontier farmers from seventeenth-century Europe, bankrupt and ringed round with hostile Bantu, were too few to hold up the march of nineteenth-century progress. In 1876 he annexed their country in an attempt to force them into an imperial federation dominated by the far wealthier, more populous and more reliable Cape Colony. But like the Egyptians and Tunisians, the Transvaalers rose three years later to fight the invaders for their independence; and the illusion of federation was consumed in the smoke of the first Boer War of 1881. More than that, the image of imperial aggression awakened among the Afrikaans-speaking South Africans a feeling of racial solidarity with their brothers beyond the Vaal. Gladstone's ministry realised that 'the Boers will resist our rule to the uttermost . . . if we conquer the country we can only hold it by the sword . . . the continuance of the war would have involved us in a contest with the Free State as well as the Transvaal Boers, if it did not cause a rebellion in the Cape Colony itself'. Colonial loyalty had been shaken. Afrikanerdom seemed to be uniting behind Kruger's rebellion. To avert a 'race war' between Boer and Briton, the Liberals wisely swallowed the humiliation of Majuba and gave back the Transvaalers their republic.

Out of these reactions of Carnarvon's rough-hewing emerged the modern Afrikaner national movement, with the annals of the Great Trek as its myth and 'Africa for the Afrikaners' as its slogan. Hofmeyr's Farmers' Protection Association at the Cape coupled with the spread of the Afrikaner Bond in the Free State and the Transvaal showed how the Boers' political consciousness was solidifying. Similarly, the Afrikaans language movement of S. J. du Toit and the predicants of the Dutch Reformed Church showed how they were preparing to defend their cultural heritage against anglicisation. Afrikaner nationalism, faced with an empire whose liberality toward the Bantu threatened the colonists' position as a white aristocracy, was bound to be anti-imperialist; yet its leaders were for the most part moderates, by no means unwilling to collaborate with the British authority. But in the Transvaal after the foiled annexation there developed a nationalism more self-assured and much more extreme. Increasingly, the Transvaalers turned from the need of South African unity to the assertion of a romantic particularism, from building a new nation to wrecking an old empire.

It was not going to be easy for British statesmen to turn this balkanised South Africa with its militant nationalists into another Canada. There was no United States on its borders to persuade the Boers that the empire was the best guarantee of their national identity, as the French Canadians had been persuaded. And whereas it was the English-speaking majority who were carrying Canadian colonisation westward to the Pacific, it was the Afrikaans-speaking majority which was expanding into South Africa's hinterland. Downing Street had so much to do in upholding paramount influence over three Afrikaner-dominated, autonomous governments that it could only make haste slowly toward making a dominion. Until 1895 it waited for its colonial collaborators, helped by the inflow of British capital and immigrants, to bring about an imperial union from within. It accommodated its policies to the Cape Ministry's views, so as to avoid offending its chief ally. The Transvaal was handled with kid gloves lest open quarrels with its nationalists should unite Afrikanderdom against the empire, as it had threatened to do in 1881. In conciliating the colonies and republics alike, the 'Imperial Factor' in South Africa was progressively dismantled in favour of the politics of 'moral influence', in all respects but one: London intervened to help the colonies' expansion and to hinder that of the republics, so as to ensure a preponderance of imperial elements in the ultimate federation.

Everything therefore depended on keeping the South African balance favourable to the Cape Colony's future. When Bismarck disturbed it in 1884 by proclaiming his protectorate over Angra Pequena, the British listened to the pleas of Cape Town and quickly brought Bechuanaland and St Lucia Bay under imperial control, thus blocking a German junction with the Transvaalers. Ironically, however, it was not German diplomacy but British capital, pouring into the Transvaal to exploit the gold rushes on the Witwatersrand, that turned the balance against the Cape in favour of the republic. Toward the end of the 1880's the turn was already visible. As the centre of South African prosperity began to shift from the ports to the republic's gold-mines, the colonies frantically pushed their railways northward to catch the new Eldorado's trade. It was plain that their revenue and their farmers would soon depend mainly upon the Transvaal market. Kruger's government on the other hand preferred to apply its new economic power to the strengthening of republicanism throughout South Africa. At the cost of antagonising the Afrikaner Bond at the Cape, he shut the Cape railway out of the Rand, while using his new riches on building a line to Delagoa Bay that would release the republic from the thraldom of colonial ports and dues. Out of this economic revolution, there followed the long struggle for survival, fought with tariffs, railways and territorial claims, in which the Cape financial and mercantile interests extended their system northward in search of a future. Encircled with colonial railways and new English-speaking settlements, the Transvaal was to be forced or cajoled into a favourable commercial union.

It was this surge of colonisation and capital, this commercial civil war in the south, that drove the scramble for territory northward to the Zambezi, and onwards to Lake Nyasa and the southern boundary of the Congo Free State. Here was empire-building with a vengeance, whose like was to be found nowhere else on the continent. Yet if not cyphers, the men of Whitehall were little more than helpless auxiliaries in it. They were denied by Parliament the price of a protectorate or a colonial railway. The idea, the millions, the political fixing in London and Cape Town, in short the main impetus, was supplied from the craggy genius of Cecil Rhodes. With the impregnable credit of Rothschild's, De Beers and the Consolidated Gold Fields at his back, he knew as well as Leopold II himself how to put big business to work in politics and politics to work for big business —without putting off the shining armour of idealism. He thought big without thinking twice, and yet carried out schemes much larger than his words. A financier with no time for balance sheets but with time for dreams, awkwardly inarticulate, but excelling as a politician, passing as an Afrikaner in South Africa, an imperialist in London, his passionate belief in himself and the destiny of South Africa left him innocent of inconsistency.

When his prospectors told him in 1887 that the gold of Matabeleland would prove as rich as that of Johannesburg, he set about acquiring it—as a way of 'get[ting] a united S. Africa under the English flag'. 'If', he decided, 'we get Matabeleland we shall get the balance of Africa.' That was characteristic. And he persuaded Salisbury's government of it. That was characteristic too. Hope of another Rand and a strong British colony in Lobengula's kingdom which would offset the rise of the Transvaal moved ministers to charter Rhodes's South Africa Company in 1889. Part of the bargain was that he should extend the Cape railways through Bechuanaland and relieve the burden of this pauper protectorate on the Treasury; its essence was that Rhodes under one or other of his twenty different hats should do and pay for everything. Fearful of an anti-imperialist Parliament, suspecting the loyalty of Cape ministries under the shadow of the Bond, the imperial authorities saw no alternative but to play the King of Diamonds. Only Rhodes could make the imperial counterpoise in the north: he alone, first as Hofmeyr's political ally and soon as Cape premier, could keep the Bond faithful in the struggle for supremacy in South Africa. The intransigence of Kruger and his nationalist burghers forced Rhodes to pay the piper but it allowed him to call his own tune. At his insistence Salisbury elbowed aside Portugal's claims and Queen Victoria's protests, taking northern as well as southern Rhodesia for the South Africa Company in 1890, instead of letting it go as he first intended. Moreover, it was Rhodes's cheque-book that enabled Salisbury to throw a protectorate over Nyasaland in 1891 and save the land of Livingstone from the Catholic Portuguese advance. Henceforward Whitehall clung to the coat-tails of the Colossus who had become almost an 'independent power' in southern Africa. For them the problem was not one of promoting British trade and investment, but of shaping to their fixed imperial design the intrinsically neutral movement of colonists and capital. The danger of provoking Afrikaner nationalism stopped them from doing this directly, even if they had had the money. Rhodes not only had the purse, he was the leading Cape Afrikaner. He must do it for them.

But by 1895 all the Cape premier's projecting looked like failing. The fabled gold of Matabeleland had not materialised, but in the Transvaal the deep levels had proved profitable and practically inexhaustible. The settlers who might have colonised Rhodesia were joining the Uitlanders of Johannesburg instead. For a long time to come, the counterpoise across the Limpopo would be a mere featherweight in the imperial scale. Shares in the Bechuanaland railway and the South Africa Company slumped, while Witwatersrand issues boomed. After forty years in which the empire-builders had been working for a dominion founded upon Cape colonial supremacy, it was now certain that the real stone of union lay out of reach in the Transvaal republic. In 1894 Kruger opened his Delagoa Bay railway and, though the Cape now had a line running to the Rand, the Colony's share of the traffic and trade dwindled, as the lion's share went increasingly to the Transvaal and Natal. A year later, the battle of railways and tariffs almost brought the Colony and Republic to blows in the Drifts crisis, but no threat could force the Transvaalers into a commercial union on Rhodes's terms. Kruger held every advantage and he knew it. The true Rand together with the Delagoa Railway was raising him to be arbiter over the colonies' commercial future. Rhodes and Chamberlain suspected that he would arbitrate for a republic of South Africa. They set out to topple him.

Toward the end of 1895 Rhodes organised a rising of the Uitlanders in Johannesburg. It was a fiasco. Worse than that, Dr Jameson's Raid exposed the conspiracy and implicated the imperial authorities. Throughout South Africa, Afrikaner nationalists came together once more against British aggression. At Cape Town, Rhodes fell from office and the government came into the grip of the antagonised Bond. In the Free State, the moderates were replaced by sterner nationalists who soon made a far-reaching alliance with the Transvaal. Afrikaners in the Cape, the Orange Free State and the Transvaal stood united in defence of republicanism. Germany was giving Kruger cautious diplomatic support, hoping to lever Britain closer to the

Triple Alliance. If the Rand had turned the economic balance, Rhodes had swung the political scale against an imperial future.

This cataclysmic view was not that of Rhodes alone. The High Commissioners, Robinson and Milner, and the Colonial ministers, Chamberlain and Selborne, shared it. Early in 1896 the latter were persuaded that the Transvaal must be absorbed quickly into 'a Confederacy on the model of the Dominion of Canada . . . under the British flag'; otherwise it would 'inevitably amalgamate [the Colonies] . . . into a [republican] United States of South Africa'. About this vehement thesis the rest of the cabinet were highly sceptical. Recalling the reactions of Afrikaner nationalism to the first Boer War, they suspected that, however low colonial fortunes had fallen, a second war would lose the whole of South Africa for the empire. Such a struggle, moreover, would be extremely unpopular in Britain. The Salisbury ministry resolved to bring Kruger to reason through external pressure alone—perhaps by obtaining possession of Delagoa Bay; perhaps by squaring the Germans; perhaps by using threat and bluff to get the vote for the Uitlanders; by any means short of war to bring the Rand into a South African commercial union. Their efforts to avert a crash repeated Gladstone's over Arabi. But once more events took charge, and the outcome belied the intent. In using the severer weapons of 'moral suasion' called for by Rhodes and the extreme colonial party in South Africa, whose loyalty as their last remaining collaborators they dared not lose, the British government followed them over the edge of war. And like Arabi before him, it was Kruger who finally declared it. Gladstone's ministry had not realised their blunder in Egypt until after the event; unhappily Salisbury's knew theirs in South Africa beforehand. Hicks-Beach protested: 'I hope Milner and the Uitlanders will not be allowed to drag us into war.' Ruefully the Prime Minister admitted that they had. He foresaw with pitiless clarity the vengeance that Afrikaner nationalism would take upon the imperial cause. On the eve of the second Boer War in August 1899 he predicted: 'The Boers will hate you for a generation, even if they submit. . . . If they resist and are beaten, they will hate you still more. . . . But it recks little to think of that. What [Milner] has done cannot be effaced . . . and all for people whom we despise, and for territory which will bring no profit and no power to England.'

Hence the taking of the Rhodesias and the conquest of the Transvaal came about from a process of colonisation in which the struggles between Afrikaners and British nationalists had receded beyond imperial control. Once economic development had raised the enemies of the imperial connection to preponderance over the colonial collaborators, the government in London attempted diplomatically to switch back South Africa on to imperial lines. But in trying to make it into another Canada, they only created another Ireland. From this standpoint it was a case of mistaken identity. But the mistake went deeper than this: in the end they went to war for the obsolete notion of imperial supremacy in a Dominion—for a cause which was already a grand illusion.

Despite the astounding games of partition it played with the maps of Asia and Africa at the end of the nineteenth century, the so-called new imperialism was merely a second-order effect of the earlier work of European expansion. Colonising the Americas and the other white dominions had been a durable achievement, constructed out of the manpower, the capital and the culture of the lands on the Atlantic seaboard. By this time their growth in self-sufficiency was throwing them outside the orbit of European control, whatever relics of that overlordship might still exist on paper, or might still be fleetingly reasserted by force of arms. Yet far from this being a period of decay for Europe, its energies were now developing their maximum thrust. The potential of the old colonies of settlement had matured so far that they were generating local expansions of their own. The Canadians and Brazilians had organised their backlands. The Americans and Australians had spilled out into the Pacific. The South Africans had driven north of the Zambezi. Whatever the flag, whatever the guise, the expansive energies of Europe were still making permanent gains for western civilisation and its derivatives.

None of this was true of the gaudy empires spatch-cocked together in Asia and Africa. The advances of this new imperialism were mainly designed to plaster over the cracks in the old empires. They were linked only obliquely to the expansive impulses of Europe. They were not the objects of serious national attention. They have fallen to pieces only three-quarters of a century after being thrown together. It would be a gullible historiography which could see such gimcrack creations as necessary functions of the balance of power or as the highest stage of capitalism.

Nevertheless, the new imperialism has been a factor of the first importance for Asia and Africa. One of the side-effects of European expansion had been to wear down or to crack open the casings of societies governed hitherto by traditional modes. Towards the end of the nineteenth century this had produced a social mobility which the westerners now feared to sanction and did not dare to exploit by the old method of backing the most dynamic of the emergent groups. Frontiers were pushed deeper and deeper into these two continents, but the confident calculus of early nineteenth-century expansion was over and done with.

It is true that the West had now advanced so far afield that there was less scope for creative interventions of the old kind. The Russians had as little chance of fruitful collaboration with the Muslim emirs of Khiva and Bokhara as the French and British were to have with the theocrats of the Sudan. When the time of troubles came to the peoples of China or Tong-king or Fiji, their first response was to rally around the dynasty, just as in Africa the Moroccans and Ethiopians were to group under the *charisma* of the ruler. Movements of this sort were proto-nationalist in their results, but they were romantic, reactionary struggles against the facts, the passionate protests of societies which were shocked by the new age of change and would not be comforted. But there were more positive responses to the western question. The defter nationalisms of Egypt and the Levant, the 'Scholars of New Learning' in Kuang-Hsü China, the sections which merged into the continental coalition of the Indian Congress, the separatist churches of Africa—in their different ways, they all planned to re-form their personalities and regain their powers by operating in the idiom of the westerners.

The responses might vary, but all these movements belonged to a common trend. However widely the potentials might range between savage resistance and sophisticated collaboration, each and every one of them contained growth points. In cuffing them out of the postures of tradition and into the exchange economy and the bureaucratic state, western strength hustled them into transformation. One by one, they were exposed to rapid social change, and with it came conflicts between rulers and subjects, the rise of new élites, the transforming of values. All that the West could hear in this was distress signals. But just as its ethnocentric bias has obscured the analysis of imperialism, so its Darwinism has stressed the signs of decrepitude and crack-up in these societies at the cost of masking their growth points.

In dealing with these proto-nationalist awakenings, Europe was lured into its so-called age of imperialism; from them, the modern struggles against foreign rule were later to emerge. But the idiom has hidden the essence. Imperialism has been the engine of social change, but colonial nationalism has been its auxiliary. Between them, they have contrived a world revolution. Nationalism has been the continuation of imperialism by other means.

NOTES

[1] French consul in Cairo to Freycinet, 21 February 1882: Archives du Ministère des Affaires Étrangères [henceforth, A.E.], Égypte 72.

[2] Minister of Marine to Foreign Minister, 6 January 1874, A.E., Mémoires et Documents, Afrique (henceforth, A.E.M.D.), 58. Foreign Minister to Minister of Marine, 31 January 1880, A.E.M.D. Afrique, 77.

[3] Head of West African Mission to Décazes, 19 October 1885, 25 March 1886, Archives du Gouvernement-Général, Afrique Équatoriale Française (henceforth A.E.F.), 2 B, 28.

[4] Freycinet to Brazza, 12 April 1886, A.E.M.D., Afrique, 94.

[5] Memo. no. 70, 24 January 1890, A.E.F., Rapports sur la Situation Interieure, October 1886–February 1890.

[6] Foreign Ministry memo., 15 April 1887, A.E.M.D., Afrique, 83.

[7] Memo. by Services des Colonies, 17 July 1885, Archives of Ministère de la France d'Outre Mer (Henceforth M.F.O.M.), Afrique, IV, 12B.

[8] Under-Secretary of Colonies to Freycinet, 1 March 1886, M.F.O.M., Sénégal, IV, 84.

[9] Memo. by Galliéni, 24 September 1887, M.F.O.M., Sénégal, IV, 90; Galliéni to Under-Secretary for Colonies, 30 July 1887, ibid.

[10] Memo. by Archinard, 19 August 1889, M.F.O.M., Sénégal, IV, 93 A.

[11] Vallon to Under-Secretary for Colonies, 22 March 1890, M.F.O.M., Sénégal, IV, 95 C.

[12] Memo. by Archinard, 19 August 1889, M.F.O.M., Sénégal, IV, 93 A.

[13] Etienne to Governor of Sénégal, 14 April 1891, M.F.O.M., Sénégal, 91 B.

[14] Foreign Ministry memo., 'Considérations sur le projet d'arrangement franco-anglais', 13 August 1890, A.E.M.D., Afrique, 129.

[15] Mahdi to Negus Yohannes, 1884–5, quoted in Sanderson, G. N.: 'Contributions from African Sources to the . . . History of European Competition in the Upper Valley of the Nile': Leverhulme Conference Paper, University College of Rhodesia and Nyasaland, 1960.

[16] Delcassé to Grodet, 4 December 1893, M.F.O.M., Soudan, I, 6 A.

[17] Etienne to Governor of Sénégal, 4 December 1891, M.F.O.M., Sénégal, I, 91 B.

[18] Crampel to Under-Secretary for Colonies, 12 March 1890, M.F.O.M., Afrique, 5. Dossier Crampel, 1890–1.

[19] Governor-General, Algeria, to Colonies, 19 May 1896, M.F.O.M., Afrique, 10. Dossier Foureau, 1896.

[20] Governor-General, French West Africa, to Colonies, 12 July 1898, M.F.O.M., Afrique, II. Dossier Mission Voulet au Lac Tchad.

[21] Clozel to Colonies, 26 August 1895, M.F.O.M., Afrique. 9, Dossier Clozel.

[22] Brazza to Colonies, 18 April 1891, A.E.F. (unclassified); same to same, 6 June 1891, A.E.F., 2 B.

[23] Minister of Colonies to Monteil, 13 July 1894, M.F.O.M., Afrique, III, 16–19 (dossier 19 B).

[24] *Idem;* revised draft, with emendations by Hanotaux.

[25] Minister of Colonies to Monteil, 22 September 1894, *ibid.*

[26] French *chargé* in London to Hanotaux, 22 September 1894, A. E. Angleterre, 897.

[27] Rubenson, S., 'Ethiopia in the Scramble', Leverhulme History Conference Paper, University College of Rhodesia and Nyasaland, 1960.

[28] Memo. by Archinard, 20 January 1896, M.F.O.M., Afrique, 14.

[29] Memo. by Bonchamps, 'Reasons why Junction with Marchand was Impossible', n.d., M.F.O.M., Afrique, III, dossier 36 A.

[30] Colonies to Commissioner-General, French Congo, 15 April 1897, A.E.F., 3 D.

[31] Commissioner-General, French Congo, to Colonies, 24 November 1899, A.E.F., 3 D.

Non-European Foundations of
European Imperialism:
Sketch for a Theory of Collaboration

RONALD ROBINSON

This essay elaborates the hypothesis of the 1953 article, that imperialism is a political function of the process of integrating some countries at some times into the international economy. European imperialism was as much, and often more, a function of non-European resistance or collaboration as it was of the agencies of European expansion. Thus the essay is an investigation into the nature of crisis and change in non-European societies. Robinson attempts to formulate the implication of their previous studies by examining the possibility of a general theory. The essay extends the previous model. It now covers not only the origin of empire but also the question of how colonial rule was subsequently sustained and why eventually it ended in decolonization. The essay clearly shows the influence and results of historical scholarship on Africa and Asia of the 1960s. In Robinson's judgment, other scholars have confirmed the validity of the stress on the non-European elements in European imperialism in the 1953 article.

This essay originally appeared in Roger Owen and Bob Sutcliffe, editors, Studies in the Theory of Imperialism *(Longman, 1972) and is republished with permission of the author, editors, and publisher.*

Fresh homage is paid elsewhere in this volume to the fearful symmetry of old theories of imperialism which confounded the politics of empire with the economics of capitalism. Since they were invented, nevertheless, perspective has lengthened and decolonisation has shattered many of their impenetrably Eurocentric assumptions. A more historical theory of the working of European imperialism in the nineteenth and twentieth centuries is badly needed.

The old notions for the most part were restricted to explaining the genesis of new colonial empires in terms of circumstances in Europe. The theory of the future will have to explain in addition, how a handful of European pro-consuls managed to manipulate the polymorphic societies of Africa and Asia, and how, eventually, comparatively small, nationalist elites persuaded them to leave.

There is however a more compelling reason to grope for a better synthesis than those of the old masters. Today their analyses, deduced more from first principle than empirical observation, appear to be ideas about European society projected outward, rather than systematic theories about the imperial process as such. They were models in which empire-making was conceived simply as a function of European, industrial political economy. Constructed on the assumption that all active components were bound to be European ones, which excluded equally vital non-European elements by definition, the old theories were founded on a grand illusion.

Any new theory must recognise that imperialism was as much a function of its victims' collaboration or non-collaboration—of their indigenous politics, as it was of European expansion. The expansive forces generated in industrial Europe had to combine with elements within the agrarian societies of the outer world to make empire at all practicable.

To explore this more realistic first assumption as a basis for a fresh approach, is the object of this essay. It makes no pretension to accomplishing such a theory. It does suggest, however, that researches in the subject might take a new direction. The revised, theoretical model of imperialism has to be founded on studies of the nature and working of the various arrangements for mutual collaboration, through which the external European, and the internal non-European components cooperated at the point of imperial impact. Before reflecting on this idea, it is necessary to set it in a broader context.

1. A Definition of Modern Imperialism

Imperialism in the industrial era is a process whereby agents of an expanding society gain inordinate influence or control over the vitals of weaker societies by 'dollar' and 'gun-boat' diplomacy, ideological suasion, conquest and rule, or by planting colonies of its own people abroad. The object is to shape or reshape them in its own interest and more or less in its own image. It implies the exertion of power and the transfer of economic resources; but no society, however dominant, can man-handle arcane, densely-peopled civilisations or white colonies in other continents simply by projecting its own main force upon them. Domination is only practicable in so far as alien power is translated into terms of indigenous political economy.

Historically European imperialism might be defined as a political reflex action between one non-European, and two European components. From Europe stemmed the economic drive to integrate newly colonised regions and ancient agrarian empires into the industrial economy, as markets and investments. From Europe also sprang the strategic imperative to secure them against rivals in world power politics. As the stock-in-trade of the old masters,[1] these may be taken for granted, although of course they were indispensible to the process.

Their role however has been exaggerated. They did not in themselves necessitate empire. If they had done, the territorial scrambles of the later nineteenth century would have taken place in the Americas, where Europe was investing the bulk of its exported economic and human resources, rather than in Africa and Asia. One country can trade with another and be interested strategically in it without intervening in its politics. There was nothing intrinsically imperialistic about foreign investment or great power rivalry. European capital and technology, for example, strengthened the independence of Japan and the Transvaal, at the same time as they undermined that of Egypt. The great power rivalry that carved up Africa also stopped the 'slicing of the Chinese melon' and delayed Ottoman partition. It ought to be commonplace therefore that from beginning to end imperialism was a product of interaction between European and extra-European politics. European economic and strategic expansion took imperial form when these two components operated at cross-purposes with the third and non-European component—that of indigenous collaboration and resistance.[2] The missing key to a more historical theory perhaps is to be found in this third element.

If this triple interaction in large measure made imperialism necessary and practicable, its controlling mechanism was made up of relationships between the agents of external expansion and their internal 'collaborators' in non-European political economies. Without the voluntary or enforced cooperation of their governing elites, economic resources could not be transferred, strategic interests protected or xenophobic reaction and traditional resistance to change contained. Nor without indigenous collaboration, when the time came for it, could Europeans have conquered and ruled their non-European empires. From the outset that rule was continuously resisted; just as continuously native mediation was needed to avert resistance or hold it down. Indian sepoys and Indian revenue, for example, conquered and kept for the Raj the brightest jewel in the imperial crown. China and Japan on the other hand provided no such collaborators as India and so, significantly, could not be brought under the yoke.

It is easy to mistake the source of the power upholding these African and Asian colonial empires. Their serried panoplies might indicate that it came from Europe. But had it come thence they would have remained paper tigers. Although potentially the power was there in Europe, in reality only a tiny fraction of it was ever committed to Africa or Asia. Europe's policy normally was that if empire could not be had on the cheap, it was not worth having at all. The financial sinew, the military and administrative muscle of imperialism was drawn through the mediation of indigenous elites from the invaded countries themselves.

Its central mechanism, therefore, may be found in the systems of collaboration set up in pre-industrial societies, which succeeded (or failed) in meshing the incoming processes of European expansion into indigenous social politics and in achieving some kind of evolving equilibrium between the two.

2. The Idea of Collaborating or Mediating Elites

As the agents of large-scale industrial civilisation invaded small-scale agrarian societies, the allure of what the big society had to offer in trade, capital, technology, military or diplomatic aid, or the fear of its vengeance, elicited indigenous political and economic 'collaborators'. It should be stressed that the term is used in no pejorative sense. From the standpoint of the collaborators or mediators the invaders imported an alternative source of wealth and power which, if it could not be excluded, had to be exploited in order to preserve or improve the standing of indigenous elites in the traditional order. As the cases of Japan from 1858 to 1867[3] and of Buganda from 1886 to 1900[4] among many other examples show, if the ruling elite chose resistance there was usually a counter-elite to opt for collaboration, or vice versa. At the same time the 'bargains' of collaboration were not, and could not be too one-sided or they ceased to be effective. Collaborators or not, the social elites of Africa and Asia who made up the great majority of imperialism's involuntary partners, had to mediate with the foreigner on behalf of their traditional institutions and constituents. Too drastic concessions in sensitive areas would undermine the basis of their authority and set their forced contracts with Europe at nought. The irony of collaborative systems lay in the fact that although the white invaders could exert leverage on ruling elites they could not do without their mediation. Even if the bargains were unequal they had to recognise mutual interests and inter-dependence if they were to be kept. When mediators were not given enough cards to play, their authority with their own people waned, crisis followed, and the expanding powers had to choose between scrapping their interests or intervening to promote them directly. Nor was it possible for them later as rulers to deal with subject societies as amorphous collections of individuals. Hence the terms on which collaboration took place were critical in determining not only the political and economic modes of European expansion but also its agents' chances of achieving influence, keeping control, promoting changes, and of containing xenophobic reaction.

Two interconnecting sets of linkages thus made up the collaborative mechanism: one consisting of arrangements between the agents of industrial society and the indigenous elites drawn into cooperation with them; and the other connecting these elites to the rigidities of local interests and institutions. Collaborators had to perform one set of functions in the external or 'modern sector' yet 'square' them with another and more crucial set in the indigenous society. The kind of arrangement possible in the one thus determined the kind of arrangement possible in the other. When collaborators succeeded in solving these complex politico-economic equations, as did the modernising samurai of Japan, progress was almost miraculous; when they failed to do so, as Chinese mandarins and Egyptian pashas found, the result sooner or later was catastrophe.

Although the mediators remained integrated in local society, in their dual role they rarely formed a united interest group or a unified modern sector within that society. Of necessity they played the part of collaborator more or less with reference to their roles in their own society. Their mutual rivalries within that society cut across their common interests as intermediaries. Hence collaborative systems tended to consist of collections of mediating functions isolated and dispersed through native society rather than of unified social groups within them. This differentiation between mediating roles and groups is plain, in that the same group at times allied itself to, but at other times opposed, the imperialists. The turnover of allies in a crisis was often remarkable.

The efficiency of this system was clearly proportionate to the amount of European wealth and power committed to it. This determined the weight of externally-oriented functions within indigenous society. Where the externalised activities were small by comparison with the traditional ones, collaborators naturally attached more importance to their traditional, than to their mediatory role. The greater the resources that came from Europe the less imperialism depended on indigenous mediation. In Algeria, Kenya and the Rhodesias up to the 1950s, for example, native politics were strangled by the presence of a minority of white colonists. Imperial control could thus dispense with native cooperation to a great extent; it could not, on the other hand, be upheld without the colonists' consent. Even in these special cases native mediators later became more necessary to colonial rule as African nationalist organisation grew. In west African dependencies where there were no white colonists, mediators were always vital to their rulers. The need for intermediaries varied again with the military force available and the rulers' willingness to use coercion as a substitute for collaboration. The military element in French imperialism in North and West Africa[5] in the period before the rise of African nationalism often made it less dependent on mediators than the British, a situation which reflected the different expansive resources of a continental country with a large conscript army and an island dependent for its European security on a large navy.

Throughout the imperial era, economic inputs into Africa and Asia with the exception of India remained small, barely scratching the social surface or interrupting the implacable continuities of indigenous history. Systems of cooperation there as a result remained comparatively ineffective and unstable. In white colonies, however, where European inputs were comparatively great, collaboration proved both stable and effective.[6] Accordingly colonial rule encroached on Afro-Asia more and more directly and extensively as it attempted to construct and uphold indigenous cooperation; while in the white dominions, the more reliable collaborative mechanisms became, the more colonial rule receded.

It might almost be said that the changing bargains of collaboration or mediation define the actual working of imperialism at the point of impact at a particular time. Hence the study of them appears to offer a more comprehensive view of the factors involved than does the one-eyed analysis of European forces.

Historical flesh for these abstract bones may be taken from the case of the lone London missionary to the Tswana tribes, illustrating the mechanism at its weakest, and from that of the nineteenth-century white colonist, showing it working at its strongest.

In Bechuanaland during the 1840s and 1850s the missionary was the sole agent of European expansion. Although his spiritual resources were great, it did not appear that he had either the great powers or the industrial economy at his back. His gospel moreover had no use or meaning for most Tswana chiefs and elders, who knew that it would subvert both their religion and authority. While permitting him to teach, therefore, they assigned to this one man 'modern sector' the roles of irrigation expert, chief of defense staff, gunsmith and commercial and diplomatic agent in dealings with the outside world. He had little reward in souls. By the 1870s he was calling up imperial power from the Cape to supplement the European side of the bargain with more material resources.

This simple episode,[7] which was repeated with variations whereever the missionary first went in black Africa, illustrates the tendency of collaboration, in the absence of sufficient input, to divert the agents of European expansion to the service of traditional society. On the one side the Tswana elite stretched the bargain to exploit the European for the purpose of strengthening their position in traditional politics; on the other, they neutralised his potentially disruptive effects and so largely frustrated the European objective. The missionary conceived of a European role. The role he actually played was assigned and defined in terms of Tswana society.

3. The White Colonist: The Ideal Prefabricated Collaborator

At the other extreme is the case of the white colonist with the power of an industrial economy behind him, transplanting European attitudes and institutions carried in his head. He was the ideal, prefabricated collaborator; but by what kind of mechanism did Britain project these profitable economic satellites, these congenial imperial dominions, onto continents thousands of miles away?

In Australia, New Zealand, and to a less extent elsewhere, although original cultural affiliation played its part, political collaboration stemmed largely from economic dependence. For the greater part of the century these colonies had no alternative to Britain as a source of capital, export markets, immigrants and protection. In the early stages of growth metropolitan investment largely pre-selected the colonial economy's immigrants and governed the direction and speed of its growth. The dominant export-import sector consequently shaped colonial politics in favour of commercial and political collaboration with London. Collaborative bargains proved easy to make and to keep when commercial partnership was mutually profitable and colonists were permitted to manage their own internal affairs.

Their bread was buttered in the Mother Country. Exporter and importer, banker and docker, farmer, sheep drover and cattle herder in the colony voted for politicians who would respect the arrangements to keep export markets open and capital flowing in. Unemployment and defeat at the next election were the penalties for breaking them. Direct imperial control in such conditions was unnecessary. Indeed since it provoked violent nationalist reaction, it was a positive disadvantage and rusted into disuse. Imperial cooperation was achieved mainly by economic attraction through the normal internal political processes of the colony itself. There were sufficient economic inputs to maintain political alliance.

This platonic construction of course is too good to be absolutely true historically, even in Australasia; but the higher the synthesis, the lower the detailed historical accuracy. The white colonial model had its snags and it could also break down. There are some awkward nuts and bolts to be added in the Canadian and South African cases which did not entirely square with the classic requirements of economic dependency. The Canadians had an alternative, external trading partner in the United States. Both the Canadian and the South African colonies up to the 1890s had a small export-import sector and a large subsistence sector. French Canadians, a large minority, and the large majority of Afrikaaners in South Africa of pre-industrial European stock had historic reasons for resenting British imperialism and no close commercial connections with it. Yet in Canada, curiously enough, after 1847, the French Canadians' fear of the 'yanquees' did most to anchor the Canadian colonies politically in the empire against the pull of the United States. Canadian nationalism and the counter attraction of British capital, markets and loyalties did the rest in generating collaboration between Britain and the Canadian colonies.

In the South African colonial mechanism during the first three-quarters of the nineteenth century also, commercial partnership with Britain seems to have attracted the Cape Dutch to cooperate economically, and so politically, with the English-speaking South Africans of the export-import sector and with the imperial connection. It was otherwise with their Afrikaaner cousins, the uncooperative republican *trekboers* in the introverted up-country economies of the Transvaal and northern Orange Free State. After 1887, a geological accident gave the Transvaalers political control of the export-import sector through that of the Witwatersrand mines; and its English politico-economic entrepreneurs, divided from their Cape Dutch collaborators, lost control over South Africa and evoked Nemesis in the

Jameson Raid, the Boer War and the Afrikaaner nationalist reaction that followed.[8] It is clear from this case that greatly increased economic inputs, if they happen to hit on the weak points, can tear down, as well as build up a system of colonial collaboration. Other examples of this same type were the Argentine between 1828 and 1852[9] and Uruguay in the first half of the century. In both cases, the framework of political unification was too immature to contain the clash of politico-economic interests between the *portenos* of the export-import sector and the barons and *gauchos* of the subsistence backlands. Consequently, until the second half of the century, the *portenos* were unable to extend the political grip of the export-import sector inland quickly enough to induce the backlands to co-operate economically.

In spite of these difficulties with colonial nationalists, institutional gaps and temporary breakdowns, the collaborative mechanism of commercial partnership in white colonies converted external economic power into internal political cooperation. It worked constructively so that these colonies eventually 'took off'. Gradually as their economies diversified, local capital formation grew, the ties of political collaboration with Britain slackened and economic dependence diminished. In so far as their import-export sectors shrank in importance relative to their domestic economy, the collaborating elites associated with them lost influence to populist national movements in colonial politics. But by that time the collaborative system had done its work; for the white ex-colonies—the United States and Latin America, together with the British 'dominions'—had become expansive in their own right in pursuit of their own 'manifest destiny'.

4. Collaboration in Afro-Asia: The External or Informal Phase

A different mark of model altogether is required for Africa and Asia, although many Victorians believed at first that the white colonial model would do. Their expectations of free trade and Christianity turning Ottoman rayahs, Levantine traders, Chinese mandarins, Indian Brahmins and African chiefs into Europeanised collaborators, working to modernise their 'reactionary religions' and 'ramshackle' empires were to be disappointed.

From the 1820s to the 70s, in what might be called the external or informal stage of industrial imperialism, Europe attempted to lever Afro-Asian regimes into collaboration from outside and to reshape their institutions through commerce. Naval and diplomatic power forced their rulers to abolish commercial monopolies, lower tariffs and open their doors to the 'Imperialism of Free Trade'.[10] Later, in return for loans, or under the muzzles of high velocity guns, they were bundled into liberalising their traditional political, legal and fiscal institutions to make elbowroom for their 'productive classes' in commercial collaboration with Europe, to take over power. But in fact these 'classes' rarely succeeded in doing so. Like contemporary development planners, classical economics overestimated the power of economic inputs to revolutionise Oriental society.

The result, sooner or later, was disaster everywhere except in Japan and India, already under the white Raj. In Japan after 1869 the western samurai overthrew the Shogunate, perilously modernised its quasi-feudal institutions and exploited neotraditionalist nationalism and carefully calculated bargains with the West to protect their independence on the basis of 'rich country, strong army'. By 1914 these Japanese collaborators had achieved what otherwise only white colonists seemed able to achieve. They succeeded in translating the forces of western expansion into terms of indigenous politics. By adapting European style techniques and institutions, they managed to control them so that they strengthened, instead of destroying, Japanese government, and worked not for imperialism, but for Japan.[11]

In contrast, the collaborative mechanism in China worked superficially. Admittedly the timing of the mid-nineteenth century European break-in was unfavourable, for China was then in the grip of a demographic crisis. The mandarin bureaucracy was challenged by widespread peasant revolt from the Tai-pings[12] and Muslims; and in suppressing them, the central government lost its power to provincial warlords and gentry. They used it to defend the traditional order against collaborators' efforts to reform Chinese institutions from above. Free trade imperialism enabled European merchants in the treaty ports, in partnership with Chinese merchants, to take over the exposed riverine and maritime branches of Chinese domestic trade; but the Manchu regime rejected European capital and railways and so the export-import sector hardly dented the vast, introverted domestic economy. When K'ang Yu-wei in 1898 attempted to recentralise Manchu government and to substitute western for confucian education in imitation of the Japanese, the traditionalist bureaucracy and gentry in effect vetoed all his decrees. And when rival European powers attempted to inject capital and railways forcibly into the society between 1895 and 1900, the dramatic xenophobic reaction of the Boxers drove them back, beleagured, into the legations of Pekin.[13]

From the conservative reform period of the sixties and seventies to the abortive military recentralization of Yuan Shi-k'ai in the 1900s the indigenous modernisers and collaborators within the Manchu regime, remained prisoners of the impenetrably confucian social units that connected lower bureaucracy with provincial gentry and peasantry.[14] This had once been an imperial system of peasant control. It had turned into a system of popular defiance, cancelling Pekin's collaborative bargains with the West. Modern ideas, military technique, capital and institutions, therefore, could by no means be translated into terms of indigenous political processes. The railways planned too late to reimpose the control of Pekin, the modern artillery, the battleships and the loans, provoked deeper provincial and populist resistance; so that the Manchu régime continued to crumble until it fell in the revolution of 1911.

In the Muslim societies of the Ottoman empire, Egypt and Tunis, however, collaborating regimes were at first more successful than in China. By the 1850s and 60s international free trade and capital investment had made a considerable impression on their economies through the enforced collaboration of traditional rulers and the commercial partnership of Levantine urban classes. Rulers tried strenuously to modernise their armies and navies and to exploit railways in order to strengthen their grip on rebellious provinces or conquer new ones. But the Ottoman regime consisted of a Muslim military autocracy and a Turkish heartland ruling over a multiracial empire disrupted by Slav nationalists, Armenian Christians and Arab dissidents. A handful of cosmopolitan Turks, the majority of them in the army—the main source of modernisers in Muslim states—tried to secularise the constitution and give non Muslims equal representation and equality of opportunity within the regime. The reforms decreed by Resid Pasha in 1839 and by Midhat and Huseyin Avni after the coup of 1876 at Constantinople however, like K'ang Yu-wei's in the China of 1898, were smothered at birth in xenophobic reactions from traditional elites.[15] The Tanzimat reformers attempted to do so much more than the Chinese. They ended up doing much worse. The Hamidian traditionalist reaction of pan-Islamism and pan-Turkism after 1876 was that much more passionate. If the Turkish collaborators were eventually ineffective, European statesmen and bankers who dealt them a bad hand to play in Ottoman politics were largely to blame.

5. The Character of Afro-Asian Collaboration
Some of the reasons why Afro-Asian collaborative mechanisms worked differently from white colonial systems are obvious from

these examples. Afro-Asian economies, being largely undifferentiated from their socio-political institutions, were more or less invulnerable to the play of the international market. The institutional barriers to economic invasion proved intractable; economic reform was subject to the political veto of social conservatism; as a result the export-import sector normally remained a tiny accretion on traditional society, and this meant that commercial collaborators were few and unable to win power.

In white colonies the international economy worked through neo-European attitudes and institutions which enabled their export-import sectors to convert British economic power into colonial political collaboration with empire. In most Afro-Asian examples, institutional gaps kept industrial inputs too small to empower such a mechanism. Small as they were they had to be driven in by the hammer of European intervention. External political pressure had to supply the lack of economic leverage on the indigenous political economy before a measure of economic collaboration could be obtained. Consequently the main source of Afro-Asian collaborators was not in the export-import sector but among essentially noncommercial, ruling oligarchies and landholding elites. Again, the terms of the bargain under the imperialism of free trade permitted them to divert economic resources to the purpose of maintaining the *status quo*, in return for protecting European enterprise and a measure of political alliance.

Sooner or later consequently these collaborating Oriental regimes fell into the international bankruptcy court as did the Ottoman Sultan and Egyptian Khedive in 1876, the Bey of Tunis in 1867, and the Manchu empire in 1894. One by one they became bones of contention between European powers, subjected to increasing foreign interference to reform the management of their internal financial and political affairs. At this point Europe had forced its internal collaborators to play for high stakes with too few cards. Its demands were cutting off their régimes from the loyalty of the traditional elites which formerly upheld them—whether they were Turkish or Chinese landlords, Muslim or Confucian leaders—until eventually popular xenophobic, neotraditional uprisings confronted their impotence. The stress of free trade imperialism within and without cracked their hold on internal politics. At different times this kind of crisis wrecked collaborative systems of the informal type in most of Africa and Asia; and as they broke down European powers were compelled to change their mode of expansion from free trade imperialism into those of occupation and colonial rule. More often than not it was this non-European component of European expansion that necessitated the extension of colonial empires in the last two decades of the nineteenth century and the first decade of the twentieth.

6. The Imperial Takeover

Certainly a breakdown of this kind was the imperative behind the British occupation of Egypt in 1882 and therefore incidentally for much of the subsequent rivalry impelling the partition of Africa.[16] After the imposition of free trade in 1841 the Egyptian import-export sector based on cotton grew remarkably under the management of Levantine and European merchants.[17] Since these were extraneous to indigenous society, however, their commercial success enabled them to corrupt and exploit, but not to reform or direct, the political régime. The Khedivate overborrowed foreign capital for prestige projects, military and other non-productive purposes, and slid into bankruptcy in 1876. Europe then imposed drastic financial controls and constitutional reforms on the Khedive Ismail in return for further loans, which alienated him from the ruling elite. When he resisted the controls to regain his popularity, Britain and France had him deposed and set up Tewfik in his place. By 1881 as a result, the collaborating Khedivate had lost control of indigenous politics to a neotraditional reaction headed by Arabi and his colonels, Muslim religious leaders and landlords riding a wave of popular antiforeign feeling.[18] Confronted with the collapse, Britain and France had two choices: to scrap their commercial and strategic interest in the country, or to pick up the pieces and reconstruct the collaborative mechanism by throwing their own weight into Egypt's internal politics.[19]

Hence it was the crisis in Egyptian government provoked by heavier collaborative demands, rather than rivalry in Europe, which first set Britain and France competing for the advantage under the new arrangements; and the lack of reliable Egyptian collaborators, rather than fear of France or any increased interest in Egypt, which brought the redcoats onto the Suez Canal in 1882 and kept them there until 1956.

In the partition of China into European spheres of influence from 1895 to 1902, the breakdown of 'open door' collaboration based on an Oriental régime again played a major part. The forces which overthrew it—financial crisis, intensifying foreign intervention and anti-European reaction—looked remarkably similar to those that overthrew the Khedivate: but their Chinese sequence and combination were different. The Japanese victory over China and the war indemnity thus exacted in 1894 bankrupted the Manchu régime, making it for the first time dependent on European loans. An alteration in the eastern regional balance of power rather than European rivalry first precipitated the crisis. At bottom that alteration stemmed from the assault of Japan's revolutionary modernisation on China's reactionary resistance to modern reform. It was these essentially non-European factors which called for European imperialist action. The Japanese conquests threatened Russian strategic interests in north China. Manchu bankruptcy portended the collapse of the indigenous régime. Russia with France, her ally, felt the need, and took the opportunity, to take alternative measures for securing their stakes in the Celestial Empire. Having evicted the Japanese by diplomatic pressure, they extorted exclusive spheres of influence marked out with Chinese railway concessions from Pekin in return for foreign loans, and Britain and Germany necessarily joined in the partition to save their interests.

The antiforeign reaction to intensified imperialist intervention which had precipitated the British occupation of Egypt, helped to halt the occupation of China. The Boxer rebellion of 1900 provoked the Russians to occupy Manchuria in much the same way that Arabi's rebellion led to the British occupation of Egypt. Shortly, however, this Chinese popular resistance, together with the Anglo-Japanese Alliance of 1902 and Japan's defeat of Russia, restored the eastern power balance and halted the imperialist takeover of China. The original necessity for it having been removed, the Chinese partition was aborted. The wheel of collaboration had turned full circle—sufficiently at least to restore the international open door system, if not to save the Manchu régime from its own subjects.

To account for the imperial takeovers in Afro-Asia at the end of the last century exclusively in terms of European capitalism and strategy is to miss the point. The transition was not normally activated by these interests as such, but by the breakdown of collaborative mechanisms in extra-European politics which hitherto had provided them with adequate opportunity and protection.

7. Afro-Asian Collaboration and Non-Collaboration under Colonial Rule

If Eurocentric theory misses the crucial role of collaborative systems in the transition from external imperialism to the takeover, it also exaggerates the break with previous collaborative processes that colonial rule involved. Admittedly the transition to formal empire looks dramatic in constitutional form and proconsular heroics, and the shooting was real enough. At first sight what seemed to have happened was that the colonial power had thrown its entire weight into indigenous politics, which it was now playing from inside. But this was not the way the proconsuls saw it. Even with the colonies, European governments insisted on a policy of limited commitment in the use of metropolitan men and money. The amount of force at the disposal of colonial rulers locally seemed tiny in comparison with the possibility of disaffection and revolt. Reinforcement was usually sent with reluctance, the need for it regarded as a sign of administrative incompetence. Coercion was expensive and counterproductive except in emergency, and everyone knew that no amount of force could hold down indigenous politics for long.

Whether the official agents of imperialism were working from outside or inside Afro-Asian societies therefore, they still had to work through indigenous collaborators and political processes. Their own power was limited. It was enough to manipulate, but not to abolish them. The substance of ruling authority had to a great extent to be extracted from their subjects. Essentially, therefore, colonial rule represented a reconstruction of collaboration. This form of imperialism worked even more than in its earlier external manifestations, as a function of non-European politics.

Occupation of territory, however, made the old collaborative equations much easier to solve. With government patronage in their hands proconsuls could make better bargains with indigenous elites and enforce them. They were also able to manufacture a small modern elite of collaborators and set them in subordinate authority. The colonial régime altered the context in which indigenous political entities worked. However, because its power to maintain that context depended on their acquiescence, its ability to reform them remained slight.

Although good government and modern development were objectives of colonial rule, its first concern was to keep control. Incentives and rewards for its collaborators were partly commercial but mainly governmental—the perquisites of office, honours, contracts, social services and all the favours that could be given or taken away through its administrative land, fiscal and education policies. The rulers distributed them with the object of keeping the weightier part of the dependency's political elements on the government side. Their opponents' tactic, whether they came as at first, from traditional, or later, from modern elites, was to play on grievances and draw

this was not the way the proconsuls saw it. Even with the colonies, European governments insisted on a policy of limited commitment in the use of metropolitan men and money. The amount of force at the could make do with acquiescence if they could not obtain active cooperation. They were secure so long as traditional elites and the grass roots peasantry refused to be politicised by so-called 'agitators'. Hence the less proconsuls interfered with traditional authorities and institutions, the safer they were; and the more they attempted to alter them into modern secular shapes, the harder the collaborative equations became.

In India[20] and Africa up to 1947, there was an abundance of indigenous collaborators. They were of many kinds: some were active, but most were passive, some were modern, but most were traditional elites; some collaborated at central, others at provincial or local levels; some cooperated commercially, others administratively, ecclesiastically, or educationally. The secret of a successful system, from the European standpoint, lay in this variety of choice and combination. It is often said that this was a policy of divide and rule. More truly, rule was possible because its subjects were socially divided and could not unite. The European official bargained with traditional collaborators the more easily because their interests lay in regional politics and traditional activities, whereas he was concerned mainly with central politics and modern activities. Rulers had wide scope for action without clashing head on with the leaders of indigenous, social, religious and political establishments; and so many collaborative bargains took the form of tacit agreements for mutual non-interference and mutual support between colonial government and indigenous society. In India the indigenous political focus was provincial; in Africa, it was normally local or tribal. The miniscule nature of traditional units and their undifferentiated character usually made such bargains effective. Collaborators, on their side, were concerned to exploit the wealth, prestige and influence to be derived from association with colonial government, to increase their traditional followings or improve their modern opportunities. For these reasons collaboration, as colonial rulers well understood, could be a dangerous game. It involved dealing some of their best cards to potentially overmighty subjects. If one set of collaborators grew too powerful as a result, patronage had to be withdrawn and given to another.

In these ways, European administrators were up to their eyes in the politics of their so-called subjects, even when they did not altogether understand them. They were in the indigenous business of faction and clientage-making with zamindars and talukdars, Hindu bhadralok and Muslim jihad leaders, African clan heads, paramount chiefs and kings. The permutations on which they rang the changes, the brinkmanship involved in pushing indigenous politics in desired modern directions, constituted the true genius of colonial administration.

Collaboration as the basis of colonial rule is richly exemplified in the working of the Indian Raj and African 'indirect rule.' There is space here for but one example: that of British administration in the Anglo-Egyptian Sudan.[21] After defeating its Mahdist rulers in 1898 with Egyptian troops and money, the British controlled this dependency up to 1924 through Egyptian and Sudanese subordinate officials in collaboration with anti-Mahdist 'Notables'. Kitchener's and Wingate's arrangements were designed primarily to forestall the political revival and rebellion of the Mahdist movement. They therefore allied their administration to the interests of the rival Khatmia Muslim order, the orthodox Muslim *ulama* and the anti-Mahdist sheikhs and chiefs of the rural areas. The Khatmia and Mahdist socio-religious organisations, from the British standpoint, were the keys to indigenous politics for only they had the organisation potentially to unite town and countryside, tribe with tribe into a widespread, popular uprising. Implicitly, therefore, the bargain was that the administration exercised its patronage in favour of the anti-Mahdist elements in return for their support; while their enhanced prestige, wealth and following strengthened mutual defence against a revival of Mahdist fanaticism.

After 1924 the rulers realigned their collaborative equations to meet the emergence, in the 'White Flag' mutiny, of a radical, pro-Egyptian minority in the tiny Sudanese modern elite. In the Sudan, as in India and elsewhere in Black Africa, it was not the radical modern elite as such that colonial rulers feared. It was rather the combination of these urban malcontents with populist movements among rural peasantry and tribes through an alliance between modern urban, and rural traditional elites. To forestall this danger was the main objective of indirect rule systems of collaboration throughout the British empire between the two world wars.

Sir John Maffey's indirect rule policy in the Sudan from 1927 to 1933 bestowed official prestige, powers and patronage on the traditional chiefs and headmen of villages and tribes as 'local native authorities'. Its object was to strengthen both their loyalty to the colonial administration and their hold over local rural communities, thus cutting a firebreak to prevent urban radicals or neo-Mahdist agents from setting the grass roots of indigenous politics alight. The arrangements of indirect rule served three purposes: they strengthened local and ethnic compartmentalisation and so raised obstacles to anticolonial agitation on a national scale; they tightened the rural elite's grip on peasant and tribe against the possiblity of radical efforts to loosen it; and they reduced contact between 'graduates' in the central administration and the provincial and local rural societies to a minimum.

In the modern elite politics of the three towns of Khartoum, Omdurman and El-Obeid, meanwhile, the colonial collaborative arrangements kept the majority of 'graduates' moderate and opposed to the radical minority. The term 'graduate' signified a man who had completed at least primary education in English. Almost all this modern elite in the Sudan were in the civil service. Their Union society and later national Congress of Graduates' clubs, like the earlier Indian Congress, were more interested consequently in better professional opportunity than mass organisation against colonial rule. The eviction of Egyptian officials and army officers after 1924 provided them with more and better jobs.

After 1933 the collaborative system had to be reoriented once again to meet the threat from neo-Mahdism. Not only was its rural organisation expanding, but its leader, Sir Abdel Rahman el Mahdi was outbidding the loyal Khatmia leadership for influence over the urban graduates. To forestall this conjunction of urban and agrarian discontents through the neo-Mahdist religious organisation, the new Governor, Sir George Symes, abandoned Indirect rule to outbid the Mahdists for the support of the graduates. The new tactic offered them Sudanisation of the civil service, more higher education, consultation with the Graduates Congress on policy and, eventually, 'Sudan for the Sudanese'; and up to 1940 it succeeded in its purpose of keeping moderate graduates in control of congress, and of forestalling an alliance between the Congress and the neo-Mahdist politico-religious movement which could politicize the rural population.

After 1940, however, the pace of Sudanisation proved too slow. The Congress, divided between neo-Mahdist and Khatmia religious alliances, was captured by the radical Graduates and demanded the right of self-determination for the Sudan after the war. In 1942, as a result, the colonial rulers switched to a rapprochement with the neo-Mahdists and moderate graduates, dividing the neo-Mahdists from their alliance with the radicals, but driving the Khatmia into opposition to the British and alliance with graduate extremists.

So out of the permutations of imperial collaboration emerged the two Sudanese nationalist parties which once they could agree on a united front of non-collaboration with colonial rule, were able to persuade the British to pack their traps and go in 1956. Each party combined elements of the tiny modern elite with a neotraditional Muslim religious organisation. By this means both eventually achieved that combination of modern elite grievances with popular rural discontents which the imperial system of overrule had striven so ingeniously to prevent. Independence became possible, colonial rule impossible, when nationalism had ceased to be merely a tiny elitist movement and succeeded in allying itself to the historic, popular religious forces of Sudanese history.

The conclusions to be drawn from the Sudanese example are more or less true of modern colonial rule in most Afro-Asian dependencies. Its organisation, policy and character were more or less determined by the need to elicit indigenous collaboration and split indigenous opposition. In that sense, imperialism in the form of colonial rule was a minor function of European society, but a major function of indigenous politics. The permutations of collaboration shifted whenever a collaborating element, whether of the modern or neo-traditional elite, grew too powerful or too dissatisfied, and above all, whenever a major element in colonial politics,[22] whether cooperating or in opposition, threatened to unite an urban elite with a mass, rural following.

8. Non-Collaboration and Decolonisation

No less than colonial rule, the anticolonial nationalism of small modern elites had to be translated into broader terms of indigenous, neotraditional politics before it could challenge and overthrow the imperial collaborative system and set up a rival system of noncollaboration.[23] Nationalists had to contrive a situation in which their rulers ran out of collaborators. They had to realign against imperialism the same political elements which, hitherto, had been arrayed on the imperial side. Necessarily in pre-industrial societies, these were preponderantly neotraditionalist religious, social and ethnic units. In that sense all the national movements that won independence were more or less functions of neotraditional politics organised in the form of modern political parties. Each party was essentially a confederation of neotraditional local, ethnic, religious and status interests, managed by a small modern elite. The party, like the colonial regime before it, changed the context in which these social interests operated and integrated them with itself in new alignments. As the party became a function of them, they became to some extent a function of the party. So long as the national party was in opposition to a colonial regime, it was comparatively easy to reconcile these two roles. But when the party became the government of the nation its function as representative of neotraditional interests conflicted increasingly with its role as development agent for the nation as a whole. The experience of the 1960s shows that the reconciliation of the two roles and the problem of neotraditionalist social collaboration involved, is not much easier for new nationalists than it was for old colonialists.

9. Conclusion

The theory of collaboration suggests that at every stage from external imperialism to decolonisation, the working of imperialism was determined by the indigenous collaborative systems connecting its European and Afro-Asian components. It was as much and often more a function of Afro-Asian politics than of European politics and economics.

At the outset it depended on the absence or presence of effective indigenous collaborators, and the character of indigenous society, whether imperialist invasions of Africa and Asia were practicable or not. Secondly, the transition from one phase of imperialism to the next was governed by the need to reconstruct and uphold a collaborative system that was breaking down. The breakdown of indigenous collaboration in many instances necessitated the deeper imperial intervention that led to imperial takeover. Thirdly, the choice of indigenous collaborators, more than anything else, determined the organisation and character of colonial rule; in other words, its administrative, constitutional, land and economic policies were largely institutionalisations of the indigenous, political alliances which upheld it. Fourthly, when the colonial rulers had run out of indigenous collaborators, they either chose to leave or were compelled to go. Their national opponents in the modern elite sooner or later succeeded in detaching the indigenous political elements from the colonial regime until they eventually formed a united front of non-collaboration against it. Hence the inversion of collaboration into non-cooperation largely determined the timing of decolonisation. Lastly, since anticolonial movements emerged as coalitions of non-collaboration out of the collaborative equations of colonial rule and the transfer of power, the elements and character of Afro-Asian national parties and governments in the first era of independence projected a kind of mirror image of collaboration under imperialism.

David Fieldhouse has labelled the general idea underlying this analysis the 'peripheral theory'.[24] More truly it is what might be called an 'excentric' approach to European imperialism. To borrow a figure from geometry, there was the Eurocentric circle of industrial strategy making varying intersections with circles centred in the implacable continuities of African and Asian history. Imperialism, especially in its time scale, was not precisely a true function of either circle. It was in many ways excentric to both. It should be emphasised that the Afro-Asian crises which evoked imperialism were often not essentially the products of European forces but of autonomous changes in African and Asian domestic politics. Changing over to a mechanical analogy, imperialism was in another sense the 'centre of mass' or resultant of both circles. Hence the motivation and modes of imperialism were functions of collaboration, non-collaboration, mediation and resistance at varying intersections of the two circles. It is hardly surprising, therefore, that its European directors and agents, no less than its victims, looked on imperialism as an inevitable but random process receding out of control.

What is not evident yet is a firm answer to the critical question in assessing the third world's prospects in the 1970s and 80s. Their international frame has altered from imperialism to formal independence with foreign aid. However the importance of the external frame in deciding their fortunes is marginal. Their chances of stability depend upon indigenous politics and upon collaboration between modern and neo-traditional elites. It is this factor that is likely to determine whether they become truly independent or remain victims of 'neocolonialism'. In over-throwing colonial regimes, how far did the nationalists of Africa and Asia merely realign the traditional and neo-traditional units of indigenous politics on a temporary basis? How far did they succeed, through national party organisation, in unifying and transforming them permanently? Nationalists are more 'representative' of the historic entities than colonial rulers ever were, and national leaders are able to play their politics more intimately and organise them better. It is precisely because nationalists are more 'representative' of neo-traditional units that they may be in greater danger of becoming their political prisoners than their predecessors were. The experience of the 1960s suggests that the nationalists often realigned these units negatively rather than transforming them positively. That of the 1970s and 80s may prove otherwise.

[1] These theories are well analysed in D. K. Fieldhouse, *The Theory of Capitalist Imperialism* (London, Weidenfeld & Nicolson 1967); cf. Tom Kemp, *Theories of Imperialism* (London, Dobson 1967).

[2] Cf. the earlier formulation in J. Gallagher and R. Robinson, 'The imperialism of free trade', *Econ. Hist. Rev.* (March 1953), 5–6.

[3] See especially W. G. Beasley, *Great Britain and the Opening of Japan, 1834–1858* (London, Luzac, 1951), and *Select Documents on Japanese Foreign Policy, 1853–1868* (London, Oxford Univ. Press, 1955); A. M. Craig, *Chōshū in the Meiji Restoration* (Cambridge, Mass., Harvard Univ. Press, 1961); M. B. Jansen, *Sakamoto Ryoma and the Meiji Restoration* (Princeton Univ. Press, 1961).

[4] D. A. Low, *Buganda in Modern History* (London, Weidenfeld & Nicolson, 1971), cap. 1; M. Twaddle, 'The Bakungu Chiefs of Buganda under British Colonial Rule, 1900–1930', *Journal of African History*, 10, 2 (1969), and 'The Muslim revolution in Buganda', London Institute of Commonwealth Studies Seminar Paper (unpublished, 1971).

[5] A. S. Kanya-Forstner, 'Myths and realities of African resistance', *Historical Papers 1969* (The Canadian Historical Association 1969), and *The Conquest of the Western Sudan, A Study in French Military Imperialism*, (Cambridge, Cambridge Univ. Press, 1969).

[6] For an extreme example of what collaboration English capital could elicit outside formal empire, in Chilean politics from 1879 to 1883, without overt political intervention, see J. R. Brown, 'The frustration of Chile's nitrate imperialism', *Journal of Pacific History* (Nov. 1963).

[7] See A. Dachs, *'Missionary imperialism in Bechuanaland, 1826–1890'*. Cambridge University Ph.D. thesis, 1968.

[8] See R. Robinson, J. Gallagher and A. Denny, *Africa and the Victorians, the official mind of imperialism* (London, Macmillan, 1961), chs. 3, 7, 14.

[9] H. S. Ferns, *Britain and Argentina*, (London, Oxford Univ. Press, 1969); T. F. McGann, *Argentina, the United States, and the Inter-American System*,

1880–1914 (Cambridge, Mass., Harvard Univ. Press, 1957); see also J. F. Rippy, 'The British investment "boom" of the 1880s in Latin America', *Hispanic American Historical Review,* (May 1949).

[10]See Gallagher and Robinson, 'Imperialism of free trade' *op. cit.* 1953; B. Semmel, *The Rise of Free Trade Imperialism,* (Cambridge, Cambridge Univ. Press, 1970); A. G. L. Shaw, ed., *Great Britain and the Colonies, 1815–1865,* (London, Methuen, 1970); D. C. M. Platt, *Finance, Trade and Politics, British Foreign Policy 1815–1914* (London, Oxford Univ. Press 1968) and 'The imperialism of free trade: some reservations', *Ec. Hist. Rev., xxi,* (1968).

[11]See E. O. Reischauer, J. Fairbank, and A. M. Craig, *East Asia: The Modern Transformation,* (Cambridge, Mass., Harvard Univ. Press, 1965).

[12]F. Michael, *The Taiping Rebellion,* (Seattle, University of Washington Press, 3 vols, 1966).

[13]E. S. Wehrle, *Britain, China and the Antimissionary Riots: 1891–1900,* (Univ. of Minneapolis Press, 1966); Paul A. Cohen, *China and Christianity: The Missionary Movement and the Growth of Chinese Antiforeignism 1860–1870,* (Cambridge, Mass., Harvard Univ. Press, 1963).

[14]See M. C. Wright, *The Last Stand of Chinese Conservatism: The T'ung-Chih Restoration, 1862–1874,* (New York, Stanford Univ. Press, 1966) *passim.*

[15]See R. H. Davison, *Reform in the Ottoman Empire, 1839–1876* (Princeton Univ. Press, 1963); W. R. Polk and R. L. Chambers, *Beginnings of Modernization in the Middle East, The Nineteenth Century* (University of Chicago Press, 1968).

[16]*Africa and the Victorians;* R. Robinson and J. Gallagher, 'The African partition', *The New Cambridge Modern History,* xi, 1962; cf. C. W. Newbury, 'Victorians, republicans and the partition of West Africa', *Journal of African History,* 3, (1962); Newbury and Kanya-Forstner, 'French policy and the origins of the scramble for West Africa', Kanya-Forstner, *The Conquest of the Western Sudan,* E. Stokes, 'Late nineteenth-century expansion and the attack on the theory of economic imperialism,' *Hist. Jnl.,* 12, 1969.

[17]E. R. J. Owen, *Cotton and the Egyptian Economy, 1820-1914* (London, Oxford Univ. Press, 1969); G. Baer, *Land Reform in Modern Egypt, 1800–1950* (New York, 1962); P. M. Holt, *Political and Social Change in Modern Egypt,* (Oxford Univ. Press, 1968).

[18]A. Hourani, *Arabic Thought in the Liberal Age,* (London, Oxford Univ. Press, 1962); S. G. Haim, *Arabic Nationalism* (Berkeley, Univ. of California Press, 1962).

[19]See *Africa and the Victorians,* ch. 4.

[20]For examples of Indian systems see A. Seal, *The Emergence of Indian Nationalism* (Cambridge Univ. Press, 1968); R. Frykenberg, *Guntur District, 1788–1848: a history of local influence and central authority in South India* (London, Oxford Univ. Press, 1965); J. H. Broomfield, *Elite Conflict in a Plural Society, twentieth century Bengal,* (Berkeley, Univ. of California Press, 1968); G. Johnson, 'Indian politics 1895–1905' (Cambridge University Ph. D. thesis, 1969); for the micro-politics of breakdown see S. B. Chaudhuri, *Civil Rebel-*

lion in the Indian Mutinies, and E. Stokes, 'Rural revolt in the Great Rebellion of 1857 in India', *Hist. Jnl.* 12, 4, (1969).

[21]The example is taken from G. Bakheit: 'British administration and Sudanese nationalism', (unpublished Ph.D. Thesis, Cambridge University, 1966); see also M. Abd al-Rahim, *Imperialism and Nationalism in the Sudan* (London, Oxford Univ. Press, 1967).

[22]See for African examples M. Perham, *Native Administration in Nigeria,* (Oxford Univ. Press, 1936), and *Lugard,* 2 vols (London, Collins, 1956, 1960); J. D. Hargreaves, 'West African States and the European Conquest'; J. E. Flint, 'Nigeria: the colonial experience from 1880 to 1914', in *Colonialism in Africa 1870–1960,* ed. L. H. Gann and P. Duignan, i, (Cambridge Univ. Press, 1970); J. M. Lonsdale, 'Political associations in western Kenya' and other articles in *Protest and Power in Black Africa,* ed. R. I. Rotberg and A. A. Mazrui, (New York, Oxford Univ. Press, 1970); Lonsdale, 'Some origins of African nationalism in East Africa', *Journal African History,* 9, 1, (1968); T. Ranger, 'African reactions to the imposition of colonial rule in East and Central Africa', in *Colonialism in Africa, 1870–1960,* i; J. Iliffe, *Tanganyika under German Rule, 1905–1912* (Cambridge Univ. Press, 1969); M. Twaddle, ' "Tribalism" in Eastern Uganda', in *Tradition and Transition in East Africa,* ed. P. H. Gulliver, (London, Routledge, 1968); M. Crowder, *West Africa under Colonial Rule,* (London, Hutchinson, 1968), and *West African Resistance* (London, Hutchinson, 1971); A. H. M. Kirk-Greene, ed., *The Principles of Native Administration in Nigeria. Selected Documents 1900–1947,* (Oxford Univ. Press, 1965); D. Austin, *Politics in Ghana, 1946–1960,* (Oxford Univ. Press, 1964); D. A. Low and R. Pratt, *Buganda and British Over-Rule,* (Oxford Univ. Press, 1960).

[23]T. O. Ranger, 'Connections between "primary resistance" movements and modern mass nationalism in east and central Africa', *Journal of African History,* ix, 3 and 4, 1968; E. Stokes, 'European administration and African political systems, 1891–1897', Conference on Central African History, Lusaka, 1963; D. Ashford, 'The politics of rural mobilisation in North Africa', *Jnl. Mod. Afr. Studies,* 7, 2, (1969); J. M. Lonsdale, 'African politics in western Kenya: its leadership, scale and focus' (unpublished paper to Cambridge University Commonwealth History Seminar, 1967) and 'Decolonisation in East Africa', Cambridge University Commonwealth History Seminar, 1971.

[24]Fieldhouse, *Theory of Capitalist Imperialism,* xv, 193–4.

PART III

**Selected
Critical Responses**

Further Objections to an "Imperialism of Free Trade," 1830–60

D. C. M. PLATT

D. C. M. Platt is Professor of the History of Latin America at Oxford University and a Fellow of St. Antony's College. He is the author of Finance, Trade and Politics in British Foreign Policy, 1815–1914 *(Oxford, 1968),* The Cinderella Service: British Consuls since 1825 *(London, 1971), and* Latin America and British Trade, 1806–1914 *(London, 1972). He has recently completed the direction of an inquiry into the nature of business imperialism, the results of which appear as* Business Imperialism: British Experience in Latin America before 1930 *(Oxford, 1976). He is currently writing the history of the financial house of Baring Brothers of London.*

*In 1968 in an article entitled "The Imperialism of Free Trade: Some Reservations" (*Economic History Review, *XXI, 2, August 1968), Platt concluded:*

> Gallagher and Robinson carry conviction only in their emphasis on the continued importance in British government policy of the security of British trade. In this respect there was an indisputable continuity in official policy. But there was no continuity as between the mid- and late Victorians in the steps that they were prepared to take in defence of British trade. It is here that the conventional interpretation of a break in the character of British imperialism after 1880—of the emergence of a "new imperialism"— begins to make sense. For, up to this point in time (pace Gallagher and Robinson) the dominant characteristics of British commercial and financial diplomacy were non-intervention and laissez-faire, and imperialism, informal or formal, was the last thing to be expected from laissez-faire. British 'paramountcy' was the creation of our head-start in industrialization—it was the creation of the British traders and investors themselves who neither sought nor expected government intervention.

In the following essay, "Further Objections to an 'Imperialism of Free

153 Selected Critical Responses

Trade,' 1830–60,'' Platt starts from the assumption that British diplomacy was noninterventionist in the mid-nineteenth century, and goes on to ask whether the attitudes and actions of British traders and investors, 1830–60, were any closer to the notion of an imperialism of free trade. It represents his most encompassing attack on Robinson and Gallagher. The article appeared in the Economic History Review, Second Series, XXVI, 1, February 1973 and is republished here in abridged form with the permission of the author and the Review.

The "Imperialism of Free Trade," a phrase first formulated in detail nearly twenty years ago, has now passed into the historian's vocabulary as a convenient portmanteau description of British overseas expansion in the middle decades of the nineteenth century. In their well-known article in the *Economic History Review* (1953)[1] John Gallagher and Ronald Robinson, unsatisfied with the simplistic view then current of mid-Victorian anti-imperialism, set out to establish a continuity in British attitudes to the extension of trade and control, which they identified under a general title: "The Imperialism of Free Trade." They hoped to detect common factors in a century of diverse overseas activity, to explain the existence and maintenance of British control by "formal" and by "informal" means. They saw a grand design, associated more particularly with such names as Canning and Palmerston, for the establishment of British paramountcy, to which the efforts of mid- and late-Victorians alike were directed. These efforts were more successful in some areas than in others, and formal annexation tended to replace informal control as the century progressed. But a continuity existed in the development of British interests and ambitions overseas:

> British policy followed the principle of extending control informally if possible and formally if necessary. To label the one method "anti-imperialist" and the other "imperialist", is to ignore the fact that whatever the method British interests were steadily safeguarded and extended.[2]

Naturally, any theory which establishes continuity is *ipso facto* more credible than another which depends on radical change. The "Imperialism of Free Trade" offered a bridge between the apparently disparate periods of mid-Victorian anti-imperialism and the "New Imperialism" of late-Victorian Britain. It supplied a continuity of ends, even if those ends were won or lost by different means. As such, it has gained wide currency. The traditional picture of mid-Victorian anti-imperialism has been swept aside, and recent re-

search has established beyond question that anti-imperialistic sentiment, although it most certainly existed, was only of limited
significance as applied to the white colonies of settlement. Englishmen may have grumbled at the expense of administering and defending Canada, South Africa, Australia, and New Zealand. They may
have disliked the erection of colonial tariff barriers to protect infant
industries. But ultimately they favoured the preservation of the imperial connexion with each of the white colonies, both for economic
and for sentimental reasons.

However, the main issue remains undecided. Objections to an
"Imperialism of Free Trade" gain far greater force when applied to
the "informal empire", to that submerged portion of the iceberg with
which Gallagher and Robinson were primarily concerned.

Both in the 1953 article and in *Africa and the Victorians* (1961)
Gallagher and Robinson assumed an abnormal level of activity by
politicians and officials in the promotion of British trade and investment in distant non-colonial territories overseas. They claimed that
from the beginning of the last century British officials were spreading the rule of free trade from Buenos Aires to Constantinople, from
the Niger and the Oxus to the Yangtse-Kiang. The British political
arm had first to break open each area to trade before the technique
of control through collaborating classes could operate, and this, in
official thinking, was necessary work for diplomats with gunboats in
the offing. Canningites and Palmerstonians exerted their strength all
over the world to bring about political conditions favouring commercial advance and liberal awakening.[3]

This fanciful picture of official energy and activity remained un-
challenged by historians for many years. Yet more recently, work on
the relationship between H.M. Government and British trade and
finance has suggested that the role assigned to the "political arm" of
the "Imperialism of Free Trade" was based on a misunderstanding.
In a question of this nature, difference of opinion can be a matter
only of degree. Englishmen undoubtedly believed in the superior
virtues of their own political system and were unlikely to *oppose* an
extension of their trade. Furthermore, most politicians, at one time
or another, paid at least lip service to H.M. Government's obligation
to watch over Britain's economic interests. But a theory cannot be
constructed simply from the occasional expansionist phrase on the
lips of Canning or Palmerston, spoken in a moment of exaggeration
or euphoria. It is more to the point to take account of the extraordinarily limited role commonly accepted for British government intervention in private business engagements overseas.[4]

The existence of a tradition of active government intervention was undoubtedly *one* of the assumptions on which the original "Imperialism of Free Trade" was based, and it is an assumption for which the evidence is most questionable. Yet objections to the "Imperialism of Free Trade" run deeper than this, and it is with these further objections that the present article is concerned. Was there, or was there not, a "blueprint", a "grand design" for British overseas expansion during the first half of the nineteenth century? Were the British trading and manufacturing classes really so "determined if possible, to extend their influence throughout the world"?[5] Was British political and economic aggression continuous, vigorous, and uninterrupted, combining "commercial penetration and political influence as required"?[6]

Economic historians, acquainted with the distribution of overseas trade in the 'thirties, 'forties, and 'fifties and with the problems of such British traders as operated in distant markets, might wonder whether so grossly expansionist an interpretation reflects the actual pressure for markets at the time, the priorities of British businessmen, or the expectations of British politicians and officials. Rather, the attitude of British industry, except at times of unnatural excitement, might seem to have been characterized by indifference to distant markets. Indeed, an economic historian might be inclined to argue that no blue print *could* have existed for expansion into regions of informal empire because capital and effort were better employed elsewhere, and because little expectation as yet existed of substantial profits in the "long" trades. . . .

The "Imperialism of Free Trade", and the whole notion of an "informal empire" of trade and investment so far as it relates to the early and mid-Victorian periods, developed out of three assumptions: first, the readiness of British governments at all times "to establish and maintain British paramountcy by what ever means best suited the circumstances of their diverse regions of interest"; [7] second, the determination of British manufacturers and merchants to extend their influence throughout the world; third, the subordination of primary producers, as suppliers of foodstuffs and raw materials to Britain in her chosen role as "Workshop of the World". Even if such assumptions may in part be relevant to Britain's attempts to maintain her threatened position in the late-Victorian period, it is obviously unhistorical to apply them to the period 1830–60.

The British government's role, in mid-Victorian England, was limited, and it was forced into an active promotional policy towards trade and investment overseas only under international pressure in the last decades of the century. Late-Victorian governments were *not* applying the same methods, under new conditions, to achieve what remained the same goals. The whole concept of what was a "legitimate" function for the Foreign Office and the Diplomatic Service had had to be altered and transformed under the competitive conditions and active foreign diplomacy of the 'eighties. Officials were compelled to see themselves in an entirely new relationship to British traders and financiers, a relationship which they would have rejected out of hand earlier in the century.

The trade figures merely give concrete expression to commercial attitudes so evident among contemporaries. The bias and preferences of British businessmen were still towards the development of trade in home, colonial, northern European, and North American markets, and in normal times only relatively few could afford to carry on a profitable but restricted trade with remote areas outside the empire. Apart from the isolated "boom" conditions in trade, or speculative "bubbles" in investment—and there are obvious pitfalls in taking these as a measure of British interest in commerce or investment overseas—no sustained pressure existed, at this point in time, to break open and maintain new markets in distant territories. Businessmen already had as much as they cared to handle, or dared to risk, in closer, more easily worked outlets. Those who chose, through taste, experience, or capital resources, to trade in hazardous markets in Latin America, the Levant, or the Far East were often the people most likely to resent and oppose the extension of British government intervention, since it endangered their property and persons, and broke their carefully constructed contacts with local traders, officials, and politicians. It was no accident that the big opium importers, the five or six important British houses resident in China, were in general perfectly content with the corruption and inefficiencies of the Chinese authorities. Nor was it unusual for Hudson's father, during a period of violent antagonism between the British Government and the Buenos Aires dictator, Rosas, to display a portrait of Rosas in the place of honour over the mantelpiece in his *sala,* sharing as he did with most British residents the view that the dictatorship, far from the ferocity and bloodshed described in the British home press, was an interval of peace and prosperity in the midst of anarchy.[8]

Finally, an "Imperialism of Free Trade" antedates by several decades the importance of the "informal empire" both as a destination for British investment and as a supplier of foodstuffs and industrial raw materials. Before the 1860's neither Latin America nor the Levant could offer substantial openings for profitable investment, while China made no real impact on the international loan market until the mid-'nineties. As a primary producer, Latin America had nothing distinctive to give to British consumers until the railways opened Argentina, as a major supplier of grain and beef, in and after the 'eighties. The Ottoman dominions, other than Egypt, could make no significant contribution to British imports; Egypt alone was developing her exports of raw cotton, but even then only as an alternative supplier to the acknowledged prime source, the United States. Certainly, China was Britain's sole supplier of tea, and an important source of silk. But for both tea and silk the internal market in China was enormously larger than exports. In no real sense was China economically "dependent" on mid-Victorian Britain. Neale explained, in the early 'sixties, that the Chinese took British cotton manufactures "in the spirit of profitable barter, although not as necessaries which could not be dispensed with."[9] The revenue derived in the early 'thirties from English trade at Canton, said the Chinese governor with only slight exaggeration, "concerns not the Celestial Empire to the extent of a hair, or a feather's down"; English broadcloths and camlets were of no regard, in contrast to which "the tea—the rhubarb—the raw silk—of the inner dominions, are the sources by which the said nation's people live, and maintain life."[10]

Concepts of "informal empire" have their uses when applied to the relationship which subsequently developed between primary producers and industrial nations, in and after the later decades of the nineteenth century. To some degree, they applied even earlier in circumstances where producers, without benefit of a large home market, were dependent on a single foreign outlet for their staple product, and where that foreign outlet, in turn, was at liberty to buy from an alternative supplier. The dependence on the German market of the mid-century tobacco planters in Colombia is a case in point.

So far as this relationship existed for Britain, it was maintained within the "formal" empire, in sugar and coffee from the West Indies, in sugar from Mauritius, and in timber from Canada. If British "imperialism" is to be interpreted so broadly, the development of Argentina after the 'sixties might be described as such, although the British market never controlled the Argentine wool trade and could not be said to have become a leading factor in sales of Argentine grain and beef until after the beginning of the twentieth century. On the narrower definition of imperialism as a subordination of individuals to other individuals in command of superior economic resources, there is much to be said for Hobson's distinction between mid-Victorian trade on the one hand, and late-Victorian investment on the other, between a trading capital easily withdrawn and employed elsewhere, and the fixed immovable capital of railway enterprises, public utilities, and industrial plants."

As for mid-Victorian "informal imperialism," it is certainly time that attention was paid to British government attitudes to the legitimate scale of intervention on behalf of private traders, to the size of the trade, to the extent of the interest displayed in it by British traders and investors, and to the permanence or otherwise of their stakes. Similarly, some sense of proportion is necessary in estimating the degree of dependence of those distant territories on imported manufactures, and the true place of exports in their mid-nineteenth century economies. When the "Imperialism of Free Trade" first passed into common usage, little had yet been published on government policy towards trade and finance overseas, and it was perhaps understandable that a few isolated boasts by British statesmen or officials were taken to represent a standing policy of aggressive and forcible promotion of trade. Then, little account seems ever to have been taken, in this debate over mid-Victorian imperialism, of the merchants' own estimates of the value of distant markets, estimates which were perfectly familiar in turn to politicians like Canning and Palmerston at the Foreign Office, who prided themselves on their application in studying consular trade reports. It is too often assumed that mercantile attitudes to expansion remained much as they had been immediately after the capture of Buenos Aires, and, for the Levant and China, much as they were for that short, optimistic period after the Commercial Treaties of 1838 and 1843. The fact was that British businessmen very soon came to their senses. The alternative was bankruptcy.

The point is important because for nearly twenty years a catchy phrase, the "Imperialism of Free Trade", has been permitted to reshape the whole picture of mid-Victorians overseas. A period which we know to have been characterized by a general indifference under normal trading conditions to marginal markets, and by government caution in assuming new and costly burdens of any kind, more particularly in the administration of the "semi-civilized" world, is now regularly billed as the high point of Britain's "Empire of Free Trade", in which Britain practised active imperialism over the whole breadth of the world, "informal" in pattern but no less aggressive or enthusiastic for that.

The argument for an "Imperialism of Free Trade" has been directed at establishing, above all, a continuity in British enthusiasm, official and commercial, for the incorporation of the entire world into a British trading system—a continuity of attitudes which, it is claimed, spanned the nineteenth century. Yet, even while admitting the attractions of continuity in history, this is a case where a theory of continuity actually obscures the distinct phases in a simple and logical economic development. There is no denying that throughout the century individual Britons set themselves up in remote areas overseas, on the West Coast of Africa, in Central America, in South East Asia, in the Pacific, and that their presence could and did lead to imperialistic incidents and the use of force. But this is not what the argument is about. Concentration on the activities of a few aggressive individuals, activities which in any case were by no means peculiar to Britons, to place, or to period, can only confuse the issue. What must be established is the attitude of British government and business on a national scale over specific periods of time. It is here that the break in continuity in British attitudes to economic expansion is most apparent. Over the period covered by this article, 1830 to 1860, the incentives and opportunities for rapid economic expansion into those regions of "informal empire" where the trade was even remotely significant, into Latin America, the Levant, and the Far East, simply did not exist. The timing of the new period and of new attitudes is obvious. Any truly *aggressive* expansion of British trade and investment at a national level into distant, non-colonial territories had to await the development of genuine markets for British manufactured goods. It was necessarily dependent on the emergence, within the United Kingdom, of a greatly enlarged demand for imported foodstuffs and industrial raw materials, which finally spilled out into the furthest ends of the world. It was forced and promoted by strong foreign competition within the traditional outlets for British trade and investment in Europe and North America. It developed out of a reserve of British capital in search of higher yields in the newly emergent nations. It was indeed, in every respect, a product of the last four decades of the Victorian era.

NOTES

[1] John Gallagher and Ronald Robinson, 'The Imperialism of Free Trade', *Economic History Review,* 2nd ser. vi (1953), 1–15.

[2] *Ibid.,* 13.

[3] Ronald Robinson and John Gallagher, *Africa and the Victorians: The Official Mind of Imperialism* (1961), pp. 4–5.

[4] I have attempted to explain this relationship in detail in my *Finance, Trade, and Politics in British Foreign Policy, 1815–1914* (Oxford, 1968), while the implications for the "Imperialism of Free Trade" are spelt out in my article 'The Imperialism of Free Trade: Some Reservations', *Econ. Hist. Rev.* 2nd ser. XXI (1968), 296–306. Subsequently, W. M. Mathew has published a valuable case study 'The Imperialism of Free Trade: Peru, 1820–70', *Econ. Hist. Rev.* 2nd ser. XXI (1968), 562–79.

[5] Bernard Semmel, *The Rise of Free Trade Imperialism: Classical Political Economy, the Empire of Free Trade and Imperialism, 1750–1850* (Cambridge, 1970), p. 12.

[6] A. G. L. Shaw, ed., *Great Britain and the Colonies, 1815–1865* (1970), p. 5.

[7] Gallagher and Robinson, *Econ. Hist. Rev.* 2nd ser. VI (1953), 12.

[8] W. H. Hudson, *Far Away and Long Ago* (1918), pp. 108–9.

[9] *Neale's report on British Trade at the Nine New Ports* (P.P. 1862, LVIII), p. 387.

[10] Letter to the Hong merchants, 18 August 1834, printed in *The Times,* 2 February 1835, 3d.

[11] J. A. Hobson, *Richard Cobden, the International Man* (1918), pp. 405–6.

Africa, the Victorians and Imperialism

GEORGE SHEPPERSON

George Shepperson is Professor of Commonwealth and American History at the University of Edinburgh. His publications include several studies of Central African history, Afro-American history and in the history of Scots overseas. He was a pioneer in the study of resistance movements to colonial rule in his study with Thomas Price, Independent African *(1958). At present he is engaged on a survey of Imperial Britain since 1815 and in various projects on the modern history of Africa.*

Shepperson also reviewed Africa and the Victorians *in the* English Historical Review *(April 1963). He concluded:*

> *To the relatively new subject of African history, it makes important contributions. In particular, its general approach should do much to prevent two misleading tendencies from taking too firm a grip on the historians of Africa: the over-employment of the concept of 'Africa south of the Sahara', against which the authors' depiction of the intricate influences of the Egyptian situation on the rest of Africa is an obvious warning; and the isolationist, introverting tendency which, if it is to be expected in the pioneering stages of close-focus scholarship, can easily lead to historical myopia and the concealment of important evidence for African history. If it had done nothing else,* Africa and the Victorians *would have performed an invaluable service in its demonstration of the ties that have bound—and bind—Africa and Europe.*

"Africa, the Victorians and Imperialism" originally appeared in the Revue Belge De Philologie et d'Histoire, *XL, 4 (1962). It is reprinted here in slightly abridged form with permission of the author and the Revue Belge.*

In 1898, the year of the Fashoda incident, Hilaire Belloc published his satirical poem on imperialism, *The Modern Traveller*. Unlike Mr. Graham Greene who has written recently, in his sentimental way, of "the Africa of the Victorian Atlas, the blank unspoiled continent in the shape of the human heart", Belloc evoked something of the wonder with which the Victorians confronted the "Dark Continent" in such cynical lines as:

Oh! Africa, mysterious Land!
Surrounded by a lot of sand . . .
Far Land of Ophir! Mined for gold
By Lordly Solomon of old,
Who sailing northward to Perim
Took all the gold away with him . . .

Africa and the Victorians. The Official Mind of Imperialism by Ronald Robinson and John Gallagher with Alice Denny evokes none of these shades of Victorian romanticism. Rather, it is concerned with what Belloc elsewhere in his masterly satire calls

Great Island! Made to be the bane
Of Mr. Joseph Chamberlain.
Peninsula! Whose smouldering fights
Keep Salisbury awake at nights;
And furnished for a year or so
Such sport to M. Hanotaux.

It is a book which, by analysing the attitude towards the late nineteenth century extension of British rule in Africa by what the press calls today "the Establishment" and Robinson and Gallagher term "the official mind," attempts to throw light on the nature of what, for good or ill, has been known as "imperialism" since J. A. Hobson published in 1902[1] that famous study which fructified Lenin's thought on the so-called highest stage of capitalism. "The chief issue," according to Robinson and Gallagher, "is to settle why ministers decided to advance where they did and when they did" (p. 26).

That this has always been something of a problem in the history of British expansion was made clear in a much-quoted statement in a lecture delivered at Cambridge University, in the spring of 1881, by J. R. Seeley, the Regius Professor of Modern History:

There is something very characteristic in the indifference which we show towards this mighty phenomenon of the diffusion of our race and the expansion of our state. We seem, as it were, to have conquered and peopled half the world in a fit of absence of mind.[2]

A further gloss on this curious character of British imperialism is provided by the diary of the eccentric but well-connected anti-imperialist, Wilfred Scawen Blunt, who wrote, on 4 November 1892, after calling on the Chancellor of the Exchequer, Sir William Harcourt,

> I said, "I think you ought to make up your minds on general policy, and either go in for an African Empire, or leave it alone. If you shilly-shally, first one way and then another, you will get into just the same mess that you did in 1882 (a reference to the Suez crisis of that year)".[3]

Africa and the Victorians explains, with a superabundance of detail culled from official records and the private papers of such influential individuals as Lord Salisbury, how, in another spell of shilly-shallying, a second fit of absence of mind—the first to which Seeley referred was the eighteenth century extension of British territory in India and America—Britain acquired a new empire and started, in the last twenty years of the nineteenth century, the process which was to add over four million square kilometres to her possessions in Africa.

The curious almost reluctant nature of the expansion of Britain overseas, which non-Britishers often find so puzzling that charges of "hypocrisy" can spring easily to their lips, has clearly fascinated Robinson and Gallagher for some years. In 1953 they produced an article which has had considerable influence on the first post-war generation of British historians: "The Imperialism of Free Trade".[4] *Africa and the Victorians* is the logical outcome of this article and it is likely to have even greater influence on British historians. Indeed, it is interesting to note that, a year before *Africa and the Victorians* appeared, an admirer of the Robinson-Gallagher thesis on the imperialism of free trade published an article[5] in which, by his own application of the logic of the celebrated article, he drew similar conclusions to those which are presented in this book. It is equally worthy of note that, also in 1960, another writer, commenting on Robinson and Gallagher's well-known article, with its distinction between "formal" and "informal" empire, expressed much the same kind of criticism as the present writer, in spite of all his admiration of the scholarship and synthesis of *Africa and the Victorians*, feels is pertinent to this larger work:

> It tends too much to regard imperialism as all of one piece with the different imperialisms [formal and informal—G.S.] as responses to different conditions, one succeeding the other in an almost mechanical fashion. . .[6]

It is probably not accidental that Robinson and Gallagher belong to the historical school which Seeley helped to establish. The influence of Cambridge University, furthermore, may probably be felt in their reactions to the simpler models of imperialism, especially the single-factor economic version which Robinson has called elsewhere "the decrepit, mythological beast of economic imperialism".[7] From the 1930s to 1940s, the Cambridge Left cherished and popularized the Hobson-Leninist thesis on imperialism, against the cruder generalities of which it seems natural that young historians, once they have become aware of the complexities of British expansion, should react with some zeal.

Unfortunately, in their latest work, Robinson and Gallagher give little indication that the subtleties of their attack on simple models of economic imperialism build on the work of other writers.[8] This is certainly not because they are unaware of this or because they wish to make their own undoubted discoveries stand out more brilliantly; but largely because, one may suppose, although they claim they are making a contribution to the general theory of imperialism, the close-focus of the meticulous examination they make of British expansion north as well as south of the Sahara has had the effect of hiding from their eyes, temporarily, historiographical matters which were not immediately relevant to their work.

The attack on the Hobson-Leninist variety of interpretation of imperialism, however, can too easily mask the fact that contemporary agents of European expansion often gave an economic construction to their motives. Sometimes, this was done consciously as a veil for political and nationalist aims, support for which could only be obtained from reluctant but influential groups whose main spur to action was the appeal of economics. More often, however, these agents of imperialism believed sincerely that they were working for economic ends. That this was an unconscious rationalization of wider and more complicated social and individual processes may be true. (Robinson and Gallagher may have something of this in mind when they write at the start of their book—p. 25—"We must go deeper than the symbolism of the conscious calculations . . . of the policy-makers".) Nevertheless, the superficial economic motivation was present with many of the imperialists; and historians have not devoted enough energy to explaining why the rationalization of the more complex processes of European overseas expansion so often took this form.

The economic motivation for imperialism—and a motivation coming close, to the surplus capital interpretation—was uppermost in the minds of the delegates at the West African Conference of Berlin, 1884–5. They declared that the Powers found themselves in the presence of three interests; and set down as the first of these "That of the commercial and industrial nations which a common necessity compels to the research of new outlets".[9]

There are few references to the West African Conference of Berlin in *Africa and the Victorians*. Because of this, one should not be surprised to find that the role of Leopold II in the partition of Africa seems to be consistently underplayed; and some of the more important aspects of his African designs are relegated to references to recent secondary works in a couple of footnotes (p. 169, n. 2; p. 199, n. 4). It is, however, rather surprising that *Africa and the Victorians* does not mention the schemes of some Britishers (the Rhodes-Johnston axis) in the late 1880s and early 1890s to secure Katanga: schemes which had to be disavowed and discouraged by the British Government not only because they were at variance with the tenuous international law of the period but mainly because they conflicted with its wider conception of the national interest. Indeed, the short-lived flirtation of some British imperialists at this time with Katanga would seem to be an ideal demonstration of the central thesis of *Africa and the Victorians*.

Perhaps the most valuable feature of *Africa and the Victorians* is its emphasis on the importance for British policy in Africa after the 1870s of factors outside of Europe. If this leads occasionally to neglect of the traditional diplomatic interpretation of imperialism, Africa as a factor in the Balance of Power in Europe, it does stress what Mr. J. D. Hargreaves, another British writer who is making his own distinctive contribution to the history of the Scramble, has indicated in a recent article: that the process of the partition of Africa should be seen "no longer as a mere episode in later-nineteenth-century European history, but as the culmination of a whole period of Anglo-African relations".[10]

The non-European factors which Robinson and Gallagher emphasize in British African policy have one common element: the rise of nationalism. When they discuss the manner in which Britain was sucked into an African empire as a result of the growth of Egyptian and Afrikaaner nationalism, or when they examine the relevance of the Home Rule movement in Ireland for British foreign policy, they are clearly part of a current scholarly trend in the reinterpretation of imperialism. But the nationalism which they find important is on the periphery of the mother-country.

In an occasional comment on Jules Ferry, for example, Robinson and Gallagher come close to this point of view; and when, in a stimulating footnote (p. 347) on Italy, they comment "It is noteworthy that here was another country where expansion was unpopular during the so-called age of imperialism", they seem to be suggesting that there are factors in Italian nationalism which are more important for the imperialism of the late nineteenth century than is commonly recognised.

Nowhere, however, do they examine the factor of nineteenth-century European racialism in this imperialism. Here one must note the important—but by too many historians neglected—contribution to the re-interpretation of imperialism made by Hannah Arendt in her *Origins of Totalitarianism.*[11] Part Two of this stimulating work is devoted entirely to imperialism. What she has to say, for example, on the "Phantom World of the Dark Continent" represents an ideological approach which can easily be abused. But it does indicate that the history of ideas—to use an American methodological expression—has a part to play in the historiography of the Scramble for Africa and the subject of imperialism in general which few historians have troubled to investigate. Certainly, there is nothing of this approach in *Africa and the Victorians,* except, perhaps, in the last chapter, "Nationalism and Imperialism."

Indeed, one might suggest to prospective readers of this book that they should start with this stimulating last chapter which has the effect of making some of the re-interpretations of late nineteenth century British imperialism which are offered in the earlier chapters less mechanical in their implications. There is, for example, the strategical factor. The importance which Robinson and Gallagher attach to this may be seen when they say, "If the papers left by the (British) policy-makers are to be believed, they moved into Africa, not to build a new African empire, but to protect the old empire in India. What decided when and where they would go forward was their traditional conception of world strategy" (p. 464). The importance of the protection of British interests in India and the East as a factor in the spread of British power in the east of Africa, to mention but one area, deserves emphasis. But it must also be pointed out that such an emphasis, warranted though it undoubtedly is, can, in effect, be creating a new type of economic interpretation of imperialism. Was this, perhaps, in the authors' minds when, in a few pages from the end of their book (p. 470), they write:

Perhaps at the deepest level the causes of the British share in the African partition are not found in strategic imperatives, but in the change from Canning's hopes for liberalism to Salisbury's distrust of nationalism, from Gladstone's old-fashioned concern not to turn South Africa into another Ireland, to Chamberlain's new-fangled resolve to forge it into another Canada.

This statement not only stresses again nationalism; it also is something of an after-thought. These two elements may serve to draw to a conclusion these remarks on an important British book.

In the re-interpretation of imperialism which is now in progress amongst scholars of the West, the influence of nationalism probably cannot be stressed too much. There is a multitude of books and pamphlets on the subject: but, as Karl W. Deutsch observed in 1953 —and his remarks are still largely true—"There has seemed to be no answer to the question why nationalist ideas met with wide and strong response at certain times and places, and with almost no response at others".[12] Deutsch's statement suggests the importance of the chronological approach which is clearly in Robinson and Gallagher's minds when they write, "We must turn from the sophistications of social analysis to the humbler tasks of chronology" (p. 25). Yet they are not as completely anti-sociological as this remark seems to imply. They have a good word to say (p. 21) for the analyses of imperialism which were made during the 1914–1918 War by Joseph Schumpeter[13] at much the same time as Lenin's although, of course, independently of his. Schumpeter's approach to imperialism, with its subtle employment of the over-lag of institutions and attitudes from one period to another, in spite of changed economic circumstances, naturally appeals to historians.

One hopes, however, that they will not fail to notice that this approach was also employed—and earlier—by the pioneer American sociologist, Thorstein Veblen. Although Veblen was an admirer of Hobson he added a potentially new dimension to his theory of imperialism, first of all, in a few lines, in his *The Theory of Business Enterprise* which was originally published in 1904. While he felt that the new imperialism might have, as Hobson had supposed, economic origins, he anticipated Schumpeter when he wrote:

The barbarian virtues of fealty and patriotism run on national or dynastic exploit and aggrandizement, and these archaic virtues are not dead . . . The eventual outcome should be a rehabilitation of this ancient patriotic animosity and dynastic loyalty to the relative neglect of business interests. This may easily be carried so far as to sacrifice the profits of business men . . .[14]

Veblen developed these ideas in greater detail in his *Imperial Germany and the Industrial Revolution* (New York, 1915). Thus, from Veblen and Schumpeter to the present day, the solution to the problem of the nature of imperialism has awaited an understanding of the complex character of nationalism. The present writer has suggested elsewhere that "as the historian puzzles over the nature of the new political forces at work across Africa, he may find basic clues to the understanding of that vague and explosive process called 'nationalism' in Europe".[15] He is grateful to *Africa and the Victorians* for showing the importance of Egyptian and South African nationalism in the partition of Africa. Yet he feels that some attention must also be paid to the factor of black nationalism in the partition which is, in his opinion, much older than is commonly realized. This, presumably, is what Basil Davidson has in mind when, in speaking of the states of the Niger delta in the mid-nineteenth century, he writes, "Each developed its own exclusivist 'citizenship': to the point, indeed, that one may well see in these little states the first thoroughgoing application in West Africa of the ideas of modern nationalism".[16] The role of a potential black West African proto-nationalism as a neglected factor in the partition of Africa by the European Powers, furthermore, is suggested by John Hargreaves when, in a reference to K. O. Diké's *Trade and Politics in the Niger Delta, 1830–1885* (Oxford, 1956), he writes:

Professor Diké's analysis of European-African relations during the earlier nineteenth century in the Niger Delta (whose people Keltie[17] dismissed as 'all pagans and barbarians') marked a new stage in West African historiography: among other things, it means that the dramatic "scramble" which began in 1884 must be viewed as the climax to an extended period of Anglo-African relations, though a climax which sometimes involved a break in historical continuity.[18]

As Robinson and Gallagher's after-thought quoted above suggests, the whole subject of imperialism is terrifyingly complicated and desperately in need of historical re-interpretation. Their contribution to this is a distinguished one. But, as the present writer, in echoing Bernard Semmel, has stated earlier, it is sometimes almost as mechanical as the simpler models they are seeking so rightly to destroy. In all this welter of conflicting interpretations, is there no room for the individual, the maladjusted European individual who, biding his time and place, made his mark on the partition of Africa? O. Mannoni's work[19] has provided a starting-point for the analysis of such persons. But the prototype and his essence—the projection of personal fantasies on to what appeared to be the *tabula rasa* of Africa—can be found as early as 1867, in Ibsen's Peer Gynt, who, standing on the edge of the Sahara, anticipated by two decades the megalomania of Cecil Rhodes' Cape-to-Cairo dream, but in reverse.[20]

NOTES

[1]Hobson's *Imperialism. A Study* was reprinted in London in 1938 with a new introduction and some important revisions. It is curious that he did not take the opportunity of this revision to refer to Lenin's *Imperialism* which had given his own book such an important position throughout the Marxist world.

[2]J. R. Seeley, *The Expansion of England* (London, 1883), p. 8.

[3]Wilfred Scawen Blunt, *My Diaries. Being a Personal Narrative of the Events 1888–1914* (London, 1932), p. 82.

[4]*Economic History Review* (London), second series, VI, 1, 1953, pp. 1–15. One must note here Robinson's article, "Imperial Problems in British Politics, 1880–1895", *Cambridge History of the British Empire* (Cambridge, 1959), III, pp. 127–180, which forms a bridge between the 1953 article and *Africa and the Victorians.*

[5]Eric Stokes, "Great Britain and Africa: the Myth of Imperialism", *History Today* (London), X, 8, 1960, pp. 554–563. See also Eric Stokes, *The Political Ideas of English Imperialism.* Inaugural Lecture (London, 1960).

[6]Bernard Semmel, *Imperialism and Social Reform. English Social-Imperial Thought, 1895–1914* (London, 1960), p. 143.

[7]*Journal of African History* (London), II, 1, 1961, p. 158.

[8]W. H. B. Court, "The Communist Doctrines of Empire" in *Survey of British Commonwealth Affairs* (London, 1946), II, Part I, pp. 293–305; William Keith Hancock, *Wealth of Colonies* (Cambridge, 1950); R. G. Hawtrey, *Economic Aspects of Sovereignty* (London, 1952), p. 148, etc.

[9]Protocols and General Act of the West African Conference of Berlin (London, 1885; Africa, No. 4; cf. 4361), p. 78.

[10]J. D. Hargreaves, "Towards a History of the Partition of Africa", *Journal of African History,* (London), I, 1, 1960, p. 109.

[11](London, 1958); first edition, 1951. The factor of racialism, of course, was realised early in the discussion of imperialism but no attempt was made to put it into a definite theory: cf. Hobson, *op. cit.,* p. 9; Gilbert Murray, "The

Exploitation of Inferior Races in Ancient and Modern Times" in Francis W. Hirst, etc., *Liberalism and the Empire* (London, 1900), pp. 118–157; etc.

[12]Karl W. Deutsch, *Nationalism and Social Communication. An Inquiry into the Foundations of Nationality* (New York, 1953), p. v.

[13]Joseph Schumpeter, *Imperialism and Social Class* (Oxford, 1951), edited by Paul M. Sweezy. Sweezy's own neo-Leninist contribution to the theory of imperialism may be found succinctly expressed in his *The Theory of Capitalist Development* (London, 1946), pp. 307–328.

[14]Veblen, *Theory of Business Enterprise, op. cit.,* quoted from Mentor Books edition, New York, 1958, p. 187 (Chapter X). Cf. John M. Robertson, *Patriotism and Empire* (London, 1899).

[15]George Shepperson, "External Factors in the Development of African Nationalism, with particular reference to British Central Africa," *Phylon* (Atlanta, Ga.), XXII, 3, 1961, p. 224.

[16]Basil Davidson, *Black Mother* (London, 1961), p. 186.

[17]J. S. Keltie, *The Partition of Africa* (London, 1893).

[18]Hargreaves, *op. cit.,* p. 108.

[19]Dominique Otare Mannoni, *La Psychologie de la Colonisation* (Paris, 1950).

[20]Henrick Ibsen, *Peer Gynt,* translated by R. Ellis Roberts (Oxford, 1947), pp. 149–50.

Imperialism and the Scramble for Africa:
The New View

ERIC STOKES

Eric Stokes is Smuts Professor of the History of the British Commonwealth at Cambridge University. His books include The British Utilitarians and India *(1959), and with Richard Brown he has edited* The Zambesian Past *(1966). His inaugural lecture at Cambridge, "The Voice of the Hooligan: Kipling and the Commonwealth Experience," has been published in N. McKendrick, ed.,* Historical Perspectives: Studies in English Thought and Society in Honour of J. H. Plumb *(London, 1974). He is presently writing a book entitled* The Peasant Armed: The Agrarian Background of the Indian Mutiny and Great Rebellion 1857–59.

"Imperialism and the Scramble for Africa: The New View" appeared as a Local Series pamphlet of the Historical Association of Rhodesia and Nyasaland in 1963 and is now reprinted with the permission of the author and the Central African Historical Association.

A revolution of attitudes has occurred of recent years in the conception of imperialism, a revolution which is partly the outcome of closer historical study and partly the product of time and distance and the new sense of proportion these have effected concerning the historical significance of the world outside Europe. The modern historian enjoys the advantages of greater detachment and cooler appraisal, the release from ideological and ethno-centric preoccupations. The older views of imperialism, indeed the term itself, took their origins in contemporary political emotions, and whether Marxist or otherwise shared this dominant political emphasis. The essence of imperialism was thought to be the scramble for colonies, that is the extension of Western political control over dependent territories. Held fast within their own national settings it was perhaps to be expected that Western historians should have remained preoccupied with the political process of painting the map red, or yellow, or green. Yet even the Marxist version, which regarded imperialism as economically determined and which possessed at least the groundwork of an embracing sociological explanation free from the narrowing nationalism of 'bourgeois' historiography, did not depart from this emphasis on the political factor. To the Marxists the emergence of imperialism denoted a vital change in the character of capitalism. In its earlier stage, when the units of production were numerous and small, progressive capitalism was marked by free competition and free trade. From about 1870 the growth of giant combines and trusts began to crush out the competition of smaller units and introduced monopoly capitalism, with its attendant feature, the attempt to secure exclusive possession of markets, raw materials, and investment areas. Following on the rapid development of advanced capitalist forms in newly industrialised countries like Germany and the United States, the competition among large-scale productive units took on the character of a national struggle for markets. The exclusive control of markets sought by monopoly capitalism was most perfectly realised in the form of political control. Hence the political subjection and subordination of colonial territories to a national metropolitan economy remained the ideal type-instance of capitalism in its highest stage.

A further approximation of the Marxist and non-Marxist views followed from their reading of late nineteenth century expansion in terms of the scramble for colonies. For it suggested that the acquisition of colonies became the supreme objective of national policies, and that the Western powers propelled themselves into the unpartitioned regions of the earth—particularly into Africa—driven by some compulsive force from within Europe itself. The non-Marxist historians were not prepared to accept the economic motive as a sole and sufficient cause of the Scramble for Africa, but the spell cast by the English Liberal, J. A. Hobson's book, *Imperialism* (1902), made it regarded as the greatest single influence. Lenin's rigid determinism was, however, rejected by the non-Marxists, who followed Hobson's line that imperialism represented a voluntary choice to develop an extensive overseas market as against an intensive home market. Hence non-Marxist historical writing has always given much greater importance to the movement of the public mind as an originating force in policy, and has therefore been prepared to allow greater weight to psychological and social influences. Yet, whatever the differences of emphasis, it was common to both views that the springs of action lay wholly in Europe.

Africa was in consequence regarded as almost a blank map on which the Europeans were free to write their will. In face of the imperialist tide the dark continent seemed to play an inert and passive role, powerless to offer anything but a token and ineffectual resistance; the process of expansion was conceived as a purely one-way relationship.

In every one of these points the traditional views have been challenged. Dr. Ronald Robinson and Professor John Gallagher, the principal architects of the historiographical revolution, have developed their plan of argument around a subtle philosophical re-interpretation of the character of European expansion. That character they see as remaining constant throughout the nineteenth century, a spontaneous outpouring of money, men and goods, spilling beyond the confines of Europe. As that character stayed constant, so also did the policy of governments towards it—especially that of the greatest expansionist power, Britain. The fixed aim of statesmen was to ensure the security of economic growth at minimum cost. A kind of Benthamite attitude towards the function of government action passed over into overseas policy. Political power, whether exercised momentarily as military force, or in a more sustained form as political control, was at best a necessary evil, justifiable only when the free flow of energies had encountered artificial check or was threatened by external menace.

To divide the nineteenth century into two sharply distinguished periods—firstly an anti-colonial period from 1815 to 1870, and then a succeeding era of 'earth-hungry' colonialism, is to miss the essential character of Western expansion, and to reverse the true order of relationships between the economic and political factors. If the ordinary role of political power was to provide security for the pattern of trade and settlement which had established itself spontaneously, then its main concern lay with the economic links between self-governing, and mostly white, states, that dominated the pattern.

We are presented with something like the following model. Western 'capitalist' expansion in its highest stage stood typified by the relations between two advanced industrial economics, politically independent of one another. Political power entered into the relationship merely for the regulation of tariffs and for the external defence of the trading pattern. Where the relationship between the two economies was less equal, as between a metropolitan and different forms of colonial economy, then political power had to be more extensively exerted. Where white settler states were concerned, they would enjoy full internal self-government but would rely on the metropolitan power (Britain) either for the defence of the trade routes (the U.S.A.) or for the entire external defence of their land area (Canada, Australia, New Zealand). Below this level came the exercise of varying degrees of political influence and control over the internal government of states, the true colonial and semi-colonial territories. Since political maturity usually went hand in hand with economic maturity, it was normally the rule that the least valuable a territory economically the more dependent it was politically. Hence the principle of parsimony in extending political control.

The older historians misconceived the relationship between the economic and political factors and were led into placing undue emphasis on the formal empire of the political maps rather than on the informal but real empire of trade, settlement, and investment. The dramatic extension of formal empires after 1870, particularly in Africa, caused historians to postulate an equally profound change in the conditions of Western economic activity and of the policy of Western governments. No such revolution, we are told, in fact occurred. The expansion of the Western economy after 1870 continued along the same lines of thrust, the overwhelming proportion of activity being directed into the existing framework—that is, into the links with North America and the white dominions, and secondarily, into those with S. America, S. Africa, and India. Above all, there was no economic drive worth the name into Tropical Africa, the region where the bulk of political expansion took place. To argue that the partition of Africa was the direct product of the pressure of capitalism in full vigour turning its main strength into the colonial field, is to fly in the face of the simplest statistics. Neither before nor after the partition was there any really significant expansion of trade and investment with Tropical Africa, which remained the Cinderella of the international economy.

It may be urged that the European nations were not looking for immediate returns but were 'pegging out claims for the future', carving out estates which would for long lie undeveloped but which had to be acquired as reserve areas for future growth in a world where the expanding frontier had at last reached its term. Alternatively, the scrambling powers can be regarded in the light of historical hindsight as dupes of a great illusion, their competing greed and rivalry jostling them into a gold rush for an imaginary Eldorado. But the documentary evidence would suggest that the statesmen of the great powers were perfectly aware of the limited economic possibilities to be found in Tropical Africa, and that it was only after more than a decade of barren and costly possession that they began to make a virtue out of necessity and encourage some measure of economic development. It is true that they had long been pressed by small groups of their nationals—traders, explorers, missionaries, officials—to embark on schemes of colonial acquisition in Africa, and such local expansionist elements might include figures as big as Leopold of the Belgians or Rhodes. But the partition was necessarily a matter for decision in the European capitals, and without the consent of London, Paris and Berlin, even Leopold was powerless to found his Congo empire.

If therefore the main tide of economic expansion after 1870 continued as before to by-pass Tropical Africa, and the statesmen of the great powers had coolly appraised the realities of the position, how is their action in setting on foot so rapid a political partition of the entire continent to be explained? The explanation must lie, argue Robinson and Gallagher, in the relation that African questions bore to their constant concern, the security of the existing framework of trade and power in the rest of the world. Africa was a matter of political and military strategy and not primarily of economic concern. Its northern and southern extremities flanked the British sea-routes to Australasia and the East, while for France North Africa was part and parcel of her Mediterranean security problem. Robinson and Gallagher set themselves to explain how a disturbance of the position in these strategic areas touched off the scramble. How was French or British security endangered? Was the threat deliberately directed or provoked by the move of one or other of the great powers? Far from it. The notion of the diplomatic historians like A. J. P. Taylor and W. L. Langer that the Scramble is to be explained in terms of the extension of European rivalries to the rest of the globe is of a piece with the old assumption that the Scramble originated in Europe. Instead Robinson and Gallagher put forward the claim that its origin was fortuitous, prompted by no change of attitude or purpose in the European capitals but springing wholly from local events within Africa. It was the local crisis firstly affecting Egypt and the Suez Canal, and secondly, the Cape, which extorted the reluctant intervention of England and France and involved them inextricably in an ever widening circle of activity on the African continent.

This conclusion is of the profoundest importance. It reverses the old notion of the Scramble as the product of drives originating within Europe, whether economic or otherwise. Instead it suggests that the powers so far from thrusting themselves eagerly into Africa were drawn in hesitantly step by step as the result of a chain of local crises, which beginning at the northern and southern extremities of the continent led them on until European rule was established (barring Ethiopia) over the whole of Africa. The conception of the 'local crisis' restores to African history its own identity and importance. It can now be regarded not as a mere appendage or extension of European history, but as an autonomous element which plays its part in that interaction between Europe and the rest of the world which is the truly universal history of the modern age.

The primary local crises in Egypt and South Africa in the 1880's admittedly had economic roots. But the economic interests at stake were not sufficiently imperilled, to prompt direct military intervention from Europe on their own behalf. The French had the greater economic stake in Egypt but it was the British under Gladstone who in 1882 put in the troops. The overriding motive was apprehension—apprehension lest in the prevailing instability of Egypt the Canal might be endangered and above all, another major power might throw itself across the route to the East. In South Africa (between 1885 and 1889) Britain had a larger financial stake which promised to grow rapidly after the discovery of the Witwatersrand gold reefs in 1886. Yet the concern of British statesmen was not directed to economic interest. That the Rand should fall within the political domain of Kruger's South African Republic was not of vital moment, since the Transvaalers were capable of providing an adequate, if rudimentary, system of law and order. The real threat to British interests lay in the danger that the Rand gold might supply the sinews of a hostile expansionist nationalism which, leagued perhaps with Germany, could transform the Transvaal into the de facto paramount power in South Africa and cast a menace over the British strategic hold on the Cape. To neutralise the potential threat, British ministers chartered Rhodes's schemes of expansion and encirclement in Central Africa, consenting to throw the mantle of legality (and so international standing) over a local expansive force which appeared to serve not Britain's economic but its strategic interests.

In both Egypt and South Africa the crises were local in origin, and both arose from the emergence of indigenous movements hostile to British purposes. The headlong intensity of Ismail Pasha's attempt to modernise Egypt in the 1860's and early 70's had led him captive into the hands of his European moneylenders, who when he defaulted on his bonds prevailed upon their governments to place Egypt's finances under close international control. When Ismail tried to wriggle free the powers secured his replacement in 1879 by a more pliant Khedive, Tewfik. But Britain and France were not to be left to enjoy power without responsibility; and having weakened the indigenous political structure so far they found themselves powerless to control the course of Egyptian politics. Discontent at the dictated economy measures and at the growing foreign domination of the country came to a head in the quasi-nationalist movement of Ahmed Arabi which soon took over the reins of government. The challenge of nationalist movements, in Egypt and South Africa, viewed against the wider background of the rise of nationalism in Ireland and India, evoked the defencive, defiant reaction of opinion manifested as the imperialism of the 90's. But imperialism was the consequence rather than the cause of the African partition.

The British occupation of Egypt in 1882, sincerely avowed as a purely temporary measure, proved the fulcrum on which the whole partition turned. France found that in a moment of weakness and vacillation she had allowed herself to be ousted from a region which had traditionally formed a key point in her Mediterranean security system, and where she had been the foremost agent in the process of modernisation, including the engineering triumph of the Canal itself. To recover the vital position in Egypt, it became necessary to harass and threaten British interests elsewhere in Africa. She resolved to play for power and influence on the Congo, backing de Brazza's private empire, seeking a dominant voice in Leopold's International Association, and thwarting British counter-measures against the threat of French commercial hegemony by exploding the Anglo-Portuguese Congo treaty of 1884. At the same time French activity in the Niger was stepped up.

Bismarck seized the opportunity to widen the Anglo-French rift over Egypt in the interests of his European diplomacy. To give him a *locus standi* and to increase his nuisance value for Britain he gave the signal to German merchants or adventurers like Peters to take possession of Togoland, the Cameroons, Angra Pequena, and the Tanganyika coast (1884–5). Tied down in Egypt, Britain was not prepared to resist the German claims but felt bound to take precautionary measures so as to prevent damage to her interests in regions where she possessed established strategic or economic footholds. In face of French and German moves she threw a protectorate over the Niger delta and chartered Goldie's Niger Company for the up-river regions. To remove the bogey of a German link-up with the Transvaal through S.W. Africa she took Bechuanaland under protection and appropriated the unannexed coast-line between the Cape and Natal. Likewise Bismarck's recognition of Peters' treaties evoked a resolve not to be driven off the East African coast altogether. It was decided to hold out for the possession of Mombasa, the nearest good harbour to the south of the Horn of Africa and the Suez route. All these moves meant a reluctant abandonment of the older methods of exercising informal political influence rather than direct authority. Yet so little did the major scrambling powers wish to become deeply involved in the African interior that Britain and Germany whenever they could threw the costs of the requisite political establishments on the local expansionist groups; and the French ministers constantly sought to rein in their soldiers in West Africa by withholding the necessary votes of credit.

The overriding priority of denial rather than acquisition in the policy of the powers was naturally most marked among the British who started from a position of informal hegemony. To deny control to another foreign power, the British had occupied Egypt. To render that position secure, they deemed it necessary to deny access to its river life-line so that eventually they found themselves laying their hands on the whole of the Nile Valley, Uganda and its corridor to the sea, Kenya. For the sake of this supreme object Salisbury deliberately renounced the lion's share of W. Africa where the best possibilities of commercial development were to be found. The French acted from similar motives. To deny Egypt to the British, French ministers were ready to back their expansionist element—the French army—in order to obtain pressure points on the British elsewhere. Later in the 90's when it was clear that the British were entrenching themselves indefinitely in Egypt, Paris gave partial countenance to the wildcat schemes of those who dreamed of a French east-west axis across Africa as a counter to the Cape-to-Cairo fantasy on the British side. For the French policy-makers it was not intended as a bid for empire; but for the most part was seen as no more than a means of obtaining a purchase on the Nile Valley to force the British to renew the idea of evacuating Egypt.

The persistence of the Egyptian problem was the most important factor in urging the powers to extend their spheres of influence ever deeper into the interior of the continent. But the urge remained prompted by the wish to deny rather than acquire. Hence the partition was regarded as no more than a paper partition; originally there was no intention to occupy and administer. That within a short space the powers found themselves shouldering the costs of governing the African peoples was an unexpected development springing again from events within Africa. The 'local crises' in Egypt and South Africa were the product of local resistance movements to outside influences, and reproduced themselves in a lengthening chain, forcing the powers to counter by military means and then compelling them to govern because the indigenous system of government had been swept away. Resistance came most fiercely from Islamised or Arabised groups. The British quickly discovered that they had destroyed khedival authority not merely in Egypt but in the Sudan as well, and found themselves embroiled with the most powerful of the Islamic *jihads.* The French army in West Africa became engaged with Ahmadu and Samori, drawing it into a deepening zone of occupation. In the Eastern Congo Leopold was anxious to make use of Tippu Tib's extensive sway, but his officials, chafing to assert their supremacy, became involved in a costly war to the death with the Arabs in the early 90's. German heavy-handedness involved them in the Bushiri rising of 1888 with its unwished for consequence of large-scale punitive operations, direct rule of the Crown, and the establishment of effective administration. The pattern was repeated on smaller scale in numerous other instances, notably in Buganda and to some extent in Nyasaland.

Once the movement for occupation was under way by the early nineties, it developed a momentum of its own, and the local expansionist elements with gathering support in the metropolitan territories were able to play an increasingly influential role. The French army colonels, 'with one hand on their Maxims and the other on their next set of proofs' became a pressure group of their own, increasingly difficult for Paris to contain. And statesmen arose in the metropolitan countries—the Chamberlains and Delcassés—ready to justify African empire on its own account and to plough capital into the undeveloped tropical estates. The idea of trusteeship germinated. At all events, having found themselves involuntarily drawn into the work of administration, they were compelled to frame measures by which the colonies would ultimately be enabled to sustain their own administrative costs. Hence in the 90's, when at last imperial sentiment became a genuine force, African empire in some measure came into its own:

> 'By now the manoeuvres and blunders of the partition had been rationalised into apologies for African empire. But the crux of this imperialism lies in its sequence. It was not businessmen or missionaries or empire builders who launched the partition of Africa, but rather a set of diplomats who thought of that continent merely as a function of their concerns elsewhere. But once started off, this paper partition was turned into occupation and

colonisation by the clashes between the European and the proto-national-ists, the religious revolutionaries of Africa. Only at the end of the process did the businessmen arrive—when Europe had to foot the bill for having dealt with Africa as though it was uninhabited. The sequence is quite the reverse of that postulated in traditional theories. Imperialism was not the cause of the partition. It was the result.[1]

The admission that imperialism enjoyed even a short-lived reign on the African scene (roughly between 1895 and 1900) is an important concession, and closes an awkward gap in the original argument.[2] Imperial connivance in the Jameson Raid, the struggle with France over the delimitation of frontiers on the Niger, the great crisis over Fashoda, and finally the Boer War, these were clearly phenomena of a different order and demonstrated a willingness to proceed to extremities over African questions which was absent from the main partition period in the 80's. Even so, argue Robinson and Gallagher, while the policy makers were finding their African lobby possessed of a new obstreperous force, they never lost control of the position and ensured that Africa was kept subordinate to their larger strategy. They continued to think and act defensively though outwardly their moves looked more blatantly aggressive. It was the local crisis that continued to draw them on. The Fashoda incident which for the first time threatened a major European war over an African issue, sprang from the unexpected resurgence of Ethiopian power. Menelik's defeat of the Italians at Adowa removed the client power which had debarred the Ethiopians and their French allies from access to the Upper Nile. It was the immediate signal for Kitchener to advance for the reconquest of the Sudan. Yet at bottom the dramatic clash with the French at Fashoda remained not a struggle for African empire at all 'but for what that lonely place symbolised: to the British, safety in Egypt and India; to the French security in the Mediterranean'. The Boer War likewise sprang from the internal breakdown of the South African political system due to 'the collision of two internal waves of colonisation'. Once again the collaborating element—in this case, the Rhodes group—broke down (due to the fiasco of the Jameson Raid) and impelled imperial intervention. The British Cabinet allowed itself to be pushed by Chamberlain and Milner beyond remonstrance into war. Yet even the war party was not fighting to rule South Africa but to unify it as a self-governing friendly dominion from which the Imperial factor could be safely withdrawn.

In the final analysis, Robinson and Gallagher see the colonial empires in Africa as 'produced by a series of phenomena which were eventually to destroy them'. They arose in response to the challenge of colonial nationalisms or proto-nationalisms that threatened European security systems and the balance of power; and they fell when the processes of modernisation threw up a fresh and more powerful wave of nationalism in our own time. They were at best 'gimcrack creations' built without the *gout de permanence,* and dismantled once it was clear that modern nationalism had taken over from imperialism the work of the modernising process. . . .

Taken in its full sweep the argument cannot fail to strike as a powerful, compelling, and deeply-meditated construction that lifts the old-style colonial history and new-style African national histories to a new level of intellectual significance. Although it asserts that the partition of so large a continent cannot be ascribed to any single factor the unity of the argument tends to suggest that the problem is susceptible of a single connected explanation. On this the authors may have drawn the chain of logic too tightly. It is of the essence of their argument that the powers were scrambling in Africa and not for Africa, and that their true concern was directed towards their security systems in Europe, the Mediterranean, and along the Suez and Cape routes to the East. While Robinson and Gallagher are prepared to emphasize the importance of other local crises for bringing on the effective occupation and administration of spheres of influence, the partition itself originated, they argue, from a single source—the Egyptian crisis, and later became generalised through the spilling over of an independent local crisis in S. Africa. They are therefore led to play down the influence of developments in other areas, since these had no extra-African strategic importance and would infer the importance of African considerations on their own account. While the reader is given the impression of mounting economic activity in Egypt and South Africa, which eventually promoted internal conflict and anti-foreigner movements, Tropical Africa in contrast is depicted as static, with trade stagnant and unimportant and local rivalries of trivial consequence. *Africa and the Victorians* suggests a substantial continuity of conditions and policy for three or four decades up to the eve of the scramble; with trade, so far from buoyant, encountering increasing economic depression and political difficulties towards the end of the period.

One must seriously doubt whether this picture does justice to the transformation of Europe's relations with Africa in the age of exploration and penetration after 1860, and particularly after 1870. More narrowly, the account of West African trade exposes itself to considerable criticism. The fall in palm oil prices needs to be looked at against the general fall in world prices that characterised the so-called 'Great Depression' of the European economy between 1872 and 1895, for this feature is known to have masked a constant increase in the physical volume of trade. It is also far from axiomatic that trading difficulties and competition make for a weakening of political impulses to expansion, as the history of relations with China amply illustrates.

All the facts taken by themselves would suggest that in the later 70's and the beginning of the 80's swift changes were taking place in the West African scene well before the Egyptian crisis broke. Some branches of trade, such as German liquor imports or British commerce with the Congo, were showing rapid growth. The emergence of trade competition on national lines is well known; and there were signs that local officials and even home governments were prepared to give their merchants limited backing. The French had begun active probing from Senegal towards the Upper Niger in 1879, and Paris had given some measure of support to De Brazza to counter the threat of Leopold's International Association (1879) staking too large a claim to Congo trade. French firms were also making a bid for commercial expansion on the lower Niger, at the same time (1879) as Goldie merged the British firms into the United African Company. International competition was a symptom of mounting trading conflict. The fall in palm oil prices necessitating monopoly organisation to keep buying prices down and selling prices up, also quickened the impulse on the Niger and in the Cameroons to break through the 'crust' of African middleman trading states and obtain direct access to the producer regions. All the elements of a 'local crisis' were to hand.

Robinson and Gallagher refuse to give it more than minor status. To them West Africa entered the partition simply as an extension of the Egyptian crisis. Until that point Britain and France were in broad agreement to prevent petty trading disputes in the region being allowed to become inflamed to the damage of their international relations at large. After that point Paris was only too willing to pursue a policy of pin-pricks in West Africa to improve its bargaining position over Egypt. There is, however, a critical ambiguity in the argument. While the general tenor goes to suggest that all the actions of French ministers elsewhere stemmed from a root obsession to recover 'the blue line of the Nile', there is a possible hint that they were also seeking 'compensation' independently. As one version has it:

> 'As long as Baring was puppet-master in Cairo, so long did the French seek to prise him out and take compensation by unleashing their military

proconsuls against exposed British interests in unclaimed Africa, in South-east Asia and the South Pacific; while the Germans did likewise hoping to extort more British support in their European affairs. Once the Powers for these diplomatic purposes began to back their nationals' private enterprise against each other, commerce and strategy inevitably changed from a matter of restrained footholds and influence on the coast, into a business of extended territorial claims. In this roundabout fashion Arabi's revolution and Gladstone's blunder inflated the importance of intrinsically trivial squabbles in tropical Africa and generated its division among the Powers.'[3]

Was it then a scramble in Africa or for Africa? In what ways did expansion in West Africa give France any stronger purchase on the Egyptian problem? Britain for the most part gave ground elsewhere with little demur; no evidence is led to show that she was ever influenced in her Egyptian policy by French or German pressure on her West African interests. Conversely, one critic has asserted quite categorically: 'throughout the records of the French ministries for these years there is not a shred of evidence to connect West Africa with Egypt'.[4] That is not to say, of course, that the Egyptian crisis did not have a decisive influence on the partition in West Africa. As a recent study acknowledges, it quickened the whole process immeasurably.[5] But it was rather that the rupture of relations between Britain and France over Egypt allowed the local expansionist elements greater play, by rendering it difficult to negotiate standstill agreements.

In view of these considerations one must conclude that in addition to pure *pique,* French ministers were motivated by a desire for compensation in West Africa in its own right. Now it may be urged that such compensation was still reckoned in terms of diplomatic makeweights, in intangible 'cold war' calculations of spheres of influence and supposed political advantage. This indeed is what the diplomatic historians have been arguing all along. But any such admission weakens the whole case made out by Robinson and Gallagher that the partition was rationally directed and controlled, that the European statesmen were contending about real interests, and were not led astray by fantasies. Once an insubstantial element like prestige is introduced it becomes difficult to draw the line between rational and irrational motivation. The strength of the local expansionist element (represented by the French army) is readily acknowledged. It therefore becomes a question as to when Paris was persuaded into going beyond the search for diplomatic compensation to a regard for a West African empire as an object of intrinsic value. Generally speaking, Robinson and Gallagher take the line that at least before 1896 there was 'little substance in the West African quarrels', and that while therefore the French colonial group exercised increasing sway the attention of Paris continued to be absorbed by the struggle for the Nile Valley as part of the Mediterranean security problem. Yet this attempt to keep quite separate the motives of the local expansionist element and the motives of the Paris policy-makers craves wary walking. To some it will appear an intellectual tight-rope that cannot sustain the weight of the argument.

By placing the whole emphasis on the Egyptian crisis, the partition is regarded as completely fortuitous:

> 'For all the hindsight of the social scientists there was no comprehensive cause or purpose behind it. In all the long annals of imperialism, the partition of Africa is a remarkable freak. Few events that have thrown an entire continent into revolution have been brought about so casually.' [6]

This is again to emphasise the view that the powers stumbled unwittingly and unwillingly into Africa out of preoccupation with their non-African interests. History affords no exact parallels, but many of the features of the African partition bear comparison with the 'break-up' of China into European spheres of influence over the last years of the nineteenth century. Admittedly this occurred in the middle nineties in the high imperialist age and in a region where economic interests were rather more valuable. But the pattern is similar. The appropriation by one major power of a sphere of special influence (after the Sino-Japanese War had demonstrated the extreme weakness of China) prompted a rush by the other powers for compensating spheres. China was only of marginal importance to the world economy but considerations of the delicately poised power balance were sufficient to initiate a European scramble for railway, telegraph and loan concessions that were wildly speculative from any sober commercial viewpoint. Once more it was a question of governments giving rein to their local expansionist interests because they were unable to agree to contain them and were fearful of immediate losses of prestige and ultimate damage to prospective economic and political interests. Once it became clear that a partition could be effected which did not disturb the power balance, the China question like the Africa question lapsed back as an issue of secondary economic and strategic importance. In this sense the 'break-up' of China was as much a freak as that of the African partition. That the result in terms of political control was different does not alter the character of European motivation.

The argument of fortuitousness also raises the question of the character of the local crises in the Africa of the 80's. On closer examination their fortuitousness is seen to reside not in their ultimate origin—the erosion of indigenous systems by European economic activity—but in their contemporary unexpectedness and the unpremeditated nature of the European response. What has to be considered, therefore, is the relation between the immediate consciousness of statesmen and the deeper levels of social and economic impulses. Such levels did not register themselves automatically in policy; indeed the specialised aims of statesmen were primarily strategic rather than economic. Economic interests it is true were inadequate to produce the Scramble, but that was true of political expansion elsewhere. Governments were rarely moved merely at the promptings of economic appetite. To say that in Africa 'the powers were advancing not the frontiers of trade but the frontiers of fear'[7] is to state the general law of colonial expansion. Territorial expansion usually occurred at the economic margin and European powers acted immediately from motives of security. This, of course, was peculiarly true of a power like the British; even in regions where there were fair prospects of economic growth—as in the Western Malay States in the early 70's—it was only fear of German or French straddling of the strategic route through the Straits of Malacca that induced the Colonial Office to agree to protection.[8] Robinson and Gallagher tend, on the other hand, to postulate the absolute identity of strategic and economic motive in regions of paramount economic concern and their complete disseverance elsewhere, whereas it would appear that statesmen never distinguished them clearly and never renounced the primacy of the strategic motive. Great play is made with the importance of India—the partition is seen from the British side as 'a gigantic footnote to the Indian Empire'—but for all the reinforcement of gathering trade and capital investment it seems the statesmen were primarily bent on preserving the existing structure of power and influence rather than the promotion of manufacturing and capital exports. This much, indeed, is belatedly admitted, and India classed along with Africa as an area of only secondary economic importance.

> ... the gaudy empires spatch-cocked together in Asia and Africa. ... were linked only obliquely to the expansive impulses of Europe. They were not the objects of serious national attention ... It would be a gullible historiography which would see such gimcrack creations as necessary functions of the balance of power, or as the highest stage of capitalism.'[9]

Beyond this is the question of the significance of conscious motive as against that of objective cause. The fortuitousness of the partition extends only to the level of conscious expectation and the superficial divergence between metropolitan policy and local expansionist tendencies. Beneath this level it is admitted that the partition so far from being fortuitous had its grand sociological cause:

> 'All the processes of British expansion were reaching their peak. The metropolitan society was putting forth its strongest energies. It was at this climactic point that the social changes in its satellites were quickest and most violent. Hence it was at this time that their relations with the metropolis were breaking off towards full independence; while anti-western nationalism and social upheaval were estranging the non-European partners of British interests.'[10]

Here we have the admission that on a wider reading Africa was subjected to impulses stemming from within Europe and that the local crises within Africa were in this sense 'caused' by these external pressures. It looks very much like the old view writ large, except that in place of the one-way relationship we have a more subtle dialectic of challenge and response, and a more refined theory on the interrelation of motives.

The place of the economic factor has yet to be determined. Robinson and Gallagher refer to it *en passant,* for on their view the statistics settle its importance without further discussion. Certainly they brush aside as ridiculous any suggestion of the scramble as the highest stage of capitalism. But the economic motive was never postulated in quite the crude terms that this popular notion holds; no serious writer put out the view that the full flood of capitalist expansion turned towards Africa. The thesis propounded by Hobson accepted that in terms of trade expansion the losses on colonial acquisitions far outweighed the very limited gains which themselves never formed any really significant share of the total trade of the metropolitan powers. But certain minority and sectional interests had gained handsomely. 'The driving force of the competing Imperialism of Western nations has been traced to the interests of certain small financial and industrial groups within each nation, usurping the power of the nation and employing the public force and money for their private business ends'. These were the 'economic parasites' of capitalism, the agents of a basic mercantilist distortion. By securing quasi-monopoly conditions and inducing their governments to spend large sums on the administration and defence of colonial empire, they had artificially raised the profitability of certain branches of trade. The dominant feature of imperialism was, however, surplus capital driven to seek investment overseas because of underconsumption and oversaving in the domestic economy. The profitability of trade was as nothing to the profitability of export capital, as the relative statistics showed. Hence the presiding genius hiding quietly in the background was the financier. Hobson summed up his analysis thus:

> 'Overproduction in the sense of an excessive manufacturing plant, and surplus capital which could not find sound investments within the country, forced Great Britain, Germany, Holland, France to place larger and larger portions of their economic resources outside the area of their present political domain, and then stimulate a policy of political expansion so as to take in the new areas.'[11]

Lenin accepted the outline of this analysis and sought to link it more closely with the theory of finance capital developed by Hilferding and others. There is much imprecision in his periodization and like Hobson he makes little attempt to differentiate imperialist expansion in Africa from other regions. One feature is, however, clear. The age of finance capital did not properly set in, he acknowledges, until after 1900. Between 1870 and 1900 lay a transitional period in which the final territorial acquisitions occur. Monopoly capitalism had to some extent been averted so long as fresh territorial expansion could still be made.

> 'When the colonies of the European powers in Africa, for instance, comprised only one-tenth of that territory (as was the case in 1876), colonial policy was able to develop by methods other than those of monopoly—by the "free grabbing" of territories, so to speak. But when nine-tenths of Africa had been seized (approximately by 1900), when the whole world had been divided up, there was inevitably ushered in a period of colonial monopoly and, consequently, a period of particularly intense struggle for the division and redivision of the world.'[12]

Strictly speaking, imperialism is 'that stage in the development of capitalism . . . in which the division of all the territories of the globe among the great capitalist powers has been completed'. Lenin therefore does not differ so strikingly from Robinson and Gallagher's notion that imperialism was the consequence and not the cause of the partition. Admittedly his argument is not free from ambiguity. In another place he suggests that the partition of the world occurred according to the degree that finance rather than industrial capital was developing in particular states, so that Britain and France, and even Holland and Belgium acquired much larger colonial areas than more progressive capitalist economies like those of Germany and the United States.[13] Finally, Lenin's theory of imperialism attempted to be a comprehensive explanation of world history. In that perspective the struggle for, and exploitation of, colonies were simply a part, and not necessarily the most important part, of the world struggle for markets, raw materials and investment areas. Recent Marxist historians have made use of the hints supplied by Lenin to frame a more plausible account of economic imperialism.[14] In describing the German colonial movement they recognise that a 'splinter group' of the German commercial bourgeoisie, the Hanseatic trading interests, were apparently able to exercise a disproportionate influence on German policy, sufficient to launch Germany on a colonial career. These minority interests are similar to Hobson's 'economic parasites' and, as in his account, are manipulated by the figure of the high financier standing in the background. Yet these together were too weak to dictate policy, and Bismarck responded to the colonial demands more in the interests of his domestic and foreign policy than for any conviction in the validity of need for colonies. High finance made use of the weaker commercial elements to undertake the pioneering work and test the profitability of the new colonial regions. Allowing the commercial interests to stand the risks, it held its hand, and for the most part German finance capital on viewing the abortive attempt to win exploitable colonial regions directed its investment elsewhere. As it grew stronger within the German economy, especially after 1900, it undertook limited exploitation of colonial regions—chiefly mining, plantation, and railway enterprise—on the quasi-monopolistic basis of the concessions system by which it was armed with governmental powers to extort free labor. That phase of direct exploitation by finance capital superseded the indirect exploitation through mercantile interests, who were often displaced only after violent opposition.

The Marxist view is also prepared to admit non-economic, speculative, and purely irrational motives at work in the scramble. Lenin acknowledged the importance of the strategy of denial, the 'prophylactic' seizure of territory—as Müller terms it—designed to keep others out, and perhaps to serve as a basis for attack on another power. This admits as 'an essential feature of imperialism' 'the rivalry between a number of great powers in the striving for hegemony, i.e. for the conquest of territory not so much for themselves as to weaken the adversary and undermine his hegemony'.[15] The speculative element in finance capital induces it to strive after any sort of territory in the hope that it may hold out prospects of future development 'and fearing to be left behind in the insensate struggle for the last available scraps of undivided territory.'[16]

All this is no doubt a fanciful picture, but it has to be met on its own ground. It suggests that the driving force behind the scramble for territory was economic but acting in an oblique manner. Robinson and Gallagher cleverly dispose of the economic factor. In Tropical Africa they argue, it was too weak to be significant; in Southern Africa it was so powerful as to be beyond the responsibility or control of British ministers. A satellite economy that had reached the point of 'take-off', it had generated its own internal political order capable of providing the necessary framework for British economic interest. The problem for British policy was simply to ensure the stability and friendliness of the political order. The extension of Southern African interests up to the Congo border is readily acknowledged as a 'gigantic speculation in mining futures', but the British South Africa Company, distasteful to British opinion because of its monopolistic character, was chartered, so the argument runs for purely political and strategic reasons. The local expansionist factor in the Congo was clearly economic; but Leopold was helpless until he received international recognition on quite other grounds.

One does not have to accept the more far-fetched implications of Hobson's theory of the 'economic parasites' of capitalism to be persuaded by part of his argument. It might be that in terms of free enterprise and free trade Zambesia and the Congo were poor risks, but armed with the semi-monopoly powers that administrative rights conferred, these territories could still be regarded by relatively powerful financial groups as attractive prizes. Freed from crude misconceptions of the 'highest stage of capitalism' type, the economic factor deserves more consideration than Robinson and Gallagher allow to it. Moreover, as a constituent part of the local expansionist element, it has to be examined within the larger problem of the 'local crisis'. We have seen already the ambiguous role assigned to the local expansionist element in French policy, at one time being regarded as a mere subservient tool of Paris, and at another playing an autonomous role of its own. Officials and colonels acting on their own initiative and even in defiance of orders involved France in war à outrance with the Muslim theocracies; yet in another sense their further penetration of the Sudan was switched on or off at the dictates of the Quai d'Orsay. Similarly, the economic factor acting autonomously as a local expansionist force precipitated the local crises (as in South Africa and Egypt); but was powerless to dictate the outcome arrived at by the 'official mind' in the European capitals. At one moment the statesmen of Britain and France are regarded as supremely in control and in no way coerced by local expansionist elements; at another they are 'dragged' into Africa involuntarily because of the crises provoked by these elements. Great play is made with the purity of the strategic motive of the European statesmen, unalloyed by taint of greed or illusion of an African Eldorado; yet the expansion is effected by the elements seeking empire for the old imperialist motives of wealth and power.

The same kind of ambiguity which surrounds the role of the European expansionist element is also to be found in the account of indigenous African politics. In line with their thesis that the Scramble was brought about by events within Africa, Robinson and Gallagher lay special emphasis on anti-foreigner resistance movements which they speak of as nationalisms or proto-nationalisms. In *Africa and the Victorians* these embraced simply Egypt and South Africa; in the later *New Cambridge Modern History* chapter they extend to the whole range of resistance movements, largely Islamic, that ran in a wide arc from Samori in the Upper Niger, through Ahmadu, Rabeh, the Mahdiya, Christian Ethiopia, to the Arabs in the Congo and East Africa.

The conflation of all these different types of resistance movements raises certain problems. The original theory had relation to countries exposed to previous intrusive influences from Europe that were largely economic in character. The opposition which these countries threw up, though unexpected and unwelcome to western statesmen, was clearly in the nature of a response to external pressures and consequently must be regarded as an involuntary product of western initiatives. But this merely explains the initial intervention in Tunis, Egypt and South Africa. In order to explain the persistence of the Scramble and the transformation of spheres of influence into colonial dependencies, Robinson and Gallagher look about for a stronger support than the mere continuance of diplomatic rivalry over Egypt. They invoke the unexpected and hostile resurgence of societies in the African interior, the repression of which necessitated a much more intensive assertion of authority and control than was originally intended. But here the theory displays its ambiguity.

In one sense these resistance movements in the interior were called into existence by the threat of 'the encroaching thraldom of the white men' and are consequently classified as protonationalisms. They are placed within the larger theory which envisages the European occupation of Africa as occurring between two waves of 'nationalism', one largely traditionalist and provoking that occupation, and the other modernist and bringing the occupation to an end. In another sense, however, the protonationalisms exist independently of European pressures, and are regarded as natural products of the cyclic course of indigenous African history. From its position in the cycle can be explained the degree of resistance of any particular society: on the upswing, resistance is high, on the downswing—low. The cycle moves in terms of the integration and disintegration of large centralised states and is correspondingly linked with the rise of wide-reaching centralised religions or the fragmentation into localised animist creeds.

The movement of African history in terms of the model operates autonomously; but if it is regarded as absolute, the encounter with European expansion cannot be other than wholly fortuitous. Robinson and Gallagher leave the ambiguity unresolved, but the weight of their argument leans heavily towards the idea of African protonationalism as a response to the European expansionist challenge. This view has a respectable pedigree[17] but clearly its attraction is the intellectual coherence it offers with its possibility of framing a single, connected explanation, a grand sociological law, that brings African and European history into symbiosis.

African-centred historians will offer the criticism that such a symbiosis drains the life-blood from African history, and will emphasize that the Islamic *jihads* were a normal phenomenon of Sudanic history long before European influences were encountered,[18] or that the political explosion which threw off powerful military states like those of the Zulu, the Basuto, and Matabele, occurred independently of outside white pressures. They will argue that European motivation is of comparative triviality besides European actions, and that for the African the men on the spot completely overshadow the distant and hesitant figures in the European chancelleries.[19] Such views may be myopic, but they are levelled as an instinctual reaction to a theory that in subtle guise appears to have revamped the old notion of Africa's history as an extension of Europe's.

Robinson and Gallagher have accomplished a permanent historiographical revolution; that is no little achievement. The defects of their theory are defects of exaggerated emphasis and of an over-exuberant ambition to stand the old conception of imperialism on its head; but it would be churlish to deny that in intellectual terms they are the "fabulous artificers" who have "galvanised the last continent".

[1] 'The Partition of Africa', Chap. XXII, *The New Cambridge Modern History*, Vol. XI, pp. 632–3.

[2] 'Imperialism of Free Trade,' *Economic History Review*, 2nd Series, VI, 1953.

[3] R. E. Robinson: 'The Official Mind of Imperialism', *Historians in Tropical Africa*, University College of Rhodesia and Nyasaland, Salisbury, 1962, p. 202.

[4] C. Newbury, 'Victorians, Republicans, and the Partition of West Africa', *Journal of African History*, Vol. III, No. 3 (1962).

[5] John D. Hargreaves, *Prelude to the Partition of West Africa*, 1963.

[6] *New Cambridge Modern History*, Vol. XI, p. 593.

[7] *New Cambridge Modern History*, vol. XI, p. 616.

[8] Cf. C. D. Cowan, *Nineteenth Century Malaya*, 1961, p. 270.

[9] *New Cambridge Modern History*, Vol. XI, p. 639. This compares strikingly with the opening theme of *Africa and the Victorians* (p. 13): 'To all Victorian statesmen, India and the British Isles were the twin centres of their wealth and strength in the world as a whole'.

[10] *Africa and the Victorians*, p. 469.

[11] J. A. Hobson, *Imperialism*, p. 80; cited D. K. Fieldhouse, 'Imperialism: An Historiographical Revision', *Economic History Review*, XIV, No. 2, Dec. 1961.

[12] Lenin, 'Imperialism, the Highest Stage of Capitalism', *Selected Works*, (Two Volume Edition), Moscow, 1947, Vol. II, p. 722.

[13] Lenin, p. 689.

[14] F. F. Müller, *Deutschland, Zanzibar, Ostafrika*, Berlin, 1959.

[15] M. Nussbaum, *Vom "Kolonial-enthusiasmus" zur Kolonialpolitik der Monopole*, Berlin 1962.

[16] Cf. the variant versions above pp. 5, 8–9; also *New Cambridge Modern History*, pp. 610–11, 630.

[17] For the *jihads* in the western and central Sudan, see Oliver and Fage, *A Short History of Africa*, (Pelican), pp. 145–6. For the Mahidia, see P. M. Holt, *The Mahdist State in the Sudan*, pp. 22–3. For the Arabs in East Africa and

the Congo, see R. A. Oliver, *The Missionary Factor in East Africa*, pp. 87 ff., and R. Slade, *King Leopold's Congo*, pp. 84 ff.

[18]H. F. C. Smith, 'A Neglected Theme of West African History: The Islamic Revolutions of the 19th Century', *Historians in Tropical Africa*, Proceedings of the Leverhulme Inter-Collegiate Conference in History, Salisbury, 1960.

[19]T. O. Ranger, *Historians in Tropical Africa*, p. 2 ff.

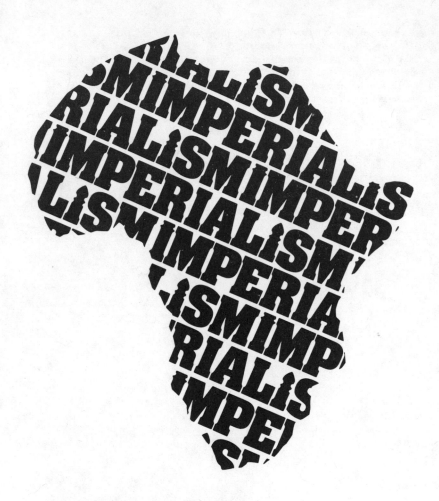

PART IV

Comments

The Meanings of Imperialism

A. J. P. TAYLOR

A. J. P. Taylor is a Fellow of Magdalen College, Oxford University. His major works include Germany's First Bid for Colonies *(1938),* The Struggle for Mastery in Europe *(1954),* Bismarck *(1955),* The Trouble Makers *(1957),* The Origins of the Second World War *(1961), and* English History, 1914–1945 *(1965).*

The Imperialism of the late nineteenth century had a special character. It had more participants: three front-runners (England, France, Germany) and two camp followers (King Leopold of Belgium, and Italy). It was more self-conscious. There were theorists of Imperialism, historians of Imperialism. Politicians made it their standby. Electorates responded to its call. All the same it was not unique, and some historians in the Robinson and Gallagher controversy have sometimes lost perspective in writing as though it were.

Imperialism is as old as civilization. It had some constant features. Though some national states (Napoleon III's French Empire, William II's German Empire) called themselves Empires for show, Empires have always meant rule over others. Here they differ from colonization where the "others" did not exist or were exterminated. The Imperial Power possessed superior strength and also superior civilization—or thought it did. The Imperial people exploited those over whom it ruled and yet at the same time thought it was doing them good. No Empire without a mission and no Empire without a profit, in reality or in imagination.

Nineteenth-century Imperialism had many strands, so much so that all the theories about it are true within their terms of reference. The European Powers were pulled into Imperialism by events in the imperial areas. They were pushed into it by enthusiasts and cranks at home. They genuinely wanted to expand European civilization. They wanted to increase their power and strategic position. They also wanted to make money. There was another special circumstance. Until the end of the eighteenth century or thereabouts, European civilization was one among many. The Chinese Empire, the Ottoman Empire, the Mogul Empire in India, were all going concerns. In the nineteenth century, thanks to Europe's industrial and financial superiority, they became derelict.

Curiously enough this Imperialism of penetration into derelict empires has been less studied than the Scramble for Africa which was a relatively trivial affair. Yet the derelict empires were the really profitable field for Imperialism and the one that provoked most conflict. The British carried off the Indian Empire after a marginally important conflict with the French. But rivalry over the Ottoman, Persian, Moorish, and Chinese Empires repeatedly caused international crises. This is not surprising. A derelict empire provided a framework for law and order, and the European Power had only to operate within this framework or sometimes take it over.

On the whole the search for markets was a false trail in the nineteenth century except insofar as a Great Power such as England did not want markets closed to it by others, as they were by France. The plums the Imperialists were after were railway concessions, banks, and capital investment generally. This was the element of truth in the theory of Economic Imperialism as developed by Hobson and Lenin. They were mistaken in equating it with political imperialism. Concessions could be gained without annexations, and annexations did not always lead to concessions. It is also a red herring to argue, as some have done, that Imperialism did not profit the Imperial Power concerned and therefore was not pursued for economic reasons. This is to formulate the wrong question. It did not matter whether the country profited as long as the Imperialists did. The Stock Exchange lists are quite enough to explain Imperialism. But the missionary tracts and even the geography textbooks explain it too. As often happens in history, once Imperialism started, everything seemed to be going the same way: explorers, missionaries, strategists, company promoters, professors of history, politicians, with the man in the street hanging on behind. Professor Stengers has grasped the sense of excitement that characterized the times better than Robinson and Gallagher.

Robinson and Gallagher have contributed to a broader understanding of the meaning of Imperialism, though they have not always been consistent in their frame of reference. For European historians, their work strengthens the argument that all the great powers found a safe channel for their exuberance outside Europe. The struggle for mastery in Europe was postponed, not abandoned: for the history of Europe before the First World War, this remains the meaning of the "age of imperialism."

The Framework of Imperialism:
An Economic Historian's Note to the
Robinson and Gallagher Controversy

W. W. ROSTOW

W. W. Rostow is Professor of Economics and History at the University of Texas. His books include The British Economy of the Nineteenth Century *(1948),* The Process of Economic Growth *(1952),* The Stages of Economic Growth *(1960),* The United States in the World Arena *(1960),* Politics and the Stages of Growth *(1971),* The Diffusion of Power *(1972), and* How It All Began *(1975).*

What kind of intellectual framework can an economic historian offer in viewing late-nineteenth-century imperialism?

As I see it, there are three phenomena involved.

First, the emergence of Germany, France, Belgium, and the United States to industrial status in the (say) three decades before 1873, as the railroad and all its works (iron, coal, engineering) permitted them more or less to match the British and surmount the precocious primacy that Britain enjoyed in the first cotton textile round of industrialization.

Second, the environment of the Great Depression (1873–96). Prices were falling in general, profit margins pinched, European agriculture pressured by the flow of cheap American grain, excess capacity developing in the heavy industries supplying the railroads (steel rails, notably), new cost-reducing technologies coming in rapidly (electricity, steel ships, machine tools, chemicals). The dramatic fall in long-distance freight rates brought about by the steel ship pulled the world closer together and made distant places of greater economic interest. It was a time of both progress and strain, of more intense domestic and foreign economic competition than, say, from 1848 to 1873. Free trade lost its charm in a good many places.

Third, in certain areas a nationalist political reaction against prior colonial and quasicolonial intrusion was generating in the third and fourth quarters of the nineteenth century, notably in India, Egypt, China, to say nothing of the Meiji Restoration in Japan. But the degree of political and economic modernization in the less developed parts of the world—and the degree of reactive nationalism—was most uneven. In each region it must be understood in terms of the timing and character of its prior experience with more advanced powers and does not lend itself well to broad generalization.

The first factor helps account for the fact that the colonial game became more competitive. There were more competent industrial nations. The French had resumed an earlier imperial thrust from, say, the wielding of the fly whisk in Algeria in 1827. But the Germans, Americans, Belgians, and Italians—all feeling in different ways a new nationalism rooted in economic progress—joined in the game in ways not likely before 1873. And, by 1895 Japan, too, was on the imperial stage in its region out of similar impulses. The British had to exert themselves more to hold what they had or to expand; the others were more assertive and energetic. The second factor gave the competition a special thrust and urgency. Governments were more inclined to commit diplomatic or even military resources to hold markets or sources of supply or to reach out for markets or sources of supply that might one day emerge. The third factor, where it existed, posed the question of negotiating or forcing new arrangements with the local authorities to assure markets or sources of supply.

From an economic historian's point of view there is a certain amount of wry humor in the African imperial Scramble.* The great climactic boom at the end of the 1880s comes in Argentina. Except for the mining outlays in South Africa, British investment in Africa is modest down to 1914. More fundamentally, all the Great Depression trends reverse after about 1896: prices are rising; capital flows to expand the world's wheat supply (Canada, Argentina, Ukraine, Australia); profits are up; competition is less intense; politics shifts towards the urban worker, hard-pressed by the rise in living costs. Joseph Chamberlain never makes it to 10 Downing Street; Free Trade survives; and across the water Bryan ultimately becomes Secretary of State.

I make this point, among other reasons, because there is a danger

---

*See Matthew Simon, "The Pattern of New British Portfolio Foreign Investment, 1865–1914," Chapter I in A. R. Hall (ed.), *The Export of Capital from Britain 1870–1914.*

of projecting the imperialist moods of the 1880s right down to 1914. They greatly waned after, say, the turn of the century, as the economic returns seemed less significant and the costs of Adowa, the Boer War, and the guerrilla struggle in the Philippines were weighed by politicians and citizens. I rate imperialist competition low among the causes of the First World War as opposed to the European balance of power.

The relations between economic factors and politics are rarely simple and direct; there are usually time lags at work, including the lags in men's minds between old concepts and current reality; and linkage often involves that most difficult of functions to deal with—interaction. The economic historian's contribution is, therefore, likely to be modest. In the problem of nineteenth-century imperialism it may, nevertheless, be useful for the political analyst to keep firmly in mind the stages of growth through which the actors were passing at particular periods; the undulating sequence of trend periods; and the timing and manner in which contacts between more and less industrialized nations triggered the long, slow, reactive process I have called the preconditions for take-off.

How does this perspective bear on the Robinson-Gallagher controversy?

I believe the element of legitimacy in the continuity view is limited and potentially misleading. It is true that the British political authorities steadily wanted the nation to enjoy its economic advantages abroad at minimum military and political commitment and cost. But that is a little like saying the United States throughout its history wished to see the balance of power in Europe maintained in ways which avoided dominance by any single power; and that the changes in U.S. policy in Europe since 1917, after Britain and France could no longer manage the job alone, were simply a matter of a changing external environment in which a continuous policy was implemented. In politics a change in means cannot be usefully distinguished from a change in ends. What Britain had to do to achieve its objectives after, say, 1870 was quite different in certain areas from what it had to do before. And I would regard that change in means as a change in policy.

With respect to the role of the political dynamics in what we would now call the developing world, it is a valuable contribution of Mr. Robinson to attempt to generalize the interplay of domestic politics and the character of the relation to the imperial powers; but he seems a bit overimpressed with what he calls "the implacable continuities of African and Asian history." He misses, it seems to me, the

sequence of modernizing generations, each wider and more assertive than the one before, making in each case a different mix of
dispositions with respect to the industrialized world beyond. There is
something excessively static about Mr. Robinson's categorization of
traditional and modern elements in the various developing societies.
And, as he is well aware, his generalization about the intermediaries
is an exceedingly limited one; for the character and extent of the
linkage depended on elements of irreducible uniqueness in the culture and history of each region intruded upon, as well as the character of the intrusion.

As for discontinuity, it is not useful to ignore the changes in the
world arena wrought by the take-offs of France, Germany, Belgium,
and the United States accomplished before 1870, and the Japanese
take-off of the 1880s. They yielded a more crowded stage at just the
time that the contours of the post-1873 trend period made the resources and markets of the less developed regions appear more
important and attractive than they had been judged earlier. For a
generation the life of the West was suffused by the heightening of a
neomercantilist strand of struggle for power and profit. It had not
been absent from the world of 1815–70; but it loomed larger for a
while, and then lifted substantially after the turn of the century, only
to be promptly supplanted by the grim maneuvering over the European power balance that yielded the First World War.

Imperialism, Scramble and Steeplechase

HENRI BRUNSCHWIG

Henri Brunschwig is Director of the Ecole des Hautes Etudes en Sciences Sociales and Professor at the Institut des Sciences Politiques, Paris. He is the author of Mythes et réalités de l'imperialisme colonial français, 1871–1914 *(1960),* L'Avènement de l'Afrique noire du XIXe siècle à nos jours *(1963), and* Le Partage de l'Afrique Noire *(1971). The following remarks are a synthesis of his views on points raised by Robinson and Gallagher that are of particular importance from the vantage point of French colonial history.*

Robinson and Gallagher, in their remarkable study, declare that the imperialist explosion at the end of the nineteenth century had really introduced nothing new. The personnel of the Foreign Office continued to react to the same stimuli, to be concerned with the route to India more than with Black Africa, and to treat with disdain the petty conflicts over boundary definitions there. This condition explains in part the relative ease with which the partition of Africa occurred. However, on one important point the authors are wrong: there was at least one change.

"Imperialism" is a political term and around 1880 signified the desire to extend the *imperium:* the sovereignty of one nation over foreign lands and peoples. It was later that men like Hobson spoke of an economic imperialism and of informal empire, ideas which would have been considered absurd around 1880.

Because imperialism was then a political term, it is in the political realm that one must look to see if there had been continuity since the beginning of the century, or whether there had been change.

Now the newness appeared to be considerable when, in the Anglo-German Treaty of April 29, 1885, the diplomats resorted to a concept that they had always rejected earlier and that the jurists had not ceased to condemn: that of the *sphere of influence*. In this instance there was a break with the modes of thought and the political and moral tradition; the diplomats in the Foreign Office did not then react as had their predecessors of 1840. Henceforth to be a classic method of procedure, the recourse to the sphere of influence, taken by the politicians at the end of the nineteenth century, might well be the best test of the imperialist mood. This change can be illustrated by drawing the distinction between the *"course au clocher"* and the "scramble."

The *course au clocher,* the French translation of the English term "steeplechase," was introduced into France in 1834. Already in 1832, Alfred de Musset gave a precise description of the sport in *A quoi rêvent les jeunes filles,* act 1, scene 4:

Avez-vous jamais vu les courses d'Angleterre?
On prend quatre coureurs—quatre chevaux sellés;
On leur montre un clocher, puis on leur dit: Allez!
Il s'agit d'arriver, n'importe la manière.
L'un choisit un ravin—l'autre un chemin battu.
Celui-ci gagnera s'il ne rencontre un fleuve;
*Celui-la fera mieux, s'il n'a le cou rompu.**

The earliest mention that I have found of the term with a political connotation is in an article by Charles Fauré, appearing in the *Revue genèvoise,* and entitled "L'Afrique explorée et civilisée," dated January 5, 1884. The author was commenting on the opening sessions of the Berlin Conference and stated: "Recently, the movement has taken on the character of a true *course au clocher.* It seems that the winner was the one who would arrive first and hoist his national flag on this or that spot on the coast of Africa not yet possessed by a European nation."

*The verse translates roughly as follows:
    Have you ever seen the races in England?
    There are four riders—four saddled horses;
    A steeple is pointed out to them, then they are told: On your way!
    The point is to get there, no matter the manner.
    One rider chooses a ravine—the other a well-worn path.
    The latter will win if he does not encounter a stream;
    The former will do well, if he does not break his neck.

Jules Ferry, in his book, on "Le Tonkin et la mère patrie," published in 1890, wrote in the first chapter, entitled, "Five Years After": "An irresistible movement seized the great European nations in their conquest of new territory. It was like an immense *steeplechase* on the route of the unknown. . . . This *course au clocher* is hardly five years old and moves on, as if pushed by already attained speed, from one year to the next. . . ." Ferry's dating moves us back also to 1885. But the term had been used before, at least in 1884, when Fauré wrote his article, published in January of 1885. At that moment the image corresponded well to the reality: the four riders were France, Leopold, Germany, and England; the steeplechase was located in the Congo.

The origin of this rivalry ought to date back to 1882 according to Robinson and Gallagher, who attach major importance to the rupture of the Anglo-French entente in Egypt; or to Stengers, who does not think Egypt at this time exerted a decisive influence on Congolese affairs, and, according to my studies, did not have a decisive influence on the mission entrusted to Brazza in the Congo.

The agreement of historians on the responsibility of France, which started the race, and on the date—1882—appeared to be unanimous until, in 1969, C. W. Newbury and A. S. Kanya-Forstner published a brilliant article in the *Journal of African History* entitled "French Policy and the Origins of the Scramble for Africa" (Volume X, pp. 253–276). The text is fundamental, even if one does not accept its conclusions, because it provides an exhaustive bibliography on the subject and because it refers to numerous documents, often unpublished—in short, because it provides the interested scholar with the synthesis of the problem in 1969. I will therefore use this excellent point of departure as the means by which to propose a compromise peace between the two parties in contention.

Newbury and Kanya-Forstner suggest a distinction of time and place. The "scramble," the English expression for the *course au clocher,* really began not in 1882, but three years before, in 1879, and occurred not in the Congo, but in West Africa. And to be sure, convincing arguments supporting this thesis are not lacking to the authors. Kanya-Forstner had only to dip into the ample documentation of his remarkable thesis, "The Conquest of the Western Sudan"; Newbury is one of the best historians of the economic evolution of West Africa. No one doubts that Anglo-French rivalry in this area was of early origin, that it perhaps dates back to the beginning of the nineteenth century, at least to the time of Faidherbe; and that it was accentuated after 1870, when Brière de Lisle and Rowe were face-to-face in the Matacong affair, and when public opinion was interested in the Transsaharan railroad. All of this history is admirably treated in the article in the *Journal of African History,* and the authors demonstrate that if the two governments constantly sought to avoid conflict until the opening of the Egyptian question in 1882, the scramble would have occurred anyway. The ratification by France of the Makoko treaty would only have created "a new front."

But a front against whom? Assuredly, not against the English. If the latter had been as active in the Congo as they were in West Africa, it is doubtful that Duclerc, President of the Council and Minister of Foreign Affairs, would have had the Makoko Treaty ratified, even faced with the repugnance of his colleague in the Marine, Admiral Jauréguiberry.

The only agency present was the International Association of the Congo, a private organization which no power had yet recognized and which did not constitute an adversary in the diplomatic conflict. It was because France was not opposed by any other power that Duclerc believed it possible to satisfy public opinion, and this done, to give the start to the *course au clocher.*

To the *course au clocher, not to the scramble.* The two terms in fact do not have the same meaning. *Course au clocher* appeared in the political vocabulary much later than "scramble." If the English term can be effectively applied to an older rivalry, whether Anglo-French, Anglo-Portuguese, or any other on any point of the globe, than to the general rush toward Africa following upon the intrusions of Leopold and Bismarck, the French expression is limited to the international rivalry which followed after the Makoko Treaty. The Anglo-French scramble in West Africa dates back to 1879 and perhaps even before that. The international *course au clocher* in the Congo dates from 1882 and thereafter spread to other regions.

German Imperialism:
Robinson and Gallagher and
Bismarck's Colonial Policy

HANS-ULRICH WEHLER

Hans-Ulrich Wehler is Professor of History, Bielefeld University. His works include Bismarck und der Imperialismus *(1969);* Geschichte als Historische Sozialwissenschaft *(1973);* Krisenherde des Kaiserreichs, 1871–1918 *(1970);* Das Deutsche Kaiserreich, 1871– 1918 *(1973);* Sozialdemokratie und Nationalstatt 1840–1914 *(1962);* Der Aufstieg des Amerikanischen Imperialismus, 1865–1900 *(1974); and* Modernisierungstheorie und Geschichte *(1975). At present he is working on a two-volume study of the interrelation between social change, economic development, and political authority in the German states, 1815–1970.*

In *Africa and the Victorians* Robinson and Gallagher uncritically endorse A. J. P. Taylor's simplistic theory about Bismarck's colonial policy. According to this interpretation, Bismarck created a colonial empire merely as a diplomatic move to provoke a quarrel with England in order to draw France closer to Germany. This theory can easily be refuted. Nor can some of Robinson and Gallagher's more general ideas be verified, at least in the case of Germany. Where could one find traditional interests and protonationalistic movements influencing German overseas policy at the time when German imperialism began? To the contrary, the fundamental point is that German imperialism must be seen primarily as the result of endogenous socioeconomic and political forces and not as a reaction to exogenous pressures or circumstances abroad.

In view of the long controversy over Bismarck's motives for entering the arena of *Weltpolitik,* one decisive point must first of all be emphasized: in Bismarck's overseas policies there is a remarkable continuity of both the ideas and the methods of free-trade commercial expansionism. He adhered to this particular policy of expansion throughout his career because he clearly recognized the financial burdens, the political consequences and the military risks that were involved in formal colonial rule. He was also influenced by the enormous success of Britain's mid-Victorian "informal empire," and at the same time he carefully calculated the importance of those interests which could be satisfied by a laissez-faire overseas policy. The years 1884–86 were not marked by a sudden revision of his basic ideas, nor by a sudden change of mind, a sudden enthusiasm for colonies. There were, however, motives contrary to his previous experience and hopes that did induce Bismarck to involve the state in the establishment of protectorates. It is indisputable that he would have preferred to hand over these territories under imperial charter to private groups and commercial syndicates, which would enjoy some form of loosely formalized imperial protection. Bismarck remained convinced that "informal empire" was preferable to fully state-administered colonies. He persisted, moreover, in the belief that economic interests should take the initiative overseas and that the state should merely follow later, eschewing the goal of formal colonial rule. It seems hardly possible to dispute this continuity in Bismarck's basic attitude. It is thus not the continuity of intention which poses the real problem but rather its relationship to the heterogeneous methods employed in the protectorate policy of the 1880s.

From the beginning of the 1860s onward, Bismarck pursued an active, if not always equally intensive overseas policy with an immediate view to promoting the exports of industrial products. The central question is: why did Bismarck decide in the mid-1880s that it was no longer possible to settle for free-trade expansion? Why—hesitantly and with many reservations—did he come round to the view that it was necessary to assume the burden of formal colonial rule? The answer is, in part, that his change of policy was a response to the exigencies of the new German Reich's socioeconomic and political system. In Germany, as elsewhere, the new period of depression which set in during 1882 had a catalytic effect on imperialist policies. Concern with a possible repetition of the grim experiences of 1873–79 which had interrupted economic growth and produced years of social and political instability, was a spur to greater involvement in the colonial world. Confronted with the effects that uneven industrial growth was producing in the economic, social and political spheres, the German government's leaders in Berlin could not stand idly by— extensive expansion overseas was one of the countermeasures designed to ease this critical situation.

The policy which led to the acquisition of colonies in Africa and in the Pacific was only one of the methods whereby the state promoted foreign trade. There is little doubt that the "open door policy" remained Bismarck's ideal—he was still able to pursue it in China and in the Congo. If England and France had guaranteed free trade in Africa, unrestricted commercial expansion of this sort would have entirely satisfied Bismarck's economic aims. It was his view that, under these circumstances, German interests engaged in overseas competition could have asserted and extended themselves with limited governmental support. But the crucial reasons which induced him from 1883–84 onward to seek a gradual formalization of imperial control in Africa and the Pacific were twofold: on the one hand internal pressures resulting from the crisis were mounting and had to be reduced; on the other, the end of the free-trade era appeared imminent, and increasing competition together with the use of protectionist methods by other powers made direct state involvement overseas seem inevitable.

In the first half of the 1880s Bismarck thus found himself caught in a pincer movement from without and within. In Africa and Asia the action of the principal colonial powers, Britain and France, aroused in Berlin fear of eventual exclusion from the commerce of those parts of the world. At home those fears were nurtured and heightened by pressure groups with vested interests. Gradually Bismarck yielded to the warnings that he should not let chances go begging during the time of the depression. The prophylactic expansionism upon which he embarked aimed at protecting present advantages and potential opportunities from the claims of rival powers in such a way that he eventually had to pay the price of formal colonial rule. In these respects his methods and the motives behind them were unquestionably similar to those of the "preclusive imperialism" then being pursued in London, particularly *vis-à-vis* Germany. It cannot be demonstrated that Bismarck would have assumed formal protectorates in overseas areas without the real or latent threat that rival states would beat him to it. Even during the critical period after 1882, Bismarck was not simply on the lookout for "unowned" territories; he preferred to have the German flag follow the country's trade. Whenever possible, merchants were to take over the administration of the protectorates and exploit them through charter companies and syndicates. The role of the state was to remain extremely limited. These intentions came to grief everywhere within the space of a few years—as a result of the weakness and reluctance of the trading interests, great-power rivalries and colonial uprisings. The long-term results were even more disastrous. As Professor Henry Turner has pointed out in an essay, the conclusions of which are similar to those of *Bismarck und der Imperialismus,* Bismarck's colonial policy contributed to the agitation for a battle fleet in keeping with Germany's status as a colonial power and thus helped to lead Germany down the ruinous path of *Weltpolitik.**

*Henry A. Turner, "Bismarck's Imperialist Venture: Anti-British in Origins?", in Prosser Gifford and Wm. Roger Louis, eds., *Britain and Germany in Africa* (New Haven, 1967).

Robinson and Gallagher
and Middle Eastern Nationalism:
The Egyptian Argument

ROGER OWEN

Roger Owen is a former Director of the Middle East Centre of St. Antony's College and a Faculty Lecturer in the Recent Economic History of the Middle East, Oxford University. He is the author of Cotton and the Egyptian Economy *(1969), and, with Bob Sutcliffe, he has edited* Studies in the Theory of Imperialism *(1972). He is presently writing an economic history of the Middle East.*

Egypt, and more specifically the events leading up to the British occupation of 1882, are given an important role in the central arguments put forward in *Africa and the Victorians*. This is not only because, for Robinson and Gallagher, it was the occupation which triggered off the "scramble" for the northern half of the African continent but also because they put forward Egyptian events as a classic example of the way in which Britain was drawn into an unplanned act of colonization as the result of something they term, variously, a "breakdown" or "a [local] nationalist crisis." Thus it follows that an examination of what they have to say about Egypt will do more than simply reveal how well they understand the particular process which led up to the British occupation; it will also say something about their general approach to the study of nineteenth-century imperialism and of the methods by which they think it ought to be analysed.

Robinson and Gallagher's account of the events preceeding the emergence of the nationalist movement of 1881–82 is a simple one. First, Egypt was bankrupted in 1875 by unwise borrowing from abroad, then, in the years which followed, the authority of the government was further undermined by Anglo-French efforts to reform the system of financial administration and by their deposition of the

Khedive Ismail in 1879. Finally, with traditional authority gravely compromised there was a nationalist reaction to foreign interference which soon threatened to upset the whole basis of Anglo-French cooperation, thus forcing a reluctant British government toward military intervention.

Details aside, and reduced to its essentials this account rests upon three basic arguments:

1. There was a fundamental "crisis" in Egypt in 1882.

2. This "crisis" had its origins in the breakdown of traditional authority as a result of years of foreign economic penetration.

Nevertheless,

3. the British response to the specific 'crisis' of 1882 must be seen in political and strategic, rather than economic terms.

I would like, very briefly, to examine each of these arguments in turn.

1. Was there a "crisis" in 1882?

Robinson and Gallagher's account of what they refer to as "the Suez Crisis 1882" assumes that the progressive undermining of khedivial authority had brought the country to a state bordering on anarchy. But this immediately raises a number of grave doubts. First, Robinson and Gallagher's account is not based on any local Egyptian sources. Second, the consensus among historians who have studied such sources would seem to suggest that far from there being a slide into anarchy the Arabi government was well able to maintain security, the only exception being the June riots in Alexandria after the provocative arrival of the British fleet.[1] Third, the sources they do refer to are almost exclusively the work of British officials in Egypt at the time, men like Sir Edward Malet the consul-general who had a particular point of view to put across. This is made very clear in a dispatch written by Malet to the British foreign secretary in February 1882:

> [It would] be necessary if it be determined that the present state of things cannot be allowed to continue, that an occupation of the country should precede its re-organization, but it would be wise to allow the experiment to prove itself clearly impracticable before such a measure is resorted to. For very clear grounds can alone justify the suppression by arms of the effort of a country to govern itself.[2]

But if the reports of anarchy or impending anarchy sent to London were exaggerated for a particular reason was there a "crisis"? The answer to this question would seem to be, as Alexander Schölch has argued so persuasively, that there was indeed a crisis but of a very different sort, one engineered by Sir Aukland Colvin and others who regarded the Egyptian government which came into office in February 1882 as a threat to the Anglo-French control over Egypt's finances.[3] This was something they were determined to prevent by any means, including a sustained effort to persuade the authorities in London that the Egyptian nationalists were not to be trusted. If this argument is true it is difficult to see how the events to 1882 can be construed as creating a vacuum into which the British were reluctantly drawn.

2. The origins of the "crisis"

In Robinson and Gallagher's account, their 1882 "crisis" had its origins in more than fifty years of European economic penetration which "eroded" existing patterns of authority. But if the account they give of the crisis is incorrect then this particular exercise in reading history backward will also have to be reworked. This is the more necessary as Robinson and Gallagher's analysis of the complex process by which Egyptian society and Egyptian political institutions were transformed through contact with Europe is so sketchy and unsatisfactory. If as a result of many decades of European penetration some traditional institutions were undermined, others were transformed or restructured to meet the increasingly complex task of administering a state bent on modernization and reform. Meanwhile, as the result of the efforts of a series of Egyptian rulers from Muhammed Ali onward the group of educated Egyptians with sufficient skills to staff the growing bureaucracy was rapidly increased. Many other developments followed to produce a system which, whatever its shortcomings, cannot be simply dismissed as "rickety." More generally, it might well be argued that the traditional historical methods which Robinson and Gallagher employ are too crude to be used in the analysis of such a process of social transformation and that this can only be done by attempting to utilize the techniques of the economic and social historian.

3. The character of the British response to the "crisis" of 1882

The central feature of Robinson and Gallagher's third, and most important, argument is contained in the following quotation:

> By 1882 the Egyptian Khedivate had corroded and cracked after decades of European paramountcy. But economic expansion was certainly not the sufficient cause of the occupation. Hitherto commerce and investment had gone on without the help of outright political control. . . . Although the

expanding economy had helped to make a revolutionary situation in Egypt, it was not the moving interest behind the British invasion.[4]

But this again raises a number of grave doubts. To begin with, even in terms of their own argument, Schölch's hypothesis about the true nature of the 1882 "crisis" would suggest that economic requirements had something to do with the events leading up to the occupation. But much more importantly there is the problem of method and the type of historical questions to which *Africa and the Victorians* is supposed to answer. As Robinson and Gallagher make perfectly clear in their first chapter the type of question they are interested in is the traditional historical one of asking why a particular historical event happened when it did. And this, as they also make clear, leads inevitably on to the question of motive.[5] If the aim of history is to discover why something happened exactly when it did it can only be done by trying to look into the minds of the actors actually involved. Several important implications follow. *First,* the investigation of the causes of the British invasion of Egypt is confined to an examination of the British officials who were immediately responsible. If there was no obvious economic dimension to their thinking then the invasion could not have any connection with the expanding British economy. Other historical topics like the effects (on Egypt), rather than the cause, of the British occupation are automatically ruled out as irrelevant. *Second,* rival accounts of the origins of the occupation (and by extension rival accounts based on general theories of imperialism) can only be considered if they can be shown to provide a precise answer to the question of why Egypt was invaded in the summer of 1882 and not either before or later. Again, if they seek to suggest that the reasons had something to do with the economy it must be shown that such ideas were present among the motives of the main officials involved.

In conclusion one final point should be made. The Robinson and Gallagher approach just described severely limits the possibility of establishing any general theory of imperialism. By defining the problem of studying empire in the way that they do, they must, if they are consistent, rule out any such theory both on account of its concern with the wrong questions and its failure to answer what they regard as the right one.

[1]Cf. Abd al-Rahman Al-Rafii, *Al-thawra al-Urabiyya wal-ihtilal al-Injilizi* (The Arabi revolution and the English occupation) (Cairo 1949); A. Schölch, *Ägypten den Agyptern! Die politische und gesellschaftliche Krise der Jahre 1798–1882 in Agypten* (Zurich 1972)

[2]Malet to Granville, 27 Feb. 1882, FO 78/3435, quoted in A. Schölch, "The 'men on the spot' and the English occupation of Egypt in 1882", *mimeo*, pp. 6 et seq.

[3]Malet to Granville, 27 Feb. 1882, quoted in *Ibid.*, p. 14.

[4]*Africa and the Victorians* (London 1963), p. 467.

[5]*Ibid.*, pp. 17–18, 25–26.

Robinson and Gallagher in Latin America:
The Meaning of Informal Imperialism

RICHARD GRAHAM

Richard Graham is Professor of History at the University of Texas. He is the author of Britain and the Onset of Modernization in Brazil, 1850–1914 *(1968). His writings also include* Independence in Latin America: a Comparative Approach *(1972), and, with Peter H. Smith,* New Approaches to Latin American History *(1974). He is presently working on a book that will deal with the relationship between socioeconomic interest groups and political decision-making in nineteenth-century Brazil.*

Many literate and informed Latin Americans today, regardless of political persuasion, would be ready to describe nineteenth-century British activity in Latin America as "imperialistic."[1] Even those who shy away from so labeling the actions of the United States—Britain's successor in the hegemony of the region—are ready to believe that Britain included Latin America within its empire. This view is not a new development. For instance, in 1941 Tenorio d'Albuquerque, a declared fascist, published a pamphlet entitled *O imperialismo britanico no Brasil.*[2] It would be easy to find similar references in the works of socialists, nationalists, and liberals. Obviously, these writers are not speaking of formal empire. Aside from areas of the Caribbean, the Guianas, Central America, and the Malvinas islands, the British have not exerted overt political control in the continent; are we to conclude, then, that Latin American writers and scholars would agree with Robinson and Gallagher's discussion of informal imperialism?

The answer to that question depends on what one means by informal imperialism. Does sheer economic power exerted by citizens of one country over citizens of another constitute imperialism? Or is it necessary to consider political, official, and governmental participation in that control before it can be considered imperialistic? Much of what Robinson and Gallagher said in their initial article of 1953 seemed to suggest that informal imperialism was precisely that kind of control in which the government intervened only when it was necessary to maintain "free trade" opportunities; when private citizens turned successfully to the government for aid, the process shaded toward formal imperialism. When they referred to British policy, they did not appear to be speaking only or principally of official policy but of the almost unconscious policy of the nation, of the British people, and especially of the British economy understood as a system—depersonalized and ahistorical as that may be. In their later works, however, Robinson and Gallagher (or at least Robinson) have become more precise but also to some degree less relevant for Latin America.[3] Other authors who do refer to Latin America have remained vague as to their meaning. D. C. M. Platt, for instance, has insisted that if the Foreign Office did not come to the rescue of beleaguered businessmen, imperialism is disproved. Clarity regarding the definition of imperialism will be essential to any future steps toward resolving the question of whether or not laissez-faire imperialism existed in Latin America.

One assumption made by many Latin American historians and one that I share at least to some degree, is that ownership by the British of ranches and plantations, mines, mills, railways, port facilities, or other economic institutions placed "control" in their hands.[4] The more such institutions they owned, the more control. It could be argued that the owners of such businesses and institutions were responding to impersonal market forces and economic imperatives inherent in the economic system itself, and that the nationality of the ownership was either immaterial or did not particularly enhance British power in Latin America. To such a stand I would retort, first, that the system was itself purposefully so structured in the nineteenth century as to benefit the British or at least an international capitalist class filled principally by the British. Any consideration of whether more Brazilians were affected by decisions made by a few Englishmen than vice versa must lead to the conclusion that the British did exert a great deal of control over Latin Americans. I believe the British had more influence on Latin America than Latin Americans had on Great Britain and that significantly more of the key decisions that affected the lives of citizens in Latin America were made by the British than the reverse. Measuring this control and evaluating its variations in time and space are beset by methodological and conceptual problems, but the general tendency is clear. It may take a hydraulic engineer to measure the flow of water, but anyone can see it flows downhill.

There is another question that also revolves around perspective. If, as is surely the case, Latin America received relatively little British trade and investment as compared to Britain's worldwide or strictly colonial interests, can it be argued, as Platt has done, that Latin America was not subjected to British imperialism? I should think it is clear that a small proportion of the total may have been quite enough to establish British control, depending on the size and nature of the local economy in question (remembering that I am not arguing that the British *government* exerted that control). Indeed, this difference in perspective that affects historians was part of the historical actors' problem too: the parameters within which Latin Americans had to make their choices were relatively narrow, compared to the wide range of alternatives available to the British. For Latin Americans to refuse to export to Britain or to refuse to accept British investments would entail "punishments" whereas the British could easily, without discomfort, shift their area of supply or the focus of their investment interests. The balance of power was thus uneven, and the preeminent position of the British only occasionally threatened.

The exact role of the British throughout Latin America has yet to be studied carefully and in detail. Latin Americans have not done as much as might have been expected to explore this facet of their past. Insofar as they have considered British imperialism, the issues that divide them are not those implicit in the argument of Robinson and Gallagher. Following the lead of André Gunder Frank, some have insisted that Latin America has always been subjected to capitalist imperialism.[5] According to this view, the phenomenon is relatively undifferentiated whether it was the formal imperialism of Spain and Portugal, or the informal imperialism of Britain and the United States. Other authors have denied this homogeneity of imperialism.[6] But they see the dividing mark not between formal and informal imperialism, but between colonialism and imperialism. The latter, by their definition, emerged only from industrial wage-labor societies that enjoyed a surplus of capital, and was the same phenomenon whether exerted in Latin America in the mid-nineteenth century or in Africa fifty years later. Thus, one may conclude that regardless of which stand they take on this debate, serious scholars in Latin America believe Britain's "informal empire" in Latin America to have been a reality.

One aspect of the Robinson and Gallagher thesis that is particularly relevant to Latin America is the stress they placed upon the collaboration of "native" elites. Some historians completely ignore this question when they insist that British businessmen had no or little ability to influence political decisions in Latin America.[7] To begin with, their method is illustrative, that is, they present an example or a series of examples purporting to show that British businessmen did not get what they wanted from some particular government. But an essential point—that the British economic system found few political obstacles to its growth and hegemony—is ignored; if the system as a whole is prospering, examples of occasional setback are not convincing. More important, the political leaders of Latin America in the nineteenth century were persuaded, on the whole, to accept the values, attitudes, beliefs, interests, and categories of the British businessmen as being best suited to their own countries. As I have argued elsewhere, the force of the imperial power is to be measured not only or even primarily by the overt acts of political control but by the degree to which these cultural features of the expansionist nation infiltrate and overcome those of the recipient one.[8] In this process the native collaborator is indispensable. It is when influential local politicians and opinion-makers become convinced that the way of life of the imperial power is the best one imaginable that the strength of that nation is at its greatest, although the evidence may then be least noticeable. Throughout Latin America one could find attitudes like those of one Brazilian publicist who believed that "the English possession of India and the English ascendancy in China constitute one of the essential bases of this benign preponderance."[9] A Brazilian politician stated, "When I enter the Chamber [of Deputies] I am entirely under the influence of English liberalism, as if I were working under the orders of Gladstone. . . . I am an English liberal . . . in the Brazilian Parliament."[10] With leaders like that in her informal empire, why should Britain extend her overt political control?

Evidently, then, I believe informal imperialism to have been a reality in nineteenth-century Latin America. I do not see it as requiring an overt governmental component at either end in order for it to be recognized. I acknowledge the need for painstaking research guided by a systematic methodology and based upon a precise theoretical formulation that will take into account such difficult historiographical questions as those of causation and motivation, of system and role, of culture and society. But until we get to that point, Gallagher and Robinson should be given credit, especially in their 1953 formulation, for putting their finger on a reality that deeply affected Latin America.

NOTES

[1] Note the unselfconscious use of the term in Roberto Tamagno's *Sarmiento, los liberales y el imperialismo ingles* (Buenos Aires, 1963).

[2] A. Tenorio d'Albuquerque, *O imperialismo britanico no Brasil* (Rio de Janeiro, 1941).

[3] See Ronald Robinson, "Non-European Foundations of European Imperialism: Sketch for a Theory of Collaboration," in Roger Owen and Bob Sutcliffe, eds., *Studies in the Theory of Imperialism* (London, 1972), pp. 117–140.

[4] Typical is Caio Prado Junior, "O imperialismo," Chapter 25 in his *História econômica do Brasil*, 15th ed. (São Paulo, 1972), pp. 270–283. This assumption is so widespread that it would be tedious to enumerate those who accept it.

[5] André Gunder Frank, *Capitalism and Underdevelopment in Latin America: Historical Studies of Chile and Brazil* (New York, 1967). Also see Caio Prado Junior, *A revolução brasileira* (São Paulo, 1966).

[6] E.g., Almir Chaiban El-Kareh, "A Companhia Estrada de Ferro D. Pedro II: Uma tentativa capitalista no Brasil imperial, 1855–1865," in Richard Graham, ed., *Ensaios sobre a política e a economia da província fluminense no século XIX* (Rio de Janeiro, 1974), pp. 129–177.

[7] E.g., W. M. Mathew, "Foreign Contractors and the Peruvian Government at the Outset of the Guano Trade," *Hispanic American Historical Review*, 52:4 (Nov., 1972), 598–620.

[8] Richard Graham, "Sepoys and Imperialists: Techniques of British Power in Nineteenth-Century Brazil," *Inter-American Economic Affairs*, 23: 2 (Autumn, 1969), 23–37.

[9] Rui Barbosa quoted by Raimundo Magalhães Júnior, *Rui, o homen e o mito* (Rio de Janeiro, 1964), p. 211.

[10] Joaquim Nabuco, *Minha formação* [?ed.]. Documentos Brasileiros, 90 (Rio de Janeiro, 1957), p. 182.

Robinson and Gallagher in the Far East: Japanese Imperialism

AKIRA IRIYE

Akira Iriye is Professor of History at the University of Chicago. His books include After Imperialism: the Search for a New Order in the Far East, 1921–1931 *(1965),* Across the Pacific: An Inner History of American-East Asian Relations *(1967),* Pacific Estrangement: Japanese and American Expansion, 1897–1911 *(1972), and* The Cold War in Asia *(1974). He is presently at work on a major book on* The Pacific War, 1941–1945.

Overseas expansion has remained a major theme in modern Japanese experience. The speed with which the Japanese in the nineteenth century absorbed Western concepts and methods of expansion was the key to their successful self-transformation, and in the twentieth-century Japanese imperialism came to define the structure of Far Eastern politics. After it failed to create an autarkic empire by military force, the nation shifted gears after 1945 and concentrated on less formal and more peaceful expansion, to such an extent that by the early 1970s it was achieving precisely those goals—commercial supremacy, economic growth, successful waging of "peacetime warfare"—which officials and publicists had advocated before the Sino-Japanese War (1894–1895), the first of the series of wars in which the country was to be involved in its quest for empire.

There has been continuity in Japanese expansionism in that the expansionist drive has always characterized national behavior. Part of this drive was traditional; even before the "coming of the West" in the mid-nineteenth century, Japanese writers fondly recalled the experiences of their predecessors in the sixteenth and the early seventeenth centuries, when they ventured out into Southeast Asia and established outposts in the Philippines, Borneo, Siam, and elsewhere. A *kokugaku* ("national learning") scholar asserted in 1823 that the nation should create a gigantic empire incorporating the Philippines, Korea, Manchuria, and China. To such traditional expansionism was added another layer in the last decades of the century, a new consciousness born of contact with the West. It is interesting to note that Western expansionism embodied, in Japanese perception, not so much an aggressive thrust in the traditional sense but a constant quest for economic opportunities abroad. They were immensely impressed to discover that Westerners were forever waging "peacetime warfare," penetrating all corners of the earth for markets, raw materials, and spaces for settlement. Unless Japan did likewise, its survival seemed to be imperiled.

These two layers of Japanese expansionism more or less correspond to "formal" and "informal" imperialism, categories that have been utilized in discussions of British, European, and American imperialism. As with Western countries, Japanese expansion took multidimensional forms, and it is imperative to keep in mind that formal territorial control over Koreans, Taiwanese, and other Asians was only one dimension. More often than not the Japanese were far more interested in what they called "peaceful expansion," entailing trade with and emigration to as many areas of the world as possible and involving the minimum use of force. Thus the insight presented by Robinson and Gallagher on this point is enormously valuable. As a conceptual scheme, their thesis about different gradations of formal control is very useful in tracing different types of expansion undertaken by Japanese in different parts of the globe.

The expansionist thrust of Japan was not unique. But the actual manifestations of Japanese imperialism were conditioned by specific circumstances of time and place. Since the more formal aspect of Japanese expansion took place closer home, whereas a less formal and more peaceful orientation characterized Japanese activities in distant lands, it is imperative to study conditions in areas such as Korea, Taiwan, Manchuria, China, and ultimately Southeast Asia which provided a specific context producing a symbiotic relationship between Japanese imperialism and indigenous forces. For instance, internal politics in Korea during the 1870s and the 1880s created an environment which led to a period of Chinese influence in Seoul, a situation which in turn provoked a Japanese counterresponse eventuating in the Sino-Japanese War. Likewise, Japan's continental imperialism cannot be divorced from developments inside China. After 1895 various "reformers" and "revolutionaries" looked to Japan for moral and financial support, trying to draw Japanese policy into Chinese politics so as to undermine the hold of the Manchu dynasty. The "collaboration" between Chinese politics and Japanese expansionism, to be sure, was not quite the same thing as that described by Robinson and Gallagher in African-British relations. China, after all, had given Japan much of its civilization centuries earlier, and the impact of "modernization" upon Chinese society was an enormously complex intellectual phenomenon. Still, it is possible to borrow these historians' interpretative strategy and emphasize the crucial importance of the "periphery" in the development of Japanese imperialism. Recent studies have shown, for example, that there were factions in Chinese officialdom that looked to the United States for support against other countries after the turn of the century. The emergence of a pro-American group exacerbated Japanese relations both with China and the United States, coming as it did just at the time when the latter was instituting restrictionist policies toward Japanese immigration. Believing expansion to be the basic need of the country, and yet denied an opportunity for migration across the Pacific, the Japanese after the Russo-Japanese War began concentrating on continental expansion, only to be met by pro-American forces within China. The decision to counter this influence and entrench Japanese rights and prerogatives in China ultimately led to the Twenty-one Demands episode of 1915, as far-reaching a statement of Japanese imperialistic ambitions as any until the 1930s. That in turn provoked fierce Chinese nationalism, but even so, nationalism in China was not always, nor consistently, directed against Japanese imperialism. The second Sino-Japanese War (1937–1945) developed into the Pacific War in part because there were factions in China which accepted the symbolism of Japan's pan-Asianist foreign policy and collaborated with Japan in the creation of an anti-Western empire in the Orient.

The history of Japanese imperialism demonstrates the feasibility of some of the conceptual frameworks proposed by Robinson and Gallagher. They have made challenging suggestions about British and European imperialism which can readily be utilized in a study of imperialism in Asia. This is not to deny, however, that there was something unique about the emergence of Japan as an imperialist power and about the timing of this emergence. Japan was the first Asian imperialist. It was equipped both with traditional expansionist thought and with doctrines of modern Western empire. Its people remained physiologically (and to a great extent psychologically) Asian, but the tools of expansion (arms, ships, factories) were Western. The combination of these disparate elements was unique in Asia and in the world at that time. That was why some Western observers were fascinated with, and even alarmed by, the phenomenon. "In a quarter of a century," wrote Henry Norman in 1895, Japan "has sprung from an Oriental despotism . . . to a nation whose army and navy may meet those of contemporary Europe on equal terms." In the years to come "Japan is certain to be as keen a competitor in the peaceful arts of commerce as she might possibly be a dangerous enemy in the 'trampled lanes of war.' " Norman was convinced that in Japan there was "a sentiment which is seldom mentioned there, and which, as far as I know, has hardly been hinted at in Europe . . . Asia for Asiatics. Herein, I am convinced, lie the germs of the most momentous events in the relationships of nations since Napoleon Bonaparte was exiled to St. Helena."

Japanese imperialism was thus a momentous event in the history of interactions among peoples. Hitherto basically a unilinear movement of men, ideas, and influence from the West to the non-West, imperialism at the end of the nineteenth century took new turns. Asia became a land where Western imperialism met its non-Western counterpart. This, however, was part of the story of the deepening association among peoples of different races and cultures brought about by modern technological innovations and by the involvement of distant lands in world politics. Forces of cosmopolitanism as well as of particularism and racism were affecting man's thinking. Masses of Asians and Westerners became intellectually and psychologically aware of one another for the first time in history. Surely this was a qualitatively new situation: imperialism as a vehicle for intercultural communication. This legacy alone justifies the study of late-nineteenth-century imperialism as a unique chapter in the history of the world.

Robinson and Gallagher and American Imperialism

ERNEST R. MAY

Ernest R. May is Professor of History and Director of the Institute of Politics at Harvard University. His major books include The World War and American Isolation, 1914–1917 *(1959),* Imperial Democracy: The Emergence of America as a Great Power *(1961), and* American Imperialism *(1968).*

William Appleman Williams, *The Tragedy of American Diplomacy* (New York, 1962) contends that business-centered American governments developed a strategy of "open door imperialism." Resembling British policy in the early nineteenth century, as limned in the original Robinson and Gallagher *Economic History Review* article, this strategy assumed American competitive superiority. Instead of seeking, like European powers, to shut other nations out of colonial areas, the United States worked only to ensure that Americans were not excluded. Although this goal sometimes required acquisition of islands, since bases were needed both for trade and for the exercise of political and military influence, it did not require assumption of larger administrative responsibilities. Americans, by their competitive superiority, could achieve economic dominance without taking on such burdens.

According to this line of reasoning, the American annexation of Hawaii, Puerto Rico, and the Philippines in 1898–99 should occasion no surprise. Like the acquisition earlier of part of Samoa and later of a harbor in Cuba and a canal zone in Panamá, these larger landtakings were simply tactical moves. The grand strategy of American imperialism remained consistent.

Unfortunately, Williams's thesis was too broad, too undiscriminating, and too nearly tautological to lend itself to any kind of rigorous testing. Works which tried to develop it, such as Walter Lafeber's *The New Empire* (Ithaca, N.Y., 1963) and Thomas McCormick's *China Market* (Chicago, 1967), arrayed evidence that merchants had had more interest in foreign markets than previously supposed, and Williams's own *Roots of the Modern American Empire* (New York, 1969) indicated that this interest was equally keen in agricultural towns of the Middle West; but it remains to be established that there was any causal link between these expressions of generalized interest in foreign trade and the decisions made by the central government when faced with questions of whether or not to annex noncontiguous territory.

A view which is somewhat at variance with Williams's is set forth in two books of mine: *Imperial Democracy: The Emergence of America as a Great Power* (New York, 1961) and *American Imperialism: A Speculative Essay* (New York, 1968). Focusing on American intervention in Cuba in 1898, the first presents evidence that Cuban propagandists had a good deal to do with inspiring public interest and that further interest was whipped up by Protestant clergymen, principally in large cities, who were violently anti-Catholic and who were casting about for ways of counteracting declines in churchgoing and religiosity. The second book concentrates on the question of how, among a public traditionally anticolonial, there developed temporary support for the annexations of the 1890s. Crudely summarized, its argument is that the public which regularly paid attention to foreign affairs was quite small and tended to take its leadership from a tiny cosmopolitan elite. The older members of this elite identified with such heroes as Cobden, Bright, and Gladstone. Partly in reaction, the younger members developed an identification with the likes of Rosebery and Chamberlain. In doing so, they became champions of empire. The elite and the small foreign policy public were thus divided when the Spanish war came. Because of this division, there could be debate among the larger public aroused by the Cuban issue, and people in government were given the impression that there was broad support for pursuit of a new "manifest destiny." Quite possibly, an interest in foreign markets had some conscious or unconscious influence on the opinions expressed, but the whole thing was short-lived. The Philippine insurrection and the Boer War sapped enthusiasm for empire on both sides of the ocean, restored an anticolonial consensus among the American elite, and put an end to broad public discussion of alternative policies.

Both of these interpretations emphasize the inner springs of American imperialism. For the period in question, this is almost certainly right. To be sure, the American settlers in Hawaii created the question of whether or not those islands should be annexed, and their agents lobbied energetically in Washington. Nevertheless, it is in Washington or at least in the United States that one must look for an explanation of the outcome.

American experience bearing on the debate over the Robinson-Gallagher thesis is really that of a later period, for which analytical historical study is yet in its infancy. Dana G. Munro, *Intervention and Dollar Diplomacy in the Caribbean, 1900–1921* (Princeton, 1964), Michael Hunt, *Frontier Defense and the Open Door in Manchuria* (New Haven, 1973), and Peter Stanley, *A Nation in the Making: The Philippines and the United States, 1899–1921* (Cambridge, Mass., 1974) suggest that the patronizing policies of the United States toward Caribbean republics and toward China and the Philippines may have been functions more of Latin American, Chinese, and Philippine than of American politics. But there is a good deal yet to be done on the Latin American and Asian sides before anyone can speak confidently of the extent to which the history of American relations with real and would-be dependencies bears out or modifies theses based on analyses of British and European colonialism.

A Final Comment on the Value of Robinson and Gallagher

SYDNEY KANYA-FORSTNER

A graduate of the University of Toronto, Sydney Kanya-Forstner studied under Robinson and Gallagher in Cambridge during the early 1960s. Formerly a Fellow and College Lecturer in History at Gonville and Caius College, Cambridge, he is currently Associate Professor of History at York University, Toronto. He is the author of The Conquest of the Western Sudan: A Study in French Military Imperialism *(Cambridge, 1969), and of several articles on French expansion. He is presently working, with C. M. Andrew of Corpus Christi College, Cambridge, on a study of French colonial war aims and peace diplomacy during and after the First World War and on the history of the French colonialist movement.*

What has always struck me most about the corpus of Robinson and Gallagher's work is the neat, logical—almost irresistible—extension of a line of argument, both conceptually and in terms of its scope.* It began in 1953 with what was basically an attempt to turn conventional ideas about mid-Victorian imperialism on their head—but which already contained in embryo the elements of a much more general theory. In *Africa and the Victorians* the argument was refined

---

*The remarks which follow have been extracted from a letter which I wrote Roger Louis in reply to his request for comments about his draft introduction. My letter was not, of course, intended for publication. However, Professor Louis and I have decided to reproduce the comments in their original form, except for the correction of several grammatical errors, the deletion of a few personal references, and the addition of one or two sentences where the argument was too compressed or allusive. I hope that the spontaneity with which my remarks were written will excuse their lack of polish.

and extended into the late-Victorian period, through a case study, with the emphasis shifting to the analysis of British policy-making. Having dealt with the British—and it is important to remember that *Africa and the Victorians* was intended not so much as an interpretation of the partition as an analysis of the motives and attitudes of British statesmen during the partition—they took the logical step, in "The Partition of Africa," of extending the theory to cover all European powers, at the same time developing the African context and the theory of the local crisis. This really was a large step beyond the book and what made "The Partition" such an intellectually exciting, though ultimately I think an unsound, piece of work. Finally we have Robinson the social scientist, complete with his mathematical analogies, bringing together all the ideas into an attempted general theory —not merely of imperialism, nationalism or small questions like these—but about the relationship between European and non-European, advanced and backward, dynamic and tradition-bound societies during the past five centuries. A truly remarkable progression, you must admit.

I do not consider either "universality" or "continuity" to be the crucial themes of the original argument. The article itself made no claim to universality—only "The Partition of Africa" did that—although the theme of continuity was of course stressed. But if the objective was to attack conventional theories about a mid-Victorian era of anti-imperialism followed by a late-Victorian era of imperialism, with a sharp break around 1870–80, then the obvious line of attack was to deny the existence of the break and to posit a mid-Victorian era as expansionist as its late-Victorian counterpart. The essence of the argument, it seems to me, lay in the reinterpretation of the mid-Victorian era and the introduction of the concept of informal empire. The continuity they emphasised was not chronological so much as thematic, between formal and informal empire as means to the same end—and this end was economic, though more than that too. Surely the fundamental continuity is between the two pieces of their famous iceberg.

My interpretation of "The Imperialism of Free Trade" in turn affects my view of *Africa and the Victorians*. If the objective of the original exercise was to turn existing interpretations on their head, why stop at half measures? Why not go further and deny the imperialistic character of the late-Victorian age? In a sense this is what I think Robinson and Gallagher try to do, especially in the conclusion of the book. They argue that there *was* a change between the two periods, but that this change ran directly counter to the old view of late-Victorian imperialists, aggressive, self-confident, technological-ly invincible, establishing their mastery over the world. The change Robinson and Gallagher see is that between the dynamism, self-confidence, and expansiveness of mid-Victorian Britain, and the pessimistic, frightened, neurotic men like Salisbury who presided over the end of the era. What brought this change about was not just changed circumstances on the diplomatic stage but also the recog-nition that it might not after all be possible to reshape the world in Britain's image (a central feature of the imperialism of free trade), that lesser breeds might react violently against attempts to transform them into Englishmen, and that it might therefore be better to forget about social engineering on a global scale and concentrate instead on global security. This implicit theme, though not fully spelt out even in the conclusion, seems to me the fundamental theme of the book itself, much more important than the detailed arguments about Egypt and South Africa, which are all most critics ever look at. This too, by the way, is the reason why the change of the subtitle in the American edition to 'The Climax of Imperialism in the Dark Conti-nent' was such a crime.

The extension of the theory in "The Partition of Africa" is relatively simple. All they have to do is make the "local crisis" the focus of their analysis and apply their conclusions about British policy to the policies of other powers, especially France. After all, why stop with an interpretation of the British role in the partition when the same basic arguments can be used to explain everything—and not just European expansion but the African forces which gave rise to it as well? Indeed the chapter is the most Afrocentric interpretation of the partition ever advanced—quite ironical given some of the attacks which have been leveled against it.

Finally, Robinson's essay extends the theory to its ultimate limits, seeking to provide a unified interpretation of the whole process—informal empire, its breakdown, colonial rule, its breakdown, until we come back to where we started, all neat and symmetrical, com-posed of essentially simple elements capable of infinite sophistica-tion, and for this reason so attractive. Indeed, this approach is what I find so attractive about all the pieces in the corpus. Each one can be seen, at least in part, as an intellectual exercise, a *jeu d'esprit* whose object is to turn received ideas upside down, to work out simple, symmetrical interpretations and then extend their scope as far as one dares. It may not always come off, but you must admire the two of them for trying, just as it is difficult not to share some of the obvious enjoyment with which they do it.

231 **Comments**

As for the critics, most I think have missed the point. Half the attacks on "The Imperialism of Free Trade" are on the title, which has precious little to do with the article. Once the semantics are cleared away, Platt does have valid criticisms to make, but the differences of opinion are of degree rather than of kind—as Platt himself admits in his most recent article, although he would argue that these differences are crucial. My own criticism of "The Imperialism of Free Trade" concerns the new summing up: "trade with informal control if possible; trade with rule when necessary." Yet almost all the annexations which Robinson and Gallagher cite are concentrated on the frontiers of India and South Africa, the two key points on the East of Greenwich imperial route. Turbulent frontiers are not a sufficient explanation—many turbulent frontiers provoked no annexations— what mattered was clearly strategic security. What mattered even more, however, was where geographically these strategic considerations came into play. One could argue that there were two British empires, each comprising a formal and informal element, one Atlantic, the other Afro-Asian. The relative importance of the formal and informal elements varied, as did the relationship between them. But the exercise of force was largely restricted to one of these empires, for reasons which are implicit in Robinson's "Non-European Foundations. . . ." In this respect two points can be made. The first is that there was some shift in the interpretation between "The Imperialism of Free Trade" and *Africa and the Victorians,* in which the special position of India and its impact on the whole east of Suez arc was more clearly spelt out. The second concerns the shift in the analysis of the Atlantic empire between "The Imperialism of Free Trade" and "Non-European Foundations." British policies in Latin America, for example, were given some prominence in the first; in the second, this theme hardly gets a mention.

Similarly, most criticisms of *Africa and the Victorians* seem to me irrelevant and often misguided. Newbury and Stengers attack the book as an interpretation of the Partition, which it was not intended to be. They concentrate on West Africa, and largely on the analysis of the French response to the Egyptian occupation, which after all was a quite unimportant part of the thesis. Demolishing this part of the interpretation certainly won't bring the whole structure down— though they do cause a lot more damage to the chapter in the *New Cambridge Modern History.* Criticisms which focus on theories of imperialism seem positively misguided. The book's contribution to the theory of imperialism surely lies in the questions asked and the kind of research undertaken to answer them. Robinson and Gallagher actually tried to come to grips with what happened, using policy-making and the official mind as their frame of reference, instead of imbuing themselves with "the spirit of the times," reading libraries of fifth-rate literature and wasting their time with Shepperson's "maladjusted European individuals."

My own criticism of *Africa and the Victorians* comes from a different perspective, although I think it respects the intentions of the authors more than most. It is in fact about the book's scope. If the purpose was to analyze the formulation of official policies toward Africa, then the frame of reference should have been relevant to this purpose. But for West Africa they allowed the Partition as a diplomatic process to determine the cut-off date. Choosing 1898 did let them turn one more traditional idea on its head and argue that British imperialism in West Africa was a product of the Partition rather than its cause, but this argument would have been much more difficult to sustain had they chosen some later date more relevant to the actual processes of British expansion. Chamberlain's doctrine of tropical African estates may have inspired the beginnings of West African development (however abortive these beginnings might have been); it also inspired the occupation of Northern Nigeria, by far the largest territorial addition ever to this part of the empire.

Robinson and Gallagher's achievement is obvious. Twenty years after its publication, "The Imperialism of Free Trade" is still provoking responses, and while it is true that nobody can fail to take account of their work, the remarkable thing is how many historians have taken account of it and have been influenced by it. Indeed, you could argue that they virtually singlehandedly rescued "The Expansion of Europe" as an academic field and turned it into a subject attractive enough to hold the interest of bright young historians and not so bright young undergraduates alike. None of this would have happened if they hadn't set out to be provocative and if they hadn't managed to be provocative with such panache. In the end, what carries "The Partition of Africa" is the style as much as the argument, just as what makes *Africa and the Victorians* a work of art is, not least, its series of pen portraits. It was this ability to provoke, to play with ideas, to write so well, and to do it all with such a sense of fun that made the greatest impression on me when I studied under them, and I think on most of my contemporaries too. I always resent it a little when people refer to me as a "disciple" of Robinson and Gallagher, especially since I've tried—like so many of us—to knock various parts of their interpretations down. But we sure as hell could have done worse for masters.

PART V

**Suggestions for
Further Reading**

The Controversy as of March 1975—
Platt versus Fieldhouse

The central point at issue in the controversy continues to be continuity. D. C. M. Platt's recent article, "The National Economy and British Imperial Expansion before 1914," in the *Journal of Imperial and Commonwealth History* (II, 1, October 1973) argues that British policy as late as the 1840s was fundamentally protectionist. Platt denies the reality of the expansive impulse even in its economic form before the late nineteenth century. This is reaffirmation with a vengeance. Platt is out to destroy the concept of the "informal empire" and the "continuous or universal" explanation of Robinson and Gallagher. Economic ambitions may have motivated men on the frontier to move beyond the formal Empire, but this impetus for expansion did not come from the mother country. Britain satisfied the need for raw materials and foodstuffs by trade with Europe, the United States, and the Empire. Indeed, Britain remained essentially indifferent to remoter regions until about 1860, when the expansion of railway systems in such places as Argentina created favorable trading conditions. The competition with the new industrial powers of France, Germany and the United States caused British manufacturers to look to less attractive fields such as Latin America and ultimately Africa. British expansion went through distinct phases, from mercantilist at the beginning of the nineteenth century to the "New Imperialism" at the end of the century, "separated by at least half a century of imperial expansion for which it would indeed be difficult, except at the most local and personal level, to find convincing economic explanations." On the other hand, for the mercantilist period as for the "New Imperialism," "To argue that . . . economic motives for imperial expansion were of minor significance takes a degree of special pleading unusual in scholarship, if characteristic enough of the political climate in which this argument is normally conducted." The economic factor must be seen in the perspective of the period. Platt's article should thus be regarded as part of his progressive effort to replace the idea of "The Imperialism of Free Trade" with a structured explanation of imperial expansion in which the economic motives for empire did not remain constant. The question of eras is vital: economic circumstances changed so remarkably over the nineteenth century that it would be surprising if policies and attitudes did not change. Contemporaries clearly saw these changes. The reader may rightly infer from Platt's writings that he regards Hobson as a more reliable guide to the late nineteenth century than either Robinson and Gallagher or Fieldhouse. Platt's work is fundamental reappraisal of the expansive impulse, and he concludes that earlier writers on the whole correctly associated it with the decades of the "New Imperialism."

While Platt has moved progressively in the direction of affirming the idea of the "New Imperialism," David Fieldhouse has moved closer to Robinson and Gallagher. In *Economics and Empire* (London, 1973)* he extensively examines the proposition that there was a basic discontinuity between the imperialism of the middle and later nineteenth century. After weighing the evidence in the course of the book, his conclusion is unequivocal: "It was the end of an old story not the start of a new one." The only novelty about the "New Imperialism" was the speed and the universality of the European advance. Fieldhouse's explanation puts forward a "general crisis" hypothesis. It views the imperialism of the 1880s and 1890s as a series of crises throughout the world to which Europeans responded with *ad hoc* solutions.

> The important fact is that, for the first time in modern history, these local problems were so widespread and the European powers concerned so numerous that collectively they constituted a 'general crisis' in the relations between Europe and the less-developed world. . . . These multiple crises and their timing were merely symptoms of a profound change in the pathology of international relationships. The world crisis was real and a solution had to be found. By about 1880 there was a fundamental disequilibrium between Europe and most parts of the less-developed world. (pp. 460–461)

*As this volume goes to press, the most important review that has appeared of *Economics and Empire* is in the *Historical Journal* (18, 2, June 1975), where Eric Stokes acclaims it as "the most sustained study of nineteenth-century imperialism since the appearance of Professor D. C. M. Platt's *Finance, Trade and Politics in British Foreign Policy, 1815–1914* in 1968."

His conclusion is fundamental: "In the most general terms it must be concluded that Europe was pulled into imperialism by the magnetic force of the periphery." In this process of peripheral expansion, the economic factor played a variable role. Fieldhouse considers his conclusion in this regard to be the most important of the book: "European governments were normally prepared to use political methods to solve problems associated with European economic enterprise on the periphery only when and because this came up against some otherwise insurmountable non-economic obstacle; or, alternatively, when economic activity gave rise to some strictly non-economic problem which again demanded political action." In other words, the link between economics and empire was not in the need for colonies by the metropolitan country, nor the requirement of economic interests, but the consequence of problems created on the periphery. The "New Imperialism" to Fieldhouse can be considered as a distinct era only in the sense that diverse economic and noneconomic problems in the "outer world" produced a world crisis in the last two decades of the nineteenth century. European statesmen responded with political solutions such as the partition of Africa. His conclusion that it was the end of an old story is thus in line with Robinson and Gallagher. Here the three of them stand in opposition to Platt.

Nevertheless Fieldhouse's book is by no means a general endorsement of Robinson and Gallagher, and on specific issues Fieldhouse comes closer to Platt. The case against Robinson and Gallagher is not the main purpose of *Economics and Empire,* so it is important to make clear the major differences. Fieldhouse rejects the "Egyptian theory" of the partition; he does not accept the "nationalist" argument, which he sees as weak anywhere but North Africa and possibly South-East Asia; and he sees the problem of imperialism as global in scope and by necessity having to take account of most parts of the world and the major European states, which is an implicit rejection of the case-study approach of Africa and Victorian statesmen—to a greater degree than Robinson and Gallagher he attempts to differentiate between the reactions of European statesmen to problems in various places. On the whole, however, the conclusions about the "local crises" and the "periphery" should be seen as original and independent support for Robinson and Gallagher.

Fieldhouse's *magnum opus* is disguised as a textbook, which must not be allowed to obscure its importance. Unfortunately it has no bibliography, though the references form a more or less comprehensive list of important sources. The following comments are offered as a convenient means of pursuing the ramifications of the Robinson and Gallagher controversy.

One good way of gaining perspective on the problems of British imperialism and the themes of continuity and universality is to examine the literature on the colonial expansion of Britain's major rivals, Germany and France. For Germany, see the bibliographical essay by Hartmut Pogge von Strandmann and Alison Smith, "The German Empire in Africa and British Perspectives: A Historiographical Essay," in Prosser Gifford and Wm. Roger Louis, eds., *Britain and Germany in Africa: Imperial Rivalry and Colonial Rule* (New Haven, 1967); and a further essay by von Strandmann, "The German Role in Africa and German Imperialism," *African Affairs*, 69, 277 (October 1970). See also the extensive bibliography in Hans-Ulrich Wehler, *Bismarck und der Imperialismus* (Cologne, 1969). For France, see the bibliography in Henri Brunschwig, *Le Partage de l'Afrique Noire* (Paris, 1971); and by the same author, "L'impérialisme en Afrique noire," *Revue Historique*, 505 (January–March 1973). See also the bibliography in Jean Ganiage, *L'Expansion Coloniale de la France* (Paris, 1968). For a survey of the literature on the 1880s and 1890s, see M. E. Chamberlain, *The New Imperialism* (Historical Association pamphlet G. 73, 1970). For the Free Trade era, see the bibliography in C. C. Eldrige, *England's Mission: The Imperial Idea in the Age of Gladstone and Disraeli, 1868–1880* (London, 1973). For the subject of economic imperialism, the bibliography in Roger Owen and Bob Sutcliffe, *Studies in the Theory of Imperialism* (London, 1972) is excellent. See also V. G. Kiernan, *Marxism and Imperialism* (London, 1974). For the worldwide scope of imperialism in relation to Japan and the United States, see the bibliography in Akira Iriye, *Pacific Estrangement: Japanese and American Expansion, 1897–1911* (Cambridge, Mass., 1972). The most recent comprehensive bibliography is *Colonialism in Africa* (volume 5): *A Bibliographical Guide to Colonialism in Sub-Saharan Africa*, eds. Peter Duignan and L. H. Gann (Cambridge University Press, 1974). See also John D. Hargreaves, *West Africa Partitioned: The Loaded Pause* (London, 1975); and Ronald Hyam and G. W. Martin, *Reappraisals in British Imperial History* (London, 1975), which includes an expanded version of Hyam's critique of *Africa and the Victorians*.

As this volume goes to press, E. H. Carr has delivered the most recent attack on Robinson and Gallagher in the *Times Literary Supplement* on March 7, 1975. Commenting on their "able and much quoted" book, Carr gives this verdict:

The writers seemed so frightened of being taken for disciples of Marx, Hobson or Lenin that they were unable to produce any coherent analysis of imperialism, British or other, and were content to depict a series of empirical, often rather muddled, responses to successive crises. The ultimate impression left on the mind of the reader is not so far removed from the old Victorian adage that the British Empire was acquired in a fit of absence of mind.

However one judges the value of Robinson and Gallagher's work, this clearly was not the sole impression they intended to give. If the present volume has at least clarified the underlying unity of their views, then it will have served a useful purpose.

INDEX

doctrine of tropical estates, 30, 233; policy in West Africa, 114–15; and Jameson Raid, 122; and origins of the Boer war, 123; poem about, 163; proposal to forge South Africa into another Canada, 168; and trusteeship, 181; purpose in South Africa, 182

China, 18, 21, 25, 26, 65, 80, 85, 125, 130, 131, 184, 198, 210, 220, 228; and the collaboration theory, 137–38; economic imperialism in, 140–41; and Platt on trade, 157–60; rivalry in, 186

Christianity: its part in the Scramble, 102–103; and nationalism, 125

Clarendon, Lord, 65

Cobden, Richard, 18–19, 227

Collaboration, theory of, 8, 26, 61, 82; the vital key to the work of R&G, 36–37; in relation to the nature of African societies, 101–102, 125; failure of, during Scramble, 116; in South Africa, 124; the theme of Robinson's 1972 essay, 128–48; breakdown of collaborative mechanisms the cause of imperial takeovers, 141; as the basis of colonial rule, 144; assessed by Rostow, 202–203; in Latin America, 219–20; between China and Japan, 224

Colombia, 63, 64

Congo, 8, 27–28; rivalry of great powers in, 86, 88–90, 116, 179, 184, 206

Congo Free State, 96, 108, 120; creation of, 87–89

Crispi, Francesco, 74, 99, 110

Cromer, Lord. *See* Baring, Sir Evelyn

Cuba, 226, 227

Dahomey, 84, 93, 102, 104

Davidson, Basil, 169

Decolonization: and the collaboration theory, 128; in relation to non-collaboration, 146–47

Delagoa Bay, 57, 120, 122, 123

Derby, Lord, 95

Dernburg, Bernhard, 117

Deutsch, Karl, 12, 168

Diké, K. O., 169

Disraeli, Benjamin, 19, 69, 79, 85

Djibouti, 98

East Africa, 9, 10, 70; partition of, 94–95

Economic factor: not sufficient as an explanation, 5, 25; put in perspective by Stokes, 9–10, 178, 188–92; analyzed by Hopkins, 22–24; analyzed by Newbury, 28–29; in West Africa, 47 n.77; Shepperson on, 165; insufficient to produce the Scramble, 187; "deserves more consideration than R&G allow to it," 191; assessed by Platt, 235–36; assessed by Fieldhouse, 236–37

Egerton, Hugh Edward, 6, 55

Egypt, 10, 11, 21, 96, 106, 116, 130; crisis of 1879–82, 4, 5, 76, 78–84, 117, 164, 177–79; nationalism in, 19, 25–26, 31, 48 n.94, 75, 78–83, 95, 100, 116, 125, 166, 192; British occupation of, 25, 69, 83; in relation to the Scramble, 27–32, 85–88, 98, 113, 140, 162, 180, 184; Anglo-

French conflict in, brings division of Africa, 83, 90, 95; occupation of, affects East Africa, 94; pashas as collaborating elites, 132; and collaboration theory, 138–40; and Platt on trade, 158; R&G interpretation of, challenged by Owen, 212–15

Elites: significance of, analyzed by Robinson, 129; as collaborators, 131–34; traditional versus modern, 143; urban, mass, and rural, 146

Eritrea, 97

Ethiopia, 74, 80, 96, 97–98, 103, 182; protonationalism in, 110, 116, 125; and the Nile struggle, 111–13

Étienne (Algerian Under-Secretary for Colonies), 92, 104, 105

"Excentric" theory, xii, 147–48. *See also* Local crisis theory

Faidherbe, General, 84, 206

Fashoda crisis, 75, 83, 113–15, 182; origins of, 106–13

Ferns, H. S., 21

Ferry, Jules, 25, 75–77, 86, 88, 167, 206; colonial policy of, 89

Fieldhouse, David, xii; attack on Hobson, 9; and the R&G controversy, 13–14; labels R&G's theory "peripheral," 147; magnum opus independent support of R&G, 236–37

Flint, John E., major attack on R&G's West African thesis, 47 n.77

France: and balance of power, 4, 25, 82, 84, 87, 95, 210; and West Africa, 8, 28–30, 91–94, 104–106, 111–16; and the Congo, 27–28, 86; and Bismarck's colonial policy, 32; and Egypt, 69, 82, 179–80; and North Africa, 76–78; humiliation in Egypt worse since Sedan, 83; and the Nile question, 106–13; meaning of Fashoda crisis for, 113

Frank, André Gunder, 219

"Free Trade," concept defined by Macdonagh, 19

Freycinet, Charles de, 30, 79, 89, 90

Fulani peoples, 92

Fyfe, Christopher, 41 n.16

Gabon, 84, 85, 89

Galliéni, Joseph Simon, 88, 90, 92

Gambetta, Léon, 76, 77, 79, 97

Gambia, 84, 93

Garson, Noel, xii, 50 n.115

German East Africa, 35, 96

Germany: colonial policy of, 32–33, 208–11; and the Egyptian crisis, 84; and colonial questions of 1884–85, 86–91; and East Africa, 94–96; agrees to stay out of Nile basin, 96; and the Nile crisis, 110; supports Kruger, 122; and the question of capitalism, 174; and South Africa, 178. *See also* Bismarck, Otto von

Gifford, Prosser, 43 n.35

Gladstone, William, 19, 21, 68, 69, 74, 75, 84, 88, 94, 99, 108, 168, 178, 220, 227; and the Egyptian crisis, 79–83; "Egypt for the Egyptians," 79; stumbles into Egypt, 83; welcomes German protectorates, 95; and the Boers, 119

Gold Coast, 6, 56, 84
Goldie, George, 85, 89, 114, 179
Goodfellow, C. F., 36, 50 n.115
Gordon, General, sent to his death at Khartoum, 81
Graham, Richard: argues informal empire in Brazil, 22; on meaning of informal imperialism, 217–20
Granville, Lord, 32, 86, 87, 88, 89, 94, 95
Grey declaration of 1895, 109
Griqualand, 6, 56, 57
Guatemala, 64
Guinea, 93

Hancock, W. K., 12
Hanotaux. Gabriel, 109, 115; poem about, 163
Hargreaves, John D., xii, 42 n.28, 169; compares AV with *Ulysses,* 29; makes distinctive contribution to Scramble, 166
Harlow, V. T., 62
Hawaii, 226, 228
Heligoland, 86, 93, 96
Hewett (British consul), 86
Hobson, J. A., 5, 55, 61, 70, 159, 168, 204; writings analyzed by Stokes, 9–10, 174, 188–91; precursor of Lenin, 163; element of truth in theory, 198; a more reliable guide than R&G, 236
Hodgkin, Thomas, 35
Honduras, 64
Hong Kong, 6, 56
Hopkins, A. G., criticism of R&G, 22–24
Humanitarian influence on British policy, 21, 45 n.55, 53
Hunt, Michael, 228
Hyam, Ronald, xii, 29

Ilorin, 115
"Imperial factor" in South Africa, 120
Imperial Federation movement, 55
"Imperialism": definition of, 4, 5, 21, 129, 204; as a response to nationalism, 8, 25, 140–41, 237; as a function of non-European politics, 14, 228; in relation to nationalism, 32–36, 125; not a cause of the partition, 74, 89; a reflex to protonationalism, 103; a result of the partition, 117, 179; "a major function of indigenous politics," 146; not characterized by continuity, 153–60; essence of "the scramble for colonies," 173; A. J. P. Taylor's interpretation of, 197–99; Japanese, 222–25
"Imperialism of Free Trade": continuity basic argument of, 2–3, 5, 53, 59, 60, 67, 175; theses of, 5–7, 53–54; derives from history of British Empire, 7; universality of, 7; as a function of economic integration, 14, 59; and informal empire, 16; attacked by Platt, 16–18, 153–60, 235–36; attacked by Macdonagh, 18–20; theory applied to Peru, 20–21; theses summarized, 24–25; the two qualifications of the theory, 59; in relation to Robinson's 1972 essay, 128, 136; in relation to AV, 164; interpreted by Kanya-Forstner, 230
India, 21, 54, 58, 70, 74, 131; defense of, 11, 25, 69, 78, 82, 95, 167, 182; and economic motives for empire, 12, 41 n.21; as an

example of formal and informal empires, 61; "British Africa . . . a gigantic footnote to the Indian empire," 99, 187; related to Fashoda crisis, 113; and the collaboration theory, 137, 143; nationalism in, 179

"Informal Empire": transition to "formal empire" triggers Scramble, 9; basic arguments of R&G in regard to, 16, 54–55, 60–61, 67, 68, 73, 180, 230, 232; concept attacked by Platt, 17–18, 155–60, 235–36; objections to concept by Macdonagh, 18–20; in regard to Peru, 20–21; in Latin America, 22, 217–20; criticized by Shepperson, 164–65; Bismarck and, 209; in relation to Japan, 223

International African Association, 85, 184

Ireland, 19; important analogy with South Africa, 124; nationalism in, 179

Iriye, Akira, on Far East and the R&G theories, 222–25

Islam, 9, 76, 83, 91–92, 99, 102–103, 181; awakening of, 80. See also Jihads; Muslim rebellion

Ismail, 81, 178–79, 213

Italy: and the partition of East Africa, 97–98; defeat at Adowa, 1 March 1896, 110; and the Nile question, 110–11; imperialism unpopular in, 167

Ivory Coast, 84, 86, 91, 92, 104

Jameson Raid, 75, 122, 136, 182

Japan, 7, 130, 131, 137; modernization and imperialism, 140–41,

201–203; and the Robinson and Gallagher theories, 222–25

Jauréguiberry, Jean, 30, 207

Java, 62, 74

Jihads, 80, 102, 181, 193; as a cause of French imperialism, 91–92. See also Islam; Muslim rebellion

Johnston, Harry, 28

Kanya-Forstner, Sydney: on origins of the Scramble, 30; 51 n.120; "the most Afrocentric interpretation ever advanced," 73, 231; comment on R&G, 229–33

Kassala, 98

Kemp, Tom, attacks R&G on Marxist grounds, 41 n.21

Kenya, 116, 133, 180

Kiernan, V. G., xi; attack on R&G, 10–12; 42 n.30

Kimberley, diamond discoveries at, 118

Kirk, John, 66

Kitchener, Lord, and the occupation of the Sudan, 110–13, 182

Kowloon, 6

Kruger, Paul, 119, 120, 121, 122, 123

Labuan, 6, 56

Lado, 108

La Feber, Walter, 38, 227

Lagos, 6, 56, 66, 84

Landes, David, theory of imperialism contrasted with R&G's, 43 n.40

Langer, William L., xi, 56; summarizes age of imperialism, 6; interpretation of Egyptian crisis,

"Peripheral" theory. See "Local crisis" theory

Persian Empire, 198

Peru, 20–22

Peters, Karl, 94, 179–180

Philippines, 85, 226, 227, 228

Platt, D. C. M., 218, 219, 232; attacks on IFT, 14–18, 153–60, 235–36; purpose contrasted with R&G, 44 n.45

Portal, Gerald, 107, 108

Portugal, claims of, in central Africa, 121–22

Protonationalism, 25, 31, 35, 75, 100, 117, 182–83, 192–93; as countertheme of subimperialism, 8; in Egypt, 9; not operative in the Congo, 33–34; as a major theme of the partition, 98, 103, 112, 116; battle of Adowa, "the first victory of African proto-nationalism," 110; lures Europe into imperialism, 125; nonexistent as a cause of German imperialism, 208. See also Nationalism

"Public opinion," role of, in the Scramble, 28, 32, 37, 88, 91

Punjab, 6, 56

Queensland, 6, 56

Rabih, 103, 105, 114, 115, 116, 192

Racialism, a neglected theme in AV, 167

Ramm, Agatha, assesses controversy of Egyptian nationalism, 31–32

Ranger, T. O.: challenges R&G on African nationalism, 34–35; 46 n.74; believes resistance the key to colonial era, 50 n.118

Rases of Tigré, Gojam, Harar and Wollo, "Ethiopian proto-nationalists [who] crushed the Italians,"110

Resistance movements, 34–35, 100–102, 192–93; create "local crises," 181. See also Nationalism

Rhodes, Cecil, 4, 13, 28, 96, 123, 170, 177, 178, 182; personality of, 121; organizes uitlanders, 122

Rhodesia, 96, 123, 133

Rio de la Plata, 63

Robinson, Ronald (writings and ideas of, as distinct from collaborative work with John Gallagher): clarifies argument, 14; known as "Thinker," 14; description of "the decrepit, mythological beast of economic imperialism," 24, 165; and the argument of "Non-European Foundations," 24–27; defends Egyptian argument, 36; essay on collaboration, 128–48; speculates on imperialism in the 1970s and 1980s, 148

Robinson and Gallagher: hypotheses, of, 3; challenge Eurocentric interpretation, 3, 175; areas of controversy raised by, 7; and the "New Imperialism," 6, 27, 124; and economic exploitation, 9; as non-Leninist Leninists, 10; reduce Marxist interpretation to a footnote, 10, 40 n.14; concept of informal empire attacked by Platt, 16–18; interpretation of mid-Victorian era assessed by Macdonagh, 18–20; and West Africa, 22–24; and the Egyptian argument, 27–32; and the theorists of economic imperialism, 25; explanation of Bismarck's colonial policy, 32–33; regard Ranger as stimulating critic, 34; achievement of, 36–37; on "pseudo-nationalist" movement in Egypt, 69; ambiguities of general argument, 193; as "fabulous artificers," 193; attacked by Wehler, 208; and informal empire in Latin America, 217–20; frightened of being taken for disciples of Marx, Hobson, or Lenin, 239

Rodd, Rennell, 112

Rosas, General, 63, 157

Rosebery, Lord, 67, 227; and the Nile question, 106–109

Rostow, W. W., comments on R&G controversy, 200–203

Royal Niger Company, 89, 90

St. Lucia Bay, 57, 120

Salisbury, Lord, 3rd marquis, 8, 66–68, 74, 82, 93, 98, 99, 164, 231; and origins of Boer War, 11; and beginning of the Scramble, 27; and partition of West Africa, 93, 115; gives France "light soils," 93, 98; and East Africa, 95–96; and Nile question, 106, 109, 116; orders Kitchener to invade Sudan, 110; and Fashoda crisis, 111–13; and Rhodes, 121; distrusts nationalism, 168

Samoa, 226

Samori, 90, 92, 103, 109, 112, 181, 192

Sanderson, G. N., 50 n.120

Sanusi, 105; religious order, 77

Sardesai, D. R., 44 n.41

Schölch, Alexander, 213, 215

Schreuder, D. M., 36, 50 n.115

Schumpeter, Joseph, 13, 168–69; R&G acknowledge as brilliant, 42 n.30

Schuyler, Robert L., 5, 55, 57

Scramble: causes of, 8, 9, 23–24, 25, 29–32, 67, 75, 85, 192, 206, 212; a "scramble in Africa," not "a scramble for Africa," 100, 185; a trivial affair, 198; humorous from economic historian's viewpoint, 201; distinguished from steeplechase, 205–207

Seeley, John R., 6, 55, 164, 165; on England as an expanding society, 59; on "fit of absence of mind," 163

Semmel, Bernard, 44 n.41, 169; criticism of IFT, 164 (quotation)

Senegal, 92, 93, 104, 184

Seymour, Beauchamp, bombards Alexandria, 80, 83

Shepperson, George, 41–42 n.28, 233; criticism of AV, 12–13, 162–70; *E.H.R.* review, 162

Sierra Leone, 6, 56, 84

Sinclair, Keith, 50 n.119

Sind, 6, 56

Singapore, 62

Slave Trade. *See* Arab slave trade

Sokoto, 92, 114, 115

Soudan Francais, 104, 116

South Africa, 56, 182, 192, 201; local crisis theory and, 4, 178, 182; nationalism in, 35–36, 75; major interpretation of, by R&G, 117–24; and the collaboration theory, 135–36. *See also* Africaner nationalism; Boer War

South West Africa, 32, 87

Stanley, H. M., 85

Stanley, Peter, 228